Coingate

When Law and Fairness Collide

Garrison Walters

DEDICATION

To America's investigative journalists. Hang in there, we need you more than ever.

ACKNOWLEDGEMENTS

Thanks to the social sciences: political scientists Rich Petrick and Dan Nelson, as well as psychologist Sylvia Marotta-Walters and education professional Jon Tafel read the manuscript multiple times and made invaluable suggestions.

Cover by Jarett Walen

A Juggernaut of Legal Error

Once upon a time, a man negotiated a deal to invest some money for a government agency. The investment did very well for nearly seven years. Then, the agency decided it didn't like the arrangement and asked to dissolve it. As the lawyers worked to untangle things, they discovered that some money wasn't in the right accounts and that, even though the investor had clearly and visibly maintained legal responsibility for all the funds he had received, some money had been used temporarily for the investor's personal expenses. The government lawyers then sued the investor and reached an out of court settlement in which the investor had to pay a small amount of money for potentially lost profits as well as for legal fees.

The man in this fable was not Tom Noe, who lives in the real world. Noe had the same experience as the investor described above, but the outcome was very different. Noe was involved in politics in an extremely partisan place, and the local newspaper publisher disliked him. When problems with the investment were revealed, a blizzard of stories and editorials cried "alleged THEFT!" The newspaper was powerful and times were tense with a critical election coming up, so politicians of both sides panicked and decided to either "get Noe" (the opposing party strategy) or "get him out of the way" (his own party's approach). Together, this bipartisan alliance developed a search warrant that was completely dishonest, even containing some "recklessly false" statements. The warrant allowed seizure of Noe's business together with his business records and many of his assets. All his employees lost their jobs. Then, the cooperating parties carefully crafted an audit of the investment that singled out Noe and focused on only one aspect of his business, completely ignoring its overall operations and profits.

The county prosecutor's office, controlled by the opposing political party, charged Noe with an array of crimes, including RICO (Racketeer Influenced and Corrupt Organizations). The local judge, against whom Noe had filed ethics charges, refused to recuse himself. The state Supreme Court refused to intervene.

By the time Noe went to trial 18 months after the search warrant, the local newspaper had published some 750 articles and letters on his case. Also, there were many editorials focusing on "alleged THEFT!" Television and radio stations repeated the newspaper's message. This intensely negative coverage meant that, when interviewed, a large proportion of the prospective jurors said they were biased against Noe or had heard negative information about him. But the judge kept most of them in the pool and some of them actually served. And the judge refused to move the trial elsewhere. Finally, although the prosecution consistently but indirectly suggested to the jury that the overall investment had lost money, the judge denied the defense the right to present evidence of profitability. Just after his ruling, the newspaper gave the judge a very strong and prominent endorsement for election to a higher court.

The jury convicted Noe on RICO and theft and other charges and the judge sentenced him to far more than the minimum: 18 years with no reasonable chance of early release. The day after the conviction, the state announced that its investment would likely make a profit.

The Appeals Court, operating in the same county with the same newspaper watching, agreed entirely with the discretionary decisions of the trial judge – who was now one of their colleagues. Other courts also deferred to the trial judge, and Noe has been in state prison for nine years with nine more to go.

A careful analysis of Tom Noe's saga reveals a juggernaut of legal error. The search warrant was a deliberately misleading concoction. The prosecutor had multiple conflicts of interest and should never have had a role. The same is true for the trial judge. The state Supreme Court, with multiple conflicts of its own, including some emanating from an extremely harsh partisan environment, refused to take the long view and instead acted on expediency.

Finally, an analysis of psychological research shows that Noe could not have received a fair trial in his home region. Intense and slanted media coverage clearly biases jurors, both directly and indirectly through family, friends, and co-workers. And research on other aspects of bias, notably its impact on people like prosecutors and judges, makes clear that these individuals could hardly have escaped strong even if unconscious negative feelings against Noe. This conclusion about the distorting role of primarily media-driven bias is reinforced by the fact that a review of cases with charges similar to Noe's in the past few decades shows much lighter charges, much shorter sentences, and much less time served. In fact, it appears that similar cases have typically been taken to civil rather than criminal court.

Tom Noe is a political prisoner, and the circumstances that have left him incarcerated are still very much present. Can we prevent more cases like this? Yes, but to know what to do we have to understand what happened to Noe. That is the purpose of *Coingate*.

CONTENTS

Foreword

"Tom Noe got 18 years in prison. I don't know the details, but I do know that, even if he was guilty of the crimes he was charged with, the sentence is wildly inappropriate. I think he's a political prisoner."

I'd asked a casual question about a mutual acquaintance, but the answer was totally serious, and it came from an expert in law. I was shocked. Not only didn't I think America had or could have political prisoners, I didn't think it was possible for a legal system full of checks and balances to allow prison sentences that violated clear and well-established norms.

Really, all I knew was that Noe, a rare coin expert/dealer and active member of the Ohio Republican party, had managed an investment for a state agency and had been accused of something – theft, I thought. The affair generated a lot of press in the state. But this had been probably the busiest time of my professional life and I'd read only headlines. And then I moved to another state and didn't hear more except for short comments from friends I had worked with at the Ohio Board of Regents, where Noe had been a board member.

That was about seven years ago. I thought about looking into the issue, but was extremely busy with both writing and a regular day job. Several years, a few books, and a retirement later, I inquired through a mutual acquaintance if Noe would cooperate on a book about his case. Because the appeals were still going on, the answer was "not now." Finally, about a year ago and following the completion of another project, I asked again and the answer was "yes."

I should emphasize that my interest in the book project wasn't in any way partisan. I come from a family of "rock ribbed" Ohio Republicans, but my family and I parted ways with the GOP when Nixon executed the Southern Strategy. My centrist views are largely unchanged since I first voted, but the Republicans have moved so far right I'm now a registered Democrat.

In my first communication with Noe, I explained that I was starting from the premise that his sentence was extreme – that's what would make a book interesting and possibly important. But I emphasized that I didn't know the details and might change my opinion. Once I knew more I could very well decide that severe punishment was appropriate and the sentence was fair. In any case, while the book would attempt to accurately reflect the views of all involved parties, it would also present my unfettered conclusions. Noe agreed, without hesitation, and I began to work.

My initial reading led me to believe that there had been significant theft. But that was based entirely on reading newspapers, and historians are taught to go to original sources whenever possible. So, I learned how to get digital access to the court documents in Lucas County, Ohio. Then, Noe's current lawyer, Rick Kerger, sent me a CD copy of the transcripts. And I found other sources, mostly online, that provided key documents such as Noe's contract with the Ohio Bureau of Workers Compensation,, audits, and more.

After a few more months of work (there was a three month hiatus while I was out of the country), I realized I had been completely wrong: the checks and balances in our legal system aren't sufficient to keep sentences from violating basic norms of fairness. And the whole process of developing and presenting criminal charges has the potential for severe abuse.

It's entirely clear that a "non-political Noe," someone of no prominence and of no interest to the local media and therefore to politicians, would have been treated very differently in the justice system. The legal expert was entirely right in describing Tom Noe as a political prisoner.

America can and must do better. That's the message of *Coingate*.

Introduction: A Search Warrant That Violates American Values

It was well past midnight, and the watchers in the carefully parked car were settling in for a long surveillance when one of them saw movement at the edge of the building just across. Someone was coming out! The watchers leaned forward. Two men! And they were carrying boxes that they loaded into a nearby car!

The watchers thought it possible that the men across the parking lot were committing a criminal act – perhaps removing either key records or valuable coins or both.

One of the surveillance team's members was an officer in the highway patrol, but there was no effort to make an arrest. The watchers didn't want to prevent a crime. That wasn't their job. Instead, their role was simply to help provide the details for a search warrant.

A judge signed the warrant the next afternoon, and a raid on the targeted building occurred later in the day.

Search warrants require reasons, and judges rely on law enforcement to provide accurate information to support those reasons. However, in this case, in the story that became known in Ohio and nationally as Coingate, there was no reasonable basis to believe a crime had been committed, with the result that essentially every piece of evidence used to justify the warrant was false or misleading.

There's no disagreement that the state had a right to get materials and records from the business in the targeted building, and a handover had been agreed to and was in process. But a quiet transfer wasn't enough; the authorities wanted something dramatic and visible.

The search warrant was falsely contrived and hastily submitted because an array of Ohio government agencies was in a panic, frantically rushing to do something – *anything* that looked stern and serious – in response to a series of newspaper articles that alleged criminal actions on the part of Thomas Noe, the owner of the business that was eventually raided.

The search warrant turned out to be technically within the law – it was subsequently approved by other judges. But the story that became Coingate shows that law and fairness can go in differing directions.

The concept of fairness is so basic with respect to criminal acts that it's hard to define "fairness" without using "fair;" it's one of those things where people's first reaction is to say they know it when they see it.

Essentially, fairness describes a process that results in an outcome that is morally appropriate.

Morality is culturally determined, with religion being an important part of culture. In America, the cultural background is that of what we call Western Civilization, which itself rests strongly on Judeo-Christian principles.

The central tenet of fairness is that people receive punishment only if they are guilty and that any punishment imposed fits the crime. One of the seminal thinkers in the area of law and crime, the Enlightenment philosopher Cesare Beccaria, argues that the purpose of criminal punishment is maintenance of the social contract, and that punishment should never be about vengeance.[1]

The idea that someone could be punished for a crime they didn't commit is anathema to Western Civilization. This wasn't always true, as in the past many nations reserved this element of fairness only for the wealthy and powerful. The idea of embedding fairness in a nation's legal structure in order to protect *all* persons from arbitrary decisions or punishments is an American contribution to Western philosophy. We call it a just society. Our "justice system" is the organizational apparatus that is designed to implement fairness.

In effect, law and the legal system are organizational constructs designed to ensure fairness. From the American point of view, if the legal process isn't fair, justice isn't done.

It's obvious that in a kinetic, complicated world, law and fairness can get out of sync and a just outcome might be difficult to achieve. Some cultures accept that as inevitable. But Americans, perhaps because we were the first to connect law and fairness for all people, don't accept that. We believe that the legal system should never be allowed to be unfair, and consider that the people in the justice system have a moral as well as a legal responsibility to consistently strive to keep the two in harmony.

Giving a major part of the responsibility for fairness to members of the justice system is particularly important because our approach to law allows key players in the system a wide level of discretion.

The idea of fairness is embedded in our understanding of the word "judge." And, because of the intrinsic connection of law and fairness, the same should be true of prosecutors. Thus, a prosecutor's natural desire to have a strong record of success shouldn't allow him or her to bring biased or unbalanced charges, nor does fairness condone prosecutors presenting evidence in a misleading way, one that bends the outcome in a direction that violates justice.

The expectation for prosecutors to avoid any manipulation of charges or evidence most definitely includes keeping the law separate from politics. This is as important a principle as there is. If we allow the law to be used for political ends, we are directly undermining the fairness/justice duality that distinguishes our society.

Simply stated, justice exists only when the legal process operates with consistent fairness.

Given our strong and well-crafted legal structure and direct assignment of key responsibilities for fairness to officials in the system, how could things have gone awry in Noe's case?

The story goes like this:

First, a slew of newspaper stories that alleged criminal activity – without explicitly saying that – landed with extra power because they were dropped into the superheated partisan political environment of a fiercely contested region of a fiercely contested state.

Next, the intense partisan environment and media-fueled public outcry caused some officials to push for, and others to eventually file, charges that were out of all proportion to any reasonable, dispassionate analysis of the events.

Finally, because it too was influenced by the partisan fury and public anger, the legal system failed to correct the initial errors.

Put simply, a powerful and unbalanced media thrust caused politicians to panic and push the legal system to operate in a deeply distorted way. The result was not intentional in the sense that people set out to violate law or fairness. Rather, normally responsible and thoughtful people acted in ways they would never have done in different circumstances. It's doubtful that any of the official players in Coingate acted deliberately to pervert justice; instead, their actions can be explained by the kinds of unconscious rationalizations to which all people are prey.

But the consequences of unconscious bias are the same as those of its conscious counterpart. And, in this case, the sum of many people's rationalizations was the unjustified loss of one person's freedom.

But how can our elaborate and carefully crafted judicial structure allow this to happen?

Ordinary people believe that the US legal system works much like a computer – once received, inputs are processed smoothly and consistently according to well defined rules. And, should a mistake be made at an early level, there are additional computers, in the form of appeals courts, that will make sure the final product is what it should be.

Of course, a large part of the public does believe that juries make mistakes, that if the machine has a flaw, it's that people selected as jurors aren't always truly impartial. The recently rehashed OJ Simpson murder trial is one of the most flagrant examples. Critics of the Simpson verdict generally consider that the jurors suffered from a bias, likely an unconscious one connected to race, that caused them to overlook important information and as a result arrive at a not guilty verdict.

There is, in fact, strong evidence from social science research showing that juries can be biased in a number of ways, and research in this area will be an important topic in this book. But prosecutors and judges are people who are subject to the same biases – even if they're absolutely confident they can be completely impartial. That's especially important when you consider something that most people not connected with the law don't know: prosecutors and judges have much the same kind of discretion juries do. Jurors (in some cases) make the final decision on guilt or innocence, but the prosecutors and the judge can frame charges and focus or limit evidence in such a way that the jurors' own scope of action is in fact quite limited. And, depending on the nature of the decisions taken by prosecutors and judges, much of what they do is not appealable or very unlikely to be overturned on appeal.

Coingate isn't a traditional crime and justice story. There's no suspense about who did what and the audience starts with knowledge of what ultimately happened to all the key players.

But Coingate is a mystery of a different kind. This book asks essential questions about how justice is carried out: How is it possible that there could be a gross violation of fundamental fairness without anyone in the justice system committing violations of law or of formal ethical standards? How is it possible that actions that in most cases would have resulted in no more than a civil lawsuit could have instead led to an eighteen-year prison term – with no reasonable expectation of early release? How is it possible that extreme partisan strife could have as a consequence partisan agreement – with one man as a joint target? We'll see that the questions are easy to state but the answers are complex. And we'll also learn that the situations and structures that allowed for this extreme violation of American principles of fairness are still present and available for future use – most likely in other political situations. Until the conditions that created Coingate are resolved, every citizen has something to fear. For Americans, respect for the law most explicitly doesn't mean respect for authority. Rather, it's respect for fairness. If we undermine fairness, we lose respect for law and in consequence threaten the foundations of our democracy.

NB

- This book's website (http://coingate-ohio.blogspot.com/) provides important contextual information about the author, including perspective on *his* potential biases and how they have been dealt with. The site also includes more in-depth information on technical aspects (such as the Coin Fund contracts), and also includes links to a variety of source documents.
- Conventions in the book include: 1) *m* following an endnote mark indicates that the reference contains informational text; 2) since URLs in the references will not be easily usable by readers of the hard copy, the full reference list has been copied to the website.
- Appendix C contains a list of names of key players and organizations with identifying information.

Garrison Walters

Introduction to the Express Section

The main text of *Coingate* was written by an academic in an academic style. There are detailed descriptions of issues, including legal ones, and extensive documentation of arguments. Where possible, the reader is given unfiltered access to the words of the prosecutors, the *Blade*, judges, Noe's lawyers, Noe himself, and others. For those who want to dig even deeper, there are extensive references in the form of endnotes.

Given that many will not have the time to read this core work, the Express Section is principally limited to facts and conclusions. Readers with questions have easy access to more depth in the main text or in the references (including those on the book's website).

NB For various technical reasons, the Express Section chapters don't completely align with those in the main text. Connections should be easy to find, however.

Express Chapter 1- The Roots of Coingate

THE OHIO CONTEXT

Sometime around 1990, Northwest Ohio became a political cauldron. The region had always been divided, with the primarily blue-collar, union, Catholic and Democratic city of Toledo surrounded by an array of towns that were primarily small business, Protestant, agrarian and Republican.

But the decline of traditional manufacturing in Toledo changed the equation. Hard-working families that had for generations relied on manufacturing-related employment suddenly found that the good jobs were gone.

The Democrats advocated for job training and similar programs but didn't seem to have a clear idea how to respond to the massive employment collapse. The Republicans, confident and assertive, argued that their policies would revive economic growth, primarily by lowering taxes.

In fact, it's hard to say that either side had an answer. Each party controlled both state and national government for extended periods of time, but manufacturing in the region never fully revived and population growth effectively stopped. If Ohio had grown at just the national average from 1970 to 1990, it would have had an additional two million people vs. losing 50,000.

During the 1990s, Tom Noe, whose confident and outgoing personality matched that of his party, became a key Republican leader. Noe and his wife, Bernadette, had a central role in changing the political structure of Toledo's home county, Lucas, from one where offices routinely fell to Democratic nominees by default to one where most elections were hard fought and where Republicans often won.

National elections were an important part of the equation. Although Lucas County still voted primarily for the Democratic candidate, lowering that margin could help swing Ohio, a key pivot point in national elections where the difference between the two parties was almost always small.

The Presidential election of 2004 was an especially bitter one in Northwest Ohio and the Noes were at the center. Bernadette Noe, then head of the county Board of Elections, was heavily attacked for the board's failures to keep polling sites functioning efficiently, especially in Democratic areas. Tom Noe sharply criticized the University of Toledo's decision to allow George Soros, an outspoken advocate of John Kerry, to speak in the days before the election. Noe was then in turn harshly attacked by the local newspaper, *The Blade*, which supported Kerry.

The mood in the region became even angrier after the election as George W. Bush's poll numbers sank in the face of continued problems in Iraq and other areas. Many independents and even some Republicans felt a kind of "buyer's remorse" and vented their anger at Bush's supporters. Tensions built as both parties saw the 2006 election as a pivotal one for the state, with Republicans fearing they would lose not only the governorship but also the heavily gerrymandered legislature where they controlled both houses.

THE *BLADE*

Toledo's newspaper, the *Blade*, had (and has) an outsized role in local politics. It was the only significant newspaper and maintained an agreement with one of the local television stations for news. However, because the *Blade* was the only entity with staff who had the time and training to investigate, effectively all of the electronic media relied on it for stories that had any depth. The *Blade's* dominant role in regional news continues today.

In fact, the *Blade* has a strong record of accomplishment in investigative journalism, winning the Pulitzer in 2004 and often earning accolades for its reporting in other areas. Considered in perspective, these national recognitions are remarkable achievements for a small city newspaper.

Politically, the *Blade* had traditionally supported Democrats, but as the economic situation in the region changed, John Robinson Block, the co-publisher and effective editor, increasingly supported Republicans as well. Block was a fierce and sometimes prescient advocate for the region and was willing to work both sides of the political aisle to get leaders in the state capital of Columbus to provide the assistance he thought the region deserved.

Despite the bipartisanship, it was clear to all, especially after the Soros episode, that Block strongly disliked Tom Noe and was eager to challenge him personally.

Coingate

TOM NOE

Noe, born in 1954, grew up in a Catholic family in Bowling Green, a university town south of Toledo. He became a nominal Republican as a teenager, primarily as the result of a personal friendship.

Noe was interested in coin collecting from his teenage years and worked part-time at a collectors' shop in Toledo. He was doing so well there that he dropped out of college after a year and joined a national firm, working for it and various other businesses in South Carolina, New York, Miami, and Boston before returning to Toledo in 1981 to start his own business.

It's notable that Noe worked two stints in the 1970s -- with a couple years' leave in-between while he and a partner tried dealing coins on their own -- with what is today the largest and one of the most trusted rare coin firms in America. When Noe left that business and, as far as I can tell every other coin company he has ever worked for – he was on very good terms with its management. Indeed, even after his conviction, Noe's previous employers and coworkers have almost without exception continued to vouch for his integrity.

Of the many people who knew Tom Noe growing up, it's unlikely that any would have expected him to encounter the kind of adversity he faces now. Noe was originally known outside his immediate circle of family and friends for his work in charity. His parents, though living at the working class level of "just getting by," were active donors to Catholic schools and other charities. Noe recalls that money other families might have used for such luxuries as vacations were instead donated.

Once Noe was somewhat established in business, he and his wife gave generously to various charities and Tom took on the role of leading a school fundraising drive. This central role in charity continued until the world around him came crashing down, and critics have charged that his charity took the form of giving away other people's money. In fact, though, Noe's charitable leadership long predated any involvement with state funds – or politics.

It was a friendship with a neighbor, a senior person in the Lucas County Republican Party, that turned Noe's casual political affiliation into a serious one. His interest in political activity was cemented by an effort to get Ohio to follow neighboring states and allow a sales tax exemption for coin trading. This work extended his connections to the state level.

Noe became chair of the Lucas County Republican party in 1992 and was instrumental in finding candidates, raising money, and developing opposition research against Democrats. Though others had important roles, Noe and his wife Bernadette (a former Democrat whom he married in the 1990s and who also served as Republican party chairman) were seen as principal drivers of the party's local growth.

Politics is of course an activity that normally makes enemies of

9

opponents. Ironically, it isn't usually seen as an area where you make real friends on your own side either. This is evidenced by the popular saying in the nation's capital, "if you want a friend in Washington, get yourself a dog." In fact, the Noes' partisan energy certainly did make some enemies (including among Republicans), but Tom also made and retains a great many friends from politics. Among those who continue to support him to this day are quite a few Democrats.

THE COIN DEAL

Noe had been interested since the 1980s in developing a mutual fund-like investment vehicle for rare coins.

An important dimension of Coingate was that many people consider that items such as rare coins can't be serious investments. In reality, though, the value of everything is determined not by abstract criteria but by individuals' choices. And individuals have long considered rare items such as art and coins to have special value, with the result that there is a constant market for rare coins, one that includes frequent trading. Given the persistent viability of the market, the challenge for a mutual-fund like effort has been more in structuring and organizing than in advertising.

Noe's idea of a mutual fund-like investment wasn't original – there were several active funds in the 1990s – but his approach was unique. The plan was to have the managers – people like Noe who would buy and sell – benefit in the same way as the investors, which is to say only when profits were made rather than through fees for the recovery of operating costs. As a result, managers had the same interest in success as investors. In fact, their interest would be even stronger because the managers couldn't recover their own operating costs until profits were made – in this respect the managers would be taking more risk than the investors.

Noe tried to sell his fund idea to a number of organizations, but wasn't successful until the late 1990s when the State of Ohio's Bureau of Workers' Compensation (OBWC) deemed the fund eligible for its new "emerging managers" program and agreed to put in $25 million. The OBWC, which had some $16-18 billion under management, saw the fund, known as Capitol Coin Fund I, as a hedge against its traditional stock and bond trading.

The OBWC had a competition under the emerging managers program and proposals were reviewed and approved in public meetings. Noe's prospectus was notable in emphasizing that, while an investment in coins had considerable potential, there was also considerable risk. The prospectus stressed that this type of investment was not a good choice for those needing liquidity. In fact, the fund was to run for eleven years (1998-2009), with principal not returned until the end. The coin fund was like a mutual fund in that the investors didn't directly own any coins; rather, they (OBWC) owned a share of the overall fund's value and therefore a share of the profits (or loss).

However, the provision preventing withdrawal at any time made it more like a hedge fund. Profits could be distributed annually or earlier in smaller amounts but entirely at the discretion of the managers.

Noe had a contract written by his lawyer and the OBWC largely accepted it. Some of the provisions later became highly controversial. Notably, Noe (and his partner "manager" in this initial fund, another coin dealer named Frank Greenberg), had the right to take loans from the fund as well as advances on profits. They were also allowed to self-deal, i.e., their own businesses could buy and sell to the coin fund. There was also an odd provision that gave the managers three years to repay an advance on profits if the advance was taken "knowingly in violation" of the contract.

Noe explains the "loans and advances" section as essential to the intended role, which was to make cash available not just to the "managers" but also to other partners who could compete more effectively if they had resources available; in some cases, the coin fund managers acted as bankers in support of other traders' deals. The self-dealing provision was designed to prevent a situation in which coin fund monies could be lent to other businesses but not to Noe and Greenberg's own companies. The two managers were concerned that they would lose their own customer base and be non-competitive once the fund had expired.

The fund initially did well, transferring a profit of nearly $8 million to the state in the first seven years. As a result, OBWC invested another $25 million in 2002. There were some problems, however. An internal auditor at the OBWC objected to the fact that OBWC did not have access to an independently audited list of coin fund inventory. The reason for this, provided in the contract, was that competitors could access the inventory records, including prices paid, by making a public records request to the OBWC. This would give potential buyers an unfair advantage – businesses of all kinds avoid disclosing what they pay for something they are selling, since buyers are likely to use that as leverage to get a lower price.

The internal audit also objected to the coin fund's ownership of non-coin assets: notably "collectibles" (such as sports and political memorabilia) and real estate. This too was permitted in the contract and allowed because Noe wanted to be able to invest money productively when the coin market was slow.

Negotiations between Noe and Greenberg and the OBWC led to a compromise that included external auditing of inventory, and allowed the OBWC to keep copies of the inventory but label them as trade secrets so they wouldn't be subject to public records inquiries. Importantly, however, the key provisions of the contract –allowability of collectibles, self-dealing, three years to repay if "knowingly in violation," and the ability to take loans and advances

— were all reaffirmed in 2001.

Express Chapter 2- Coingate Erupts

Although the OBWC coin fund investments with Noe were approved in open meetings and operated successfully for some seven years, the fact of an OBWC deal with Noe wasn't well known until the *Blade* published an article on the arrangement in early April of 2005.

THE *BLADE* ATTACK ON NOE

The *Blade's* initial articles on Noe and the coin funds, beginning on April 7, weren't hatchet jobs but did convey a deep skepticism about the validity of the type of investment and about whether Noe's deal was political rather than truly competitive.

The *Blade* reinforced its skepticism in two ways. First, it regularly implied that the OBWC had become a coin collector, even though the Bureau had purchased shares in a trading company and didn't own a single coin. Second, the *Blade* focused on several trading problems that Noe had reported to the OBWC. One was the fact that a trader who had been loaned money had lost some $800,000. Another was a dispute between Noe and an affiliate in Colorado that involved some stolen coins and also possible fraudulent behavior.

While the facts of the *Blade's* articles weren't alarming, the tone was. The persistent suggestion was that some unknown Republican appointee had given Noe a vast amount of money to play with and that it had been mismanaged – and possibly lost.

The *Blade* articles quickly became fodder for politicians. Democrats seized on the insinuations in the articles to proclaim that cronyism amongst Republicans in Columbus was costing the state millions and, in what became a favorite phrase, "harming injured workers." Prodded by legislators, the state's Inspector General announced an investigation.

The Republican governor, Bob Taft, initially defended Noe by pointing out that the OBWC investment had earned nearly $8 million in profit to date.

Although the *Blade* offered no substantive evidence that the coin funds were in trouble, the unremitting wave of suspicion the paper unleashed caused the attorney general (AG) to file suit to have the funds closed and monies returned to the OBWC as soon as possible.

After some weeks of turmoil, Noe, realizing that the pressure wasn't going to go away, agreed to close the funds and told his attorneys to negotiate an orderly closure. Noe's concern, initially shared by the AG and the OBWC, was that liquidation of the funds should occur over a period of time, probably on the order of a year, so that the funds' assets could be sold in a regular market rather than dumped at fire sale prices.

The tide turned against this rational plan with two facts. First, it became known that the FBI was investigating Noe for campaign finance violations – specifically for giving money to others to give to the Bush presidential campaign. Noe had already donated the maximum amount for an individual but wanted to be a Pioneer, someone who gives and raises $100,000.

The federal charges against Noe had the effect of turning his own party against him. Republican leaders realized he would be convicted at some point and wanted him off the radar well before the November, 2006 elections. In addition, the Republican Attorney General, who was in a fierce primary fight for his party's gubernatorial nomination, realized that appearing to be weak in investigating members of his own party would make him vulnerable in the primary as well as the general election.

The second fact changing the initial rational plan to close out the funds was that the *Blade,* which had never ceased publishing critical articles on Noe and the coin funds, ratcheted up the pressure by sending a reporter to California to interview the trader who had lost $800,000 earlier. The thrust of the story was that the man, who had a previous felony charge and had served a prison sentence, was dishonest and unstable and that this was the kind of person who Noe was dealing with in investing state money. Nothing of importance in the story was actually new but, taken together with some earlier stories on the coin fund affiliate in Colorado, it was clear that the *Blade* wasn't going to let the Noe issue go. In fact, the story concluded with a quote from a Democrat mocking the Republican AG for inaction in what had now become known as "Coingate."

The news of the federal investigation appeared on April 27 and the *Blade* story on the trader in California was published on May 22nd.

The next day, Monday, the AG's office tossed the agreed-upon schedule for completing an inventory of the coin funds' assets and insisted the process begin immediately. Noe's lawyers, including a criminal team he had hired a few days earlier, agreed and a schedule was established that would allow Noe's attorneys to be present at the four sites around the country where coins and collectibles were held.

But, even as an agreement was reached and lawyers dispersed to the various locations to oversee the audits, the AG, still facing withering media pressure and criticism from Democrats and his primary opponent, abandoned the new agreement and insisted that state investigators have immediate access to Noe's Maumee, Ohio (Toledo area) business, Vintage Coins and Collectibles (VCC). Noe's lawyers did their best to accommodate but, because Noe's assistant hadn't yet completed an updated coin inventory for Maumee, the lawyers allowed investigators access only to collectibles until the inventory list was finished – requiring at most a few days. This action generated stories of Noe "refusing access" to state investigators.

THE SEARCH WARRANT

At some point in mid-May various public entities interested in the coin funds created an informal "State Task Force" (STF) to coordinate their work. Members included the offices of the AG, the Inspector General (IG), the OBWC, federal prosecutors from northern and southern Ohio, the state highway patrol, and prosecutors from Lucas and Franklin Counties (Toledo and Columbus).

The STF decided to have the highway patrol organize surveillance of Noe's business and shortly afterward, officers reported late night activity – including people removing boxes. This activity was described as highly suspicious. In fact, the boxes were part of a regularly scheduled auction run by a neighboring business, but the investigators hadn't investigated enough to know that.

Information from the surveillance, together with the inability to secure immediate access to the coin inventory, caused the STF to prepare a search warrant which was presented to and authorized by a judge on the morning of Thursday, May 26.

With the warrant in hand, a large team of state law enforcement officials raided Noe's VCC office in Maumee. The resulting media event included a photo-op for the Inspector General who was shown carrying a box out of the store. What wasn't shown and reported was the fact that the law enforcement swarm actually stopped the work of other state investigators who had been admitted that morning and who were in the process of inventorying coins. In fact, at the time when the STF members told the judge a warrant was urgently needed, they knew that investigators had been admitted and that the inventory they were pushing to begin was already taking place.

Express Chapter 3- Aftermath of the Search Warrant

The search warrant added as justification a statement attributed to Noe's new lawyer, William Wilkinson of the major national firm Thompson Hine, to the effect that there might be a "shortfall" of $10-$13 million in the coin funds. Wilkinson, who had been at work for only a few days and who had spoken only briefly with Noe, appears to have been referring to Noe's statement to him that *value* on the scale of $10-13 million could be lost if the state seized the inventory and sold it off quickly rather than in a strategic manner as had been agreed. As it happened, because the AG appeared to be panicking under intense media pressure to act decisively, a fire sale now seemed a real possibility.

But, because Wilkinson wasn't clear whether he meant loss in value or something more serious, the STF was acting within reason by interpreting it as referring to theft. This view was reinforced in the coming days by two factors: 1) the inventory did in fact show a disparity of more than $10 million between coins listed as in inventory and coins actually present at VCC in Maumee; and 2) Noe's legal team failed to explain either the inventory problem or the shortfall statement but simply waited for criminal charges to appear.

In fact, as will be explained later, Noe was justified in that he had used his contractual right to take loans and advances from the coin funds and had left a clear and publicly accessible record of his debt. But he was also unjustified in that he had tampered with the records to hide these borrowings from the OBWC in the short-term. Noe was willing to admit and explain from the outset, but the defense lawyers successfully convinced him not to.

Express Chapter 4- From Search Warrant to Indictment

With his shop closed and records and inventory in the hands of prosecutors, Tom Noe was effectively out of work at the beginning of June, 2005. Although it was obvious that charges were coming, the state didn't issue an indictment until nearly eight months later, in February of 2006. Even so, Noe remained very much in the news.

ETHICS IN THE HEADLINES

The *Blade*'s investigation into Coingate opened up an array of ethics problems in state government. It turned out that Governor Taft had accepted and failed to report a number of minor gifts, such as rounds of golf, from various people, including Tom Noe. Taft's problem was one of poor staff support, since he obviously neither needed or wanted the gifts, but there were other more serious issues. Notably, Noe had provided gifts in the form of meals to a number of Taft's staff and also provided cash loans to some former advisors who still had government appointments. All of these gifts were unreported in ethics filings, a clear violation of the law. It was the responsibility of the recipients and not Noe to report these gifts, but he should have known that these people were unlikely to face the public scrutiny that would come with reporting. Most serious of all, Noe had also used some of these former staff to funnel illegal campaign contributions, notably to candidates for the Ohio Supreme Court and to the 2004 Bush campaign.

During this time it was revealed that an investment manager at the OBWC had solicited bribes from some of those seeking to do business with the Bureau. The manager was fired and criminally charged. Finally, the OBWC belatedly acknowledged that another one of its "emerging managers" funds had lost nearly $215 million. The head of the OBWC was then quickly forced to resign.

POLITICAL ATTACKS

The advent of the primary season put Noe in the crosshairs. Democrats were continuing to use Noe as the poster child for what they described as a deeply corrupt Republican establishment. Republican leaders responded by trying to outdo the Democrats in disparaging their former activist. Both Governor Taft and the head of the Ohio Republican Party levelled harsh attacks on Noe, as did others such as those competing in the primaries for senior offices. It was common in media stories and in advertising for challengers to attack incumbents for not having done enough to find and punish Noe's crimes.

BLADE STORIES

The *Blade* used the hiatus between the search warrant and indictment to even more actively attack Noe. While the earliest stories, notably those from April of 2005, had offered some balance, there was little pretense of neutrality in *Blade* stories after mid-May of that year.

One persistent theme was that of problems with Noe's affiliate in Colorado. A long skein of stories in the summer of 2005 regularly suggested deep criminal activity, though none was ever discovered. As an example of the bias, the *Blade* repeatedly stated that Noe had not reported to law enforcement the theft of some coins. But there was good reason for this: the affiliate had reported to the appropriate authority, the local sheriff, Noe had reported to the OBWC, and the coins were in any case insured. Another theme was that Noe hadn't reported some missing coins as stolen. Again, there was a reason for this, since the coins weren't really missing but inaccurately inventoried.

A particularly striking example of anti-Noe spin came after the appearance of an anonymous letter suggesting that Noe had an illegal account in the Cayman Islands. While the federal prosecutors refused to talk to the *Blade* about an anonymous and probably fake communication, the Lucas County Prosecutor, Julia Bates, agreed to discuss it and therefore made possible a long, accusatory story.

Mrs. Bates, as it turned out, had numerous conflicts in her role as prosecutor in Noe's case: she was an elected Democrat, her husband was a judge against whom Noe had worked very actively, and her daughter-in-law and son-in-law were reporters for the *Blade*. As will be shown later, research in psychology suggests that these factors made her a very poor choice to prosecute Noe's case.

In addition to the Coingate misstatements, the *Blade* published an editorial on the Cayman Islands allegations. Few who read the various stories are likely to have doubted that Noe had an offshore account. This would be true even after the paper reportedly printed a deeply-buried retraction.

Finally, in December, when Noe's lawyers made their first attempt at a public defense by holding a press conference where they argued that the coin funds would wind up showing a profit, the resulting *Blade* story was, by comparison both to other stories and to what was presented, incomplete and one-sided. The paper followed with a scathing editorial which mocked the idea that the funds could have made a profit.

Express Chapter 5- Indictment and Audit

Sometime in the June 2005 to February 2006 time frame the State Task Force (STF) decided that Noe would face charges in the Lucas County Court of Common Pleas. This decision came despite the fact that similar cases were being tried in federal court and the obvious fact that an equally possible venue, the state capital in Columbus, would have been far less affected by local media and local political conflict.

The indictment, a mostly unintelligible document, specifies 53 counts: eleven of theft (one of which was the RICO (short for Racketeer Influenced and Corrupt Organizations Act) charge — see below); eleven of money laundering; eight of tampering with records; and twenty-two counts of forgery.

In Ohio's odd legal code, the money laundering charges are simply for spending money gained from theft (a kind of double jeopardy). The forgery relates to Noe signing other people's names when writing checks to move money from his business to himself — no outsider was harmed by this, but it may have allowed Noe to secure a tax advantage (though he wasn't charged with that).

The key to the indictment was the audit and here the STF also had a critical role.

THE AUDIT

The Auditor of State's June, 2005 charge to the external auditor, Crowe Chizek of Chicago, to:

- Participate in the identification and accounting of coin fund assets which, in addition to rare coins, may include collectibles, accounts receivable, agreements relating to real property, and other contracts. Further investigate discrepancies noted.
- Review transactions and agreements relating to CCF. Transactions reviewed

may include, but not be limited to, OBWC capital contributions, asset purchases and sales, and payments for administrative fees. Determine whether discrepancies exist relating to these transactions and agreements.

- Identify any discrepancy between the value of the CCF's assets and the approximately $55.4 million principal investment made by the OBWC.

In the circumstances, this charge was reasonable in both scope and specificity. What's remarkable, however, is that the Crowe report made public in February of 2006 ignored almost all of the Auditor's charge.

Specifically, looking at the first bullet, the special audit reported on some coin-related transactions but not all or even most of them, incorrectly described the legal status of collectibles, and did not at all look at accounts receivable, real property, and other contracts.

With respect to the second bullet, the special audit described only a slice of asset purchases and sales and ignored payments for administrative fees.

The third bullet, requiring the accountant to look at "any discrepancy between the value of the CCF's assets and the principal investment made by the OBWC," was entirely ignored in the report.

One would expect that a client who requested an audit with careful and specific language would be angry when it received such a small part of what it asked for. But that wasn't the case here. Indeed, the client was delighted because, quietly and behind the scenes, the STF had told the auditor to slice down the scope of the audit to limit its focus to a single thing – supporting a criminal case against Tom Noe.

What Crowe did find within the narrow limits of its revised charge was this:

1) There were numerous cases, involving both of the coin funds, where the books showed that Noe's business, VCC, had sold a coin to a coin fund but where records indicated that VCC did not actually possess the coin it claimed to have sold. Crowe described these as "unsupported inventory purchases" (UIPs). The total of the UIPs came to about $12 million.

2) Crowe then analyzed Noe and his business's books and asserted that deposits based on UIPs had been the basis of checks Noe wrote to cover business and personal expenses. This analysis, which Crowe called "use of cash," notably failed to account for the value of other deposits that were not based on UIPs. The "use of cash" approach as employed in this audit has no visible status as a standard in the accounting profession and appears to have been suggested by the prosecutors so they could argue that OBWC money went to Noe's personal use – and this argument was in fact central to the prosecution's case at trial.

The methodology used by the various auditors to get to the total amount of UIPs is questionable – in many cases conclusions were based on weak and unsupported assumptions. Even so, the general conclusion was sound: Noe had been recording sales from his business to the coin funds that didn't have actual coins behind them.

NOE'S EXPLANATIONS

Noe's lawyers denied the charges in the indictment but offered no alternative explanation of what happened. This is in keeping with a standard legal strategy of not admitting anything, but it appears to have been ultimately devastating in Noe's case.

Years later, after the appeals and when Noe's new counsel agreed that he could speak, he acknowledged that he had tampered with records.

Noe had originally expected a fund of $5 to $10 million, but like most people in that situation agreed he could handle $25 million when it was offered. This was a big mistake, both because of the difficulty of finding sufficient investments in a then-slow coin market and because the daily cost of managing so much money was much higher than anticipated.

Facing higher costs, Noe couldn't wait for profits to help pay his expenses, so used the "loans and advances" clause in the contract to take money. He agreed that these had taken the form of "unsupported inventory purchases," in which he claimed that his business had sold coins to the coin funds but in fact actually hadn't. The reason for the dissimulation was the fear that a lot of borrowing would alarm OBWC overseers.

Noe also agrees that, because this was an exceptionally busy time in his personal, charitable, and political life, he failed to pay as much attention as he should have to the business. In particular, he failed to replace his old, small-business and personal memory-based approach to accounting with an accounting system that could manage increased volume. He also agrees that some OBWC money, though he thinks not a lot, served to temporarily cover some of his personal expenses.

But Noe strongly denies the theft charges. His right to take loans and advances was not just in the contract but had been reaffirmed by the internal audit discussions at OBWC. Also, while the records sent to OBWC did disguise the loans and advances, the fact is that his debt was in no way hidden. As manager of the funds, he was clearly shown in the books as holding certain coins, and would have had to provide them or the cash equivalent when the funds were closed. And, Noe asserts, he would have been able to make available all of the money to cover the missing coins if given a chance to wind down the coin funds in a reasonable manner.

Noe was ready from the outset to acknowledge his mistakes and specifically the illegal tampering with records, but neither the public nor a jury ever heard this acceptance or the accompanying explanations.

Express Chapter 6- Pre-Trial Issues

The Republican judges in the Lucas County court system all recused themselves, so the random assignment system selected only from Democrats. Judge Thomas Osowik, an experienced and well-regarded jurist, was put in charge of Noe's case.

DISQUALIFICATION OF JUDGES

The first major filing from Noe's defense asked that Osowik and all Lucas County judges be forced to recuse themselves. The long affidavit provided extensive evidence of Noe's actions on behalf of Republican judges and against Democrats – including the filing of an ethics charge against Osowik personally.

The decision on the filing was made by the Chief Justice of the Ohio Supreme Court, who quickly rejected it by arguing that the situation wasn't that serious and that disqualification would set a bad precedent. All that mattered, the Chief Justice said, was whether Osowik was willing to say he could be fair. Since he'd said he could, there was nothing to discuss.

The *Blade* was strongly opposed to disqualification of Osowik, even going so far as to mock the idea. Amazingly, however, a somewhat later editorial effectively supported both the argument for recusal as well as that for change of venue (see below) by noting that, because public opinion was hostile to Noe and because he was facing a major electoral battle, Judge Osowik would likely take these factors into account when making a decision about the trial date.

With equal irony, the *Blade* not long afterward supported the use of a visiting judge and prosecutor in another case related to Noe's federal charges — the Blade took one point of view when the accused person was Noe and the opposite perspective when a different person was charged.

CHANGE OF VENUE

The next major filing was one seeking a change of venue. The defense provided evidence of an enormous, negative media onslaught against Noe and cited federal rulings, including the famous Shepard case,[2] that supported a change of venue in similar situations.

The prosecutors responded that all that was necessary was for the voir dire, the process of selecting jurors, to winnow out those with bias and find the requisite number of jurors who were willing to say they could be fair. Judge Osowik agreed.

CHALLENGE TO THE SEARCH WARRANT

The defense challenged the validity of the search warrant, arguing that it contained numerous inaccuracies and some statements that were deliberately false. Wilkinson pointed out that the premise of the warrant -- the need to act fast to secure inventory and records – was simply invalid because access had been agreed by Noe and in fact had already begun. He emphasized that the brief delay was for technical reasons and mainly because the Attorney General had changed his demands several times at the last minute.

Because the legal system gives law enforcement the benefit of the doubt in securing search warrants, the prosecution's defense of its actions was very passive. Instead of defending the validity of the arguments presented to the issuing judge, the prosecution simply argued that their statements met the (very low) legal standard. The strongest assertion by the prosecution was that Wilkinson's "shortfall" statement justified action.

The prosecution, knowing that precedent was on its side, largely ignored the numerous defense points to the effect that the statements in the warrant, including the one about Wilkinson, didn't justify issuing a warrant because law enforcement had already secured access to everything it wanted. Thus, the prosecutors never really answered the key question: why do you need a warrant when you already have or can easily get what the warrant is supposed to give you?

Although he did describe one key part of the warrant as "recklessly false" Judge Osowik, as expected, ruled for the prosecution and all the seized evidence was allowed. This was the right legal conclusion – it was appropriate for the state to have access to the evidence – but the wrong moral one since it was obvious that the only purpose of the warrant was for politicians to show the media that they were taking decisive action. The *Blade* had established Noe as a villain, and wanted something dramatic to prove its point. Public officials were more than willing to supply the requested drama with a televised raid on Noe's business.

The *Blade* story on the ruling didn't report the judge's comment that a part of the search warrant was "recklessly" false.

Another way of understanding the consequences of the search warrant is to consider what would have happened in the case of someone who had no role in politics and was of no interest to the media – just a prominent Toledo businessman who had a contract to invest some OBWC funds. We'll call this person "Non-Political Noe."

Just like the real one, Non-Political Noe (through his lawyers) would have agreed to provide immediate access to the inventory at all sites except, for the same reasons, would also have asked for the short -- few days -- delay in Maumee.

But now there's a difference. Without the *Blade* pressuring the authorities, the state's Inspector General wouldn't have issued a press release announcing an investigation. And the process wouldn't have been personally overseen by the state's Attorney General. There would have been no need for politicians to be seen as decisive. Why would the state's top law enforcement officer be involved in what was to that point a simple civil dispute? People would have seen it as absurd if he'd intervened and there would have been suspicions he was harboring some kind of personal grudge.

Instead, the process would have been left with a civil court judge, and he or she would have found the explanations given by Non-Political Noe to be quite reasonable and allowed the few days of extra time. One reason that a civil court judge would have been amenable to delay is that he or she would have taken the time to read the contract and, unlike the state investigators, would have known that the OBWC was actually seeing assets belonging to the coin fund when its investigators reviewed collectibles as well as coins.[3]

It would have been amazing if, in the case of a Non-Political Noe and the corresponding absence of pressure from the *Blade*, the OBWC had argued against a request for a delay of a few days and pushed instead for a search warrant. The civil court judge would have quickly rejected this idea as unnecessary, noting that the materials could easily be secured by other means. Further, the civil judge might well have held the authorities in contempt when he realized that they knew, but had failed to tell him, that the activity the search warrant was designed to ensure had already begun when the warrant was presented to him.

RICO

The acronym "RICO" stands for "Racketeer Influenced Corrupt Organization" and was created as a legal concept because traditional laws were failing to provide convictions of men, such as members of the New York mafia, who didn't participate directly in criminal activities but caused others to act for them. For example, a mafia chief would organize and profit from loan-sharking, but wouldn't participate directly. RICO statutes, which quickly proliferated from the federal system to the states, were designed to deal with criminals whose persistent activity over a number of years could not easily be prosecuted because of its indirect nature. These statutes, both at the federal and state levels, carried significant penalties for those convicted. The idea was to deal a profound blow to organized crime – and for the most part it worked.

But RICO was not intended to target crimes that were already easily prosecuted under existing law. In Noe's case, he and his assistant Tim LaPointe were accused of theft and related crimes over a number of years. A case like this could easily have been prosecuted without RICO.

But the Lucas County prosecutors described Noe and LaPointe as a "criminal enterprise" and added the RICO charges, which carry a minimum ten-year sentence. Although obviously contrary to the purposes of the law, the statute as written gives prosecutors the discretion to prosecute in this way and Judge Osowik rejected the defense's appeal to have the RICO element dropped.

DISQUALIFICATION OF COUNSEL

The prosecution sought to disqualify Noe's lawyers, primarily because prosecutors said they intended to call Wilkinson to the stand to testify about his "shortfall" comment. Judge Osowik denied the request and Wilkinson was never called (though it seems hardly possible in light of the media coverage that there was a single juror who was not aware of the comment).

Express Chapter 7- The Fairness Scorecard on the Eve of Trial

As emphasized in the main text the principal issue in Coingate isn't the technical legal dimension but the extent to which the law was applied fairly.

THE STRUCTURE OF THE CASE

The deck seemed stacked against Noe long before the trial began. The restricting of the original scope of the audit to just coins and just Noe's Maumee operation (even while invoking RICO) ensured that the jury would never see the whole story of the coin funds and couldn't know that the funds had been successful overall. At the same time, the blizzard of overlapping, vague, and duplicative charges, including the gratuitous RICO charge, ensured that a jury would find it very difficult to separate the serious from the unimportant. Finally. the use of Lucas County courts ensured the continuing presence of strong media, prosecutorial, and judicial bias. It also guaranteed a jury pool deeply affected by a year and a half of *Blade* and other media attacks.

Unlike Noe's original Coin contract which was negotiated in public, Noe's case was structured in secret and, significantly, it appears he was treated differently than others who also made "unsupported inventory purchases." Unfortunately, this concern of disparate treatment can't be entirely verified because records of the decisions are not available and may no longer exist.

THE RULINGS

The rationale used by Ohio Supreme Court for leaving Osowik in charge of Noe's trial has since been strongly rejected by the same court in another case (see below). Using the logic of the later ruling, the decision in Noe's case wasn't merely wrong, it was egregiously so.

The same characterization of egregious error can be made about Osowik's ruling on venue. He relied on his limited personal experience to conclude that jurors would ignore bias if they were willing to say they could. This view is explicitly refuted by extensive research in psychology (see below for more).

THE ROLE OF THE BLADE

The Blade maintained a rough appearance of impartiality for only the first month or so of the Coingate saga. After that, its constant stream of stories made little pretense of showing Noe's perspective or, in many cases, even avoided factual information that might contradict the paper's line of attack. As an example, the twisting of the audit to focus entirely on Noe was an important issue not just for the Noe case but for justice as a whole. The *Columbus Dispatch* picked up on this and tried to get the records of the external auditor (but were denied). This was the kind of story that *Blade* reporters had in the past recognized and dug into. But not in this case. The *Blade* never presented its readers with a critical view of the audit – or the search warrant, or the rulings on disqualification of judges and change of venue.

NON-POLITICAL NOE

This section has already alluded to an alternate version of Tom Noe, Non-Political Noe, and concluded that, absent the pressure of the *Blade*, there's almost no chance the authorities would have sought a search warrant for his business and none whatever that a judge would have agreed to one.

But it isn't just the search warrant that would have been different in the case of a "Non-Political Noe." The entire shape of the legal process would have been different as well.

Recall that Non-Political Noe is a prosperous Toledo-area businessman, visible in charitable circles but politically inactive (as is his family) and essentially unknown to the media. He's made the same deal with the OBWC and also made the same "unsupported inventory purchases."

The alternate scenario begins when a new administrator takes over at the OBWC in January of 2005 and, on learning of the coin fund contracts in early April, decides the investments are undesirable and orders his staff to close them down as soon as practicable. Lawyers would then have met lawyers and, in light of the contract provisions, it would have been agreed that the funds would be wound up in something like 18-24 months. Remember, a new administration in Columbus changing its mind and forcing a damaging fire sale is the kind of scenario Noe was concerned about when negotiating the initial contract. It's the reason he put buffers in the contract preventing immediate termination.

In fact, the deliberate approach to liquidation specified in the contract was originally agreed on in April-May of 2005 and would have been used if media pressure – entirely related to Tom Noe the high profile political person – hadn't forced the raid on his business.

Non-Political Noe has 18-24 months to sell assets, some of which are highly liquid, like stock, and some of which require more time, like coins and collectibles. As specified, Non-Political Noe has also used coin sales-purchases ("unsupported inventory purchases") as a vehicle to take advances on profits. But in this case he has time to use funds from sales of his more liquid assets to balance the accounts from which he's taken the advances. As a result, the books he presents to OBWC on closing appear completely clear – the loans/ advances aren't visible. And, he's able to present the OBWC with a significant profit on its original investment – likely about $13 million, including the earlier profit distribution.

OBWC auditors, in reviewing the closing books, at first don't see any problem. Since Noe put cash equal to the then current value of the missing coins into the accounts from which he'd taken advances, everything looks OK. This macro approach to accounting appears to be the standard with investments like the one OBWC made with Noe.

However, the auditors could have looked deeper and discovered the internal transfers Noe needed to make in order to cover the advances he'd taken but documented inappropriately as coin sales from VCC to OBWC.

Understand, though, that "could have looked deeper" doesn't mean "would have" – there's evidence that, even in a time of intense scrutiny, OBWC did not do this kind of retrospective and detailed analysis with other investments such as those they had made with Ohio banks. For example, a *Blade* article in July of 2005 reported on OBWC's termination of its investment in a fund run by Allegiant, a subsidiary of National City Bank. The fund lost around $70 million.

When asked how the losses at Allegiant occurred, an OBWC spokesman said he didn't know and the *Blade* reported no more questions. In our alternate scenario, in which Tom Noe is a political unknown, it seems certain the *Blade* would have shown the same lack of curiosity about the technicalities of his OBWC investment.

Back to the scenario. Assuming that the OBWC auditors did scrutinize the books, and did discover the "unsupported inventory purchases," it's extremely unlikely that, in a situation with no external media and political pressure, they would have asked for a criminal investigation. "Yes," the executives would say to each other, "some of the documents were falsified. But yes the money has been replaced. So why make a big, expensive deal out of it?"

Even in the very unlikely case that the OBWC would have pressed a prosecutor to file criminal charges, the highly probable response from that office in a non-political environment would have been "this isn't for us – take it to civil court." And, of course, there would have been no entity in the legal system to challenge the prosecutor's decision – we'll see later that the range of discretion available to prosecutors *for the same activity* goes from "don't bother us" all the way to "hit 'em with RICO." And if the person being considered for prosecution isn't a high profile politician, no one in the media and therefore in the community would pay any attention to where in this huge range the prosecutor's decision fell.

However, let's assume that for some reason the OBWC was determined to get criminal charges filed. In such a case, it would likely have had to use political connections (e.g., through the Governor's Office) to get the prosecutor's attention. But, even under political pressure, the prosecutor would have agreed to nothing more than to file a charge of tampering with records. Theft and allied offenses would have been ignored as far too difficult to prove: the jury would have seen the overall profit and said, "where's the theft?"

Would anyone have suggested a bunch of felony theft charges for a politically invisible Noe? With RICO thrown in and an (effective) no parole sentence of eighteen years? There's no evidence to support the idea. A longtime Cincinnati prosecutor observed that murderers and rapists often do less time that what Noe got.

There is another possibility: what if the Bureau had decided to parse the case in the same way as Prosecutor Bates and the State Task Force, and argue that profits from other parts of the coin funds – such as collectibles and stocks -- couldn't be used to cover the profit advances taken in coins? That's certainly a possible path. However, it's still not a criminal one because the sole issue would be debt, not theft. If taken to civil court it would have led to an interesting debate that might or might not have left Noe owing a significant sum to the OBWC. But, again, such an interpretation wouldn't have resulted in Non-Political Noe spending a single day in jail.

What would have happened in Non-Political Noe's case if the prosecutor in Toledo had said something like, "I can't investigate this case. My husband has had a business conflict with Mr. Noe?" Or, if the judge assigned to Non-Political Noe recused himself because someone close to Noe had filed an ethics complaint against him?

In these "appearance of impropriety" situations, no one would have found such withdrawals remarkable -- ethics are very important to all professionals.

Back in the real world, the one in which the *Blade* was alleging that Noe had stolen vast amounts of money and in consequence fearful politicians from both parties were lining up to attack him, none of these things happened. In the quiet shelter of the State Task Force, the civil path was dropped in favor of a criminal approach and subsequently no one was willing to recuse her or himself. In the real world, Tom Noe found himself a passenger on a train heading straight to criminal court.

Why No Plea Deal?

Noe was offered a plea deal, but it would have required him to plead to theft and accept a ten year prison term. Given that he did not accept that there was theft, and given that his lawyers were optimistic about the trial prospects, he rejected the plea.

Express Chapter 8- The Trial

Because so many key decisions were made in advance, the actual trial had a secondary role in Coingate. Still, there were some important issues.

The Prosecution's Line of Argument

Anticipating that the defense would rely on the "loans and advances" clause of the contracts as justification, the prosecutors led with the argument that a loan or advance is only valid if it's documented as such. Anything hidden from the OBWC was theft and the contract didn't allow theft.

But the prosecution's main tactic was to employ the "use of cash" analysis as a way of tracing OBWC money to support Noe's "lavish lifestyle." Witness after witness testified about Noe's purchase of a luxury good or service and the prosecutors then employed the use of cash approach to show that the source of the money was an unsupported inventory purchase.

Prosecutors scarcely mentioned money laundering, gave little emphasis to the forgery charges, and ignored RICO.

The Defense's Main Line of Argument

The defense's main theme was "consent." You can't have theft, the lawyers said, if the owner consents to your taking the money. And, the OBWC did consent with the loans and advances clause.

A secondary theme was that Noe's assistant, Tim LaPointe, was the one who kept the records so he was the one responsible for the "unsupported inventory purchases." But the prosecutors countered this by repeatedly showing that LaPointe acted under Noe's orders.

The Valuation Ruling

The defense entered the trial expecting to show that the coin funds had made a profit even after repaying Noe's debt. But the prosecution was determined to prevent the jury seeing this information and argued strenuously against it, primarily by stressing that any profit was to be attributed to the liquidating firm that took over in June of 2005, rather than to Noe himself.

In fact, the liquidators didn't accrue any assets, they only sold what Noe had assembled (and not very effectively, according to some sources). The liquidators added no value.

Judge Osowik, who seemed comfortable with the very narrow view presented by the prosecution, ruled against the defense. Osowik's decision, issued as the prosecution's case was reaching its end, took away the heart of the defense's strategy and they chose not to present a case but rested after the prosecution's last witness.

Osowik was a candidate in a closely fought election for an appeals court judgeship and, just days after his ruling on valuation, the *Blade* chose to endorse him in an unusual front page story that was, contrary to usual practice, separate from other endorsements, which were normally done as a group within the pages of the newspaper.

SUMMARY AND PERFORMANCE OF THE PLAYERS

The defense did a good job of attacking the prosecution's witnesses. Wilkinson was especially effective in shredding the external auditor's "use of cash" arguments.

But the strategy of blaming LaPointe failed -- the standard defense approach of saying "this other guy could have done it" lacked substance. And the decision not to explicitly admit to tampering with records left the jury thinking Noe was denying the obvious. Finally, without the ability to present the overall valuation argument, the defense's dry legal arguments about "consent" appear to have had little impact.

In addition to fending off the valuation issue, the prosecution was generally skillful in avoiding traps – for example, there was no substantive mention of the RICO charge and therefore no real need to defend it. There was also some questionable behavior. For example, the prosecution failed to notify the defense about a key witness statement. It also introduced a witness to testify about elements of valuation it needed to establish, but did so in a disguised way that prevented the defense from opening up that category of discussion.

In the same vein, although the prosecution never presented overall valuation directly, there were numerous inferences and suggestions during the trial to the effect that the coin funds had lost money equivalent to the amount of unsupported inventory purchases.

Thanks to the State Task Force's shaping of the audit and the charges, the prosecution had all the cards and played them well in portraying Noe as a rich man who took advantage of the public.

THE JURY

The jury delivered its verdict on November 13, issuing guilty verdicts for 29 counts, including all of the important ones relating to theft and RICO. It found Noe not guilty of 11 counts, principally relating to money laundering and tampering with records. Although the *Blade* and the prosecution made much of the not guilty verdicts, arguing that they showed a careful and thoughtful jury, an analysis of the various decisions shows no logical thread of any kind. Rather, it seems that the jurors who favored guilt were trading off a few not guilty deals in order to get those leaning toward not guilty to agree on the major charges.

In fact, any thought that the jury was careful and thoughtful was put in serious doubt by this statement, made a number of years later by the foreman, James Petiniot:

> I presided over a group of people who tried their best to decide the case, but were completely overwhelmed with the mountain of material they had been provided. We received over 20 banker's boxes of this material,[4m] and we didn't have any auditors, accountants, or lawyers as jurors. In reviewing the evidence, we had to sift through financial spreadsheets, and PowerPoint presentations, contract provisions, bank records, inventory records, tax records, receipts, adding machine tape, and other items. We didn't have to just look at these items, but had to interpret provisions and (especially with the contracts) decide what they meant. Unfortunately, it was a task that we had little or no prior experience doing. I did not understand much of this material, and I know that my fellow jurors did not either.

> In short, we didn't decide the case on the evidence. We felt that if we didn't return a verdict soon, the general public would think that we were stupid. After all, according to the media and the politicians, everybody in Ohio knew Mr. Noe was guilty. What would take the jury so long to convict him? Under that pressure, we had numerous, heated arguments in deciding the case. After spending a couple of days trying to get through the evidence, we gave up and convicted Mr. Noe of crimes he did not commit. I am sure you know Mr. Noe received a sentence of 18 years.

> I never felt that the State of Ohio had presented evidence beyond a reasonable doubt regarding the RICO count. Still, I signed the verdict oath form even though I didn't believe Mr. Noe was guilty of that offense. I violated my juror oath, and I signed a verdict form I didn't believe in. I was not alone; other jurors voiced the opinion they just wanted to get the case over, even if it meant convicting Mr. Noe of

offenses he didn't commit.

My failure as a juror has haunted me since I learned much more about the "Coin Gate" scandal after the case was concluded. First, I learned that coin funds had actually made money for the State. During the case, the prosecution focused on how Mr. Noe had supposedly looted the coin funds. The jurors were led to believe that the investment was a disaster. I learned the truth was vastly different.[5]

Sentencing

Judge Osowik did not have discretion on the RICO charge -- that was set as a minimum of ten years. But he could have collapsed other charges. Although the calculation is complicated, it seems that the eighteen year sentence Osowik gave Noe was eight more than the minimum that could have been given.

In choosing a harsh sentence, Osowik appears to have relied on the prosecution's argument that Noe's case was similar to another, recent one in Columbus where a lawyer had stolen from clients and received a comparable sentence. But a closer look suggests that the Columbus case was hardly similar at all: the lawyer had clearly stolen, had hidden his theft, had no ability to repay, and had left numerous victims with severe financial disability. Ironically, this man was pardoned after only about four years while Noe has served more than double that time.

Eight days after the trial concluded, state officials announced the status of coin fund recovery, showing (indirectly) that the coin funds would make a profit. Available evidence suggests that this fact was known much earlier, likely before the trial began.

Express Chapter 9- The Appeals

Appeals courts don't normally hear new evidence but instead limit their review to whether the trial court applied the law accurately. In doing this, they recognize that the trial judge has considerable latitude and avoid challenging his or her discretionary rulings.

It's hard to conclude that the district Court of Appeals offered a serious review of Noe's case. The judges of this court are elected and as a result are as much in the thrall of the *Blade* as the lower courts. Indeed, by the time Noe's case reached the appeals court, Osowik, propelled there by the *Blade*'s unusual endorsement, was one of its judges.

Although the defense's arguments were extremely well done, the Appeals Court found for the state on all points but one (a technical element of sentencing). Many of the decisions relied on the inability to challenge Osowik's discretion (for example with respect to change of venue), but others rested on very shaky legal interpretations.

Notably, in sustaining the theft charges, the appeals court ruled that, despite the clear language of the contract, the state was an "owner" not just of shares in the coin funds but also directly of the coin funds' assets, and that Noe's actions with coins therefore violated the state's rights. Applying the same logic would invalidate mutual and hedge fund contracts and also change the nature of mortgages – the bank could challenge your choice of paint colors in its status as "owner."

Interestingly, the appeals court did agree that the level of media attention to Noe was extraordinary and that the nature of the coverage could be seen as hostile to him.

The Ohio Supreme Court did not accept Noe's case and, although there were some dissenting votes, did not give reasons for its decision.

The judge in the federal appeal, the first truly independent court to hear Noe's case, was outspoken in describing the media circus that preceded Noe's trial as one that could have strongly biased the jury pool. He asserted that if it had been his decision he would have granted a change of venue, but also noted that the decision fell within Judge Osowik's discretion and could not therefore be reversed.

Overall, it's fair to say that the appeals didn't comprise a substantive review of Noe's case. That was in part because of the deference to the trial judge and in part because the elected judges in the county appeals court, like their peers in the trial court, operated in the shadow of the *Blade*.

Express Chapter 10- Tom Noe from Politics to Prison

The events that began in the spring of 2005 had a devastating effect on Noe, taking away core underpinnings of his life: business, politics, and charity -- everything except family and friends.

In theory, Noe could have continued his business. In practice, that was impossible because the prosecutors had taken control over everything he needed to operate, most importantly his inventory and his records. The various legal entities argued that they needed to seize all of Noe's assets in order to determine which belonged to the state. That's reasonable to an extent because Noe did comingle some holdings. But there was much that was obviously not involved in the coin funds and that could have been made available to him. Certainly, the media assault might have made it difficult for him to operate a storefront, but it's a fact that no opportunity was given. Noe wasn't the only one to suffer – all his employees lost their jobs and a number were still unemployed over a year later when the trial began.

Prior to the state trial and while negotiations on the federal case were going on, Noe was diagnosed with depression and given medication. He felt that the treatment left him lethargic, making it harder for him to contribute to his defense. A particular concern was the behavior of lead defense attorney William Wilkinson, who was then going through a bitter divorce and who Noe believed was abusing alcohol at a level that would affect most people's judgment.

Noe wanted to testify but was dissuaded by his lawyers. This is far from unusual, but the defense's decision not to present a case of any kind left Noe feeling he hadn't been effectively represented.

Noe's earliest days in the federal prison system were rough, as he was chained and moved around with violent criminals and several times housed in extremely overcrowded, vermin-infested facilities. A paperwork mix up in South Carolina caused him to spend nearly two weeks in a form of solitary, "the hole," where he was deprived of his prescriptions and experienced a kind of spiritual renewal in consequence of the ensuing medical crisis.

After adjusting reasonably over nearly two years in a federal prison in Florida, Noe was transferred to Ohio custody and sent to a medium-security prison in the southeast corner of the state.

He remained there for nearly eight years, until he was transferred to a low-security section of a high security prison at Marion, in the center of the state.

Noe has had exceptionally positive reviews from prison authorities. He is active in religious activities, teaches several courses including one on personal finance, and works with others on helping inmates prepare for their release.

Both in a 2009 newspaper interview and in a 2015 clemency application, Noe has acknowledged responsibility for his actions. With respect to the federal case, he not only repeats without qualification the acceptance of guilt in his plea, he emphasizes deep regret for the difficulties he caused others. As for the state conviction, he clearly accepts that he falsified records to cover up some of his loans and advances and also accepts that it was wrong to access these monies without full transparency. He does note that all his financial obligations were in openly accessible records and that he had the ability to repay monies gained in this way. Something that's not apparent from the documents, but eminently clear from conversations held in the long meetings in prison, is that Noe doesn't harbor bitterness or animosity toward the individuals who put him in his current situation. This includes prosecutors, judges, and even the *Blade* staff. He doesn't agree with things that were done and said, but doesn't believe that others consciously chose to harm him.

Express Chapter 11- Rewind: A Fair Trial?

Looking broadly at research in psychology and law suggests major problems with Noe's trial.

RECAP: ROLE OF THE *BLADE* AND OTHER MEDIA

To recap, the level of media coverage of Coingate was extraordinary – a total of some 750 articles and letters in the *Blade* from the initial allegations in April of 2005 until the defense moved for a change of venue in mid- 2006. There were another 250 or so articles published before the trial finally began in the fall of 2006. Television and radio coverage is impossible to count but it's evident that it was massive and pervasive and that it followed the *Blade*'s tone and conclusions. As noted earlier, the *Blade* had an agreement to share reporting with a local television station and the others lacked the resources to do more than repeat the *Blade's* stories. Judges in the state and federal appeals courts both described the coverage as strongly negative toward Noe.

Simply put, when Noe's trial began, the region from which the jury pool was drawn had been saturated for about a year and a half with an almost entirely negative narrative that characterized Noe as a high-level criminal.

PSYCHOLOGY AND DISCRETION: JURIES

There has been substantial research on media bias and jurors, and a survey article published by two university researchers in psychology in 1997 is unequivocal about the effect of pre-trial media bias on juries. The study concludes, both on the basis of mock trials and analysis of actual trials, that jurors are much more likely to perceive a defendant as guilty 1) if the media has portrayed him that way and/or 2) if there has been coverage of other criminal activity of the defendant – as there was in Noe's case, with highly publicized sentencing in the federal case happening just weeks before the jury selection began.

Interestingly, and very much to the contrary of Judge Osowik's opinion, research also shows that those who have prejudged are likely to strongly assert that they can be impartial.

The research not only shows a direct link between media exposure and an individual's prejudgment, it also finds that those who have prejudged have high confidence that they could be impartial and that voir dire is not effective in uncovering this problem.

It is also evident that bias doesn't have to appear from reading or watching news personally. Many people receive bias from hearing friends or family talk. They embrace these opinions without realizing they have done so and don't challenge them because the biased information comes from personal relationships, an avenue that often doesn't invite analysis.

Research also shows that individuals are vulnerable to "unconscious bias" where they connect a defendant with a preexisting bias. For example, a Democrat might be biased against a Republican without thinking about anything specific.

Finally, the problem of "stealth jurors," those who know they are biased and seek to get on a jury to act on their feelings, is well documented.

Juries: How Did the Actual Voir Dire Go?

In light of both media and unconscious bias, it's reasonable to ask if the phenomena observed by the researchers in psychology affected jury selection in Noe's trial. In fact, a review of the transcripts of the voir dire strongly indicates that these factors were in fact very much at play. Many of the prospective jurors had to be excused because they had formed a conclusion about Noe's guilt from the media. Many others indicated that they were probably biased by what they had read or seen but were kept in the jury pool because of Judge Osowik's belief that all that matters is whether someone believes they can be fair. All in all, the defense was forced to use most of its challenges on people who should never have been in the pool at all.

A final point about juries is the powerful role of peer pressure. Recall that jury foreman Petiniot, in a later deposition to a lawyer for Noe, said:

> In short, we didn't decide the case on the evidence. We felt that if we didn't return a verdict soon, the general public would think that we were stupid. After all, according to the media and the politicians, everybody in Ohio knew Mr. Noe was guilty. What would take the jury so long to convict him? Under that pressure, we had numerous, heated arguments in deciding the case. After spending a couple of days trying to get through the evidence, we gave up and convicted Mr. Noe of crimes he did not commit.[6]

Peer pressure is often thought of as an adolescent issue, but, as the brilliant author Tina Rosenberg points out in her book, *Join the Club*,[7] "In the face of strong public pressure to conform, most people conform."[8] The evidence strongly suggests that this is what happened with Noe's jury.

DISCRETION AND PSYCHOLOGY: PROSECUTORS AND JUDGES

Psychological research in law is important because of the freedom that key individuals in the system have to make critical decisions.

For example, the public doesn't generally appreciate the discretionary power of prosecutors. Prosecutors don't have to file charges in cases presented by law enforcement and often decline to do so. The question of exactly what charges to file is also at the discretion of prosecutors. No one has standing to challenge their decision on what to file.

Nowhere is prosecutorial discretion greater – or more controversial – than in the class of crimes introduced under the rubric of RICO. The RICO charge was Count 1 in the indictment handed down against Tom Noe and specifies the "corrupt enterprise" as including Noe and his assistant Tim La Pointe, in concert with Noe's business (VCC- Vintage Coins and Collectibles) and the other businesses Noe had engaged in the coin funds.

In light of the enormous amount of discretion available to them, did the prosecutors charge Noe as they would have anyone else in a similar case? Would Non-Political Noe have faced a RICO charge? As stated previously, the answer appears to be an obvious no. Not only would there not have been a RICO charge, there probably would not have been a criminal case at all.

A related question is whether it is reasonable to assume that this prosecutor and her team could reasonably act in an impartial manner given their multiple conflicts of interest.

Similarly, given the research, should one accept as conclusive Judge Osowik's statement that, despite personal conflicts and an impending election, he could be fair in Noe's case?

Judges, Prosecutors and Impartiality

The research on bias cited above suggests that both Prosecutor Bates and Judge Osowik should have made the decision to recuse on their own.

Of course, it will never be possible to isolate prosecutors and judges from biased information, whether from the media or from that acquired by the hard wiring that all humans experience. But the research on jurors strongly suggests that it is desirable to limit to the extent possible the exposure of all people to bias – "all people"[?] would include prosecutors and judges. In the case of Tom Noe, this would have taken the form of both the prosecutor and the judge recusing themselves from a situation in which, because of important personal factors, they were much more vulnerable to unconscious bias than normal.

This last point is strongly amplified by the fact that people are known to rationalize actions taken in their own self-interest.

Everyone rationalizes some things, and psychologists observe that we usually start the process by placing ourselves positively with reference to others, or to some important principle. Thus, when the principle is fairness, someone might start with saying, "Fairness is important," then proceed to "I'm a fair person" and then go from there to the rationalizing conclusion-- "and as a result I can ignore pressure of any kind."

The fact is that people often cannot ignore their self-interest, especially when they attend to it subconsciously. Thus, there's no reason to believe that Prosecutor Bates ever said to herself "I have to act in a certain way or my family and I will be punished by the *Blade*." Similarly, there's no basis to argue that Judge Osowik made a conscious decision to rule in a certain way because the *Blade* and *Blade*-fueled anti-Noe public opinion might punish him in the upcoming election for the Court of Appeals (even though, as mentioned earlier, the *Blade* itself did argue that the judge would take anti-Noe public opinion into account when making a ruling).[9]

Prosecutors and judges are, of course, in a very different situation from jurors. People who serve in these official roles are highly aware of the presence of biasing information and are trained – sort of – to deal with it. But knowing about the possibility of unconscious bias and subsequent rationalization doesn't make implementing such recusals easy.

Consider the example of Prosecutor Bates' attack on Noe's press conference, where Noe and his legal team attempted to describe his coin fund investments as profitable. In this case, Bates said Noe was, "trying to put spin into the world" and through that hoping to influence the public, including future jurors.[10]

Bates' vigorous condemnation of Noe's press conference sets an extremely high bar for what constitutes appropriate freedom of speech, especially when you consider that Noe had not yet been charged with any crime related to his business at the time of the conference.

But this high bar was nowhere in sight just a month earlier when, lacking any good evidence, Bates enabled the *Blade's* story about Noe having an account in the Cayman Islands. If Noe's attempt to explain his business took some modest steps toward influencing potential jurors, the *Blade* story that Bates participated in was a giant engine of bias.

So did Bates and Osowik *subconsciously* rationalize the self-interest of some of their actions? There's no way to know the answer, but we do know that, as humans, they are subject to the same pressures, including the propensity to rationalize, as everyone else.

The best solution to the problem of unconscious rationalization is to prevent people from being in highly conflicted situations. And, again, these are not cases that will appear often; most likely only a handful of judges or prosecutors will ever face a similar situation in their entire careers.

FAIRNESS SCORECARD: JUDGE, JURY, AND PROSECUTOR BIAS
MEANS THREE STRIKES AGAINST JUSTICE

Recent problems with local prosecutors' failure to indict police officers accused of brutality and even murder have caused some cities to suggest that specially appointed prosecutors should handle police misconduct cases. Arguments over the relations of prosecutors and local police will continue, but one point stands out from a very lively and increasingly emotional debate: no one really disagrees that prosecutors can be biased, including by local politics.

The same issue of potential bias clearly applies to elected judges. Consider these facts: 1) Lucas County was the focus of unrelenting political strife that affected not just the area but also the state and the nation, with Noe and his trial judge on opposite sides: and 2) the trial judge was preparing to enter what would certainly be a bitter and (indirectly) partisan race for a Court of Appeals Court judgeship (against a candidate who had been actively and visibly supported by the Noes) and would benefit enormously from the support of the newspaper that was regularly proclaiming Noe's guilt. Research in human psychology tells us that relying entirely on Osowik's sincere statement that he could be fair is flat out wrong. The Ohio Supreme Court erred egregiously in supporting this line of thinking.

The argument that this ruling was in error in 2005 is strongly reinforced by a complete reversal of the Court's philosophy in 2017.

In 2005, the *Blade* was scathingly opposed to recusal of judges in Noe's case, and the Ohio Supreme Court was literally dismissive.

But that was then. The *Blade* was OK about a year later when it endorsed a visiting prosecutor and judge in a case where the accused person wasn't Tom Noe. The Supreme Court took a little while longer to reconsider, but when it did the change was dramatic.

In a 2017 ruling, Ohio's Supreme Court heard a case in which a man who had been convicted of fraud argued that he didn't get a fair trial because the judge knew someone who was once a political opponent of the accused. The judge, named Crawford, had said that the friendship with the opponent was casual and not in any way political and, like Judge Osowik, averred that he could "impartially and fairly" preside over the case. Just saying so was enough for the 2005 Supreme Court, but not the 2017 version, when Chief Justice Maureen O'Connor wrote:

> Nevertheless, even in cases where no evidence of actual bias or prejudice is apparent, a judge's disqualification may be appropriate to avoid an appearance of impropriety or when the public's confidence in the integrity of the judicial system is at issue. [11]

And here's what the 2017 version of the *Blade* had to say in an editorial:

> We should all hope that Judge Crawford, and all our judges, have the integrity to follow the evidence and the law even when it leads them to personally unpleasant conclusions. But a casual observer can't judge a person's integrity. It's much easier to see the integrity of a system when it avoids a situation that might, in the worst-case scenario, lead to a biased result. Chief Justice O'Connor made the right call.[12]

Moral principles aren't temporal. If the "appearance of impropriety" that was completely ignored in the political and media firestorm of 2005 is not merely acknowledged but asserted in 2017, that ought to be a factor to consider in reviewing the case of someone who has served ten years in prison with eight more to go.

The evidence is also clear for juries. Given a certain level of publicity, bias will be there and voir dire will not be able to detect it. And the judge's instructions will not be enough to offset bias, especially if people don't know they have it. In fact, instructions to ignore bias could very well introduce it.

Taken together, a careful reading of the research, plus what is known of the political climate in Lucas County, demonstrates the high probability that a number of the jurors in Noe's trial were strongly biased against him before they were seated and didn't consider the evidence presented by the defense with an open mind. Consider this exchange from the voir dire:

> Prosecutor: Okay. Let me ask you. Have you watched any media coverage in regard to Mr. Noe?

> Prospective Juror: I think you'd probably have to live under a rock to say no to that. So I'm sure I've seen things, yes.[13]

It's obvious that routinely disqualifying prosecutors and judges, and regularly moving trials to a different venue, would be a huge burden on our system of justice. But it's equally obvious that the scale and intensity of bias will rarely be sufficient to require such deviations from the normal system. Prosecutors and judges don't often confront active political rivals. Nor do they often encounter a local media storm that coincides and overlaps with intense local political issues —on the order of 750 stories and letters in the space of a year is orders of magnitude beyond extraordinary – and that's before taking into account radio and television news together with the relentless wave of anti-Noe television commercials paid for by both political parties. When such extreme variances from the norm do appear, higher courts should disqualify the local players and move the trial to another community; in some cases, the move needs to occur in the investigatory stage, i.e., well before a prosecutor considers filing charges. It takes only a few simple steps to ensure that the kind of "legal perfect storm" that engulfed Tom Noe doesn't happen again.

Express Chapter 12- Comparable Cases

The political context of Tom Noe's case is highlighted by that of Paul Mifsud a short time earlier. Mifsud, a long-time senior aide to then Governor George Voinovich, was suspected of involvement with a contracts-for-donations scheme. But the investigation was dropped when the Governor replaced the leader of the office responsible for the investigation. Mifsud was later convicted of bribery, but a plea bargain dropped many charges and he spent almost no time in jail. The big difference vs. Noe? Republicans were united and solidly in control, allowing them to ignore complaints from

Democrats. Ironically, John Robinson Block of the *Blade* was outspoken in praising Mifsud, even after his conviction.

This formula appears to represent an unbroken pattern nationally. Assuming comparable criminal allegations, there are no sentences even roughly similar to Noe's. On the contrary, there is a huge archive of sentences that are radically different.

It's interesting that in calculating amounts lost for financial fraud charges, this author hasn't located a single case in which law enforcement followed Ohio's example and considered losses in one part of the business to be theft while ignoring profits in another part of the same business. Instead, prosecutors and judges in other jurisdictions appear always to use the *net* losses to calculate the gravity of a crime. Chopping business activity into pieces in order to find something that looks criminal appears to be a uniquely Ohio strategy.

Express Chapter 13- How Much Profit?

All sources agree that the OBWC's investment with Tom Noe made a net profit of $6 million. However, an analysis suggests that the liquidation process chosen by the state was not particularly effective or efficient: with lower expenses of liquidation and more effective marketing of inventory, the net profit could easily have been in the range of $14-18 million.

Please now either read Part X, Conclusions and Recommendations in the main text or continue to Part I, below.

Please now either read Part X, Conclusions and Recommendations in the main text or continue to Part I, below.

Part I- Coingate in the Ohio Context

Coingate was primarily a political event, and to understand the politics one has to appreciate the social and economic context.

OHIO'S ECONOMY AND POLITICS

If Pennsylvania is the "keystone state," Ohio might be called the "pivot state." It sits at the transition point between the US Northeast and the Midwest, and has also long served as a battleground where the Republican and Democratic parties confront each other on equal terms.

Ohio is part of a traditional manufacturing region with centers in the Northeast (Cleveland-Akron-Youngstown), Northwest (Toledo), South-Central (Dayton), and Southwest (Cincinnati). The state can be thought of as a logical extension of neighboring Pittsburgh: easy access to coal and iron ore created a steel industry that in turn fed manufacturing of an array of large and heavy products. Excellent rail, road and water transport kept everything moving smoothly.

But Ohio is also a major agricultural state, with notably high productivity everywhere except in the Southeast, which is very much a part of traditional Western Appalachia. This latter region features rolling hills that are poor for farming, and also has a legacy of collapsed industry from long-past boom years that were fueled by cheap and abundant coal.

For about a century, from about 1880 to 1980, Ohio was one of the richest places not just in the US but in the world. The recession of 1980, which hit Ohio exceptionally hard, signaled the end of that kind of prosperity. Ohio's manufacturing areas – places where simply being present was enough to get a great job — now began to struggle mightily as automation accelerated and outsourcing shifted employment growth to the Pacific rim. At the same time, US employers began to look for knowledge-based skills rather than simple muscle. Unfortunately, Ohio's workers, who had never needed more than a high school diploma and didn't really have to study much to get that, were unprepared to compete for education-related jobs.

Ohio's industrial areas have traditionally leaned strongly Democratic and were long a major center of union activity. Republicans, by contrast, dominated the suburban and agricultural areas, topping off their power with a strong base in the traditionally conservative Cincinnati area. The two parties alternated in power during the post WWII years, making this small, squarish region the quintessential "swing" state in US politics.

Although the Republicans have largely dominated state politics since 1990, Ohio has continued to be a key pivot point in US presidential elections.

Something else that hasn't changed, unfortunately, is the state's long history of political corruption. If you wanted to get something done in Columbus in 1960, money often had to change hands. That was still true in 2005, and this culture of corruption is a factor in how Coingate was perceived.

THE RECESSION OF 1980-81 AND DEVASTATION IN OHIO

The nation began to slowly shift away from low-skilled labor-based manufacturing in the 1970s, and that trend accelerated after the recession of 1980-81. Ohio was battered: its poverty rate in 1980 was 9.8% but hit 12.7% in 1981 and has never gone back below 10%. And, the state hit its population peak in 1970, losing 50,000 people in the decades 1970-1990. Ohio's stagnating population should be considered in the light of overall US growth of about 22% for the same period. Put another way, if Ohio had grown at just the national average from 1970 to 1990, it would have had an additional two million people vs. losing 50,000.

Lucas County, home to Toledo, is best known to the outside world as the "Glass City" for the many glass-related companies that started there. It's also well-known as the place where Jeeps are made. It continues to be home to many automobile parts manufacturers, including the Dana Corporation, a $6 billion plus per year business.

Prior to the crash of low skills-based manufacturing, life in Lucas County was good for people with blue collar jobs. Certainly, there was some turbulence as the auto industry went through its cycles and unions staged strikes. But people adapted to these changes just as farmers adapted to weather cycles – people understand there will be lean years and the elders show others how to prepare.

People working in manufacturing felt themselves in a life pattern that, although it had its uncomfortable episodes, was on the whole stable, predictable and good. The changes to industry that began in the 1970s altered that in a fundamental way. Suddenly, the future was unstable and unpredictable and the elders weren't able to offer the young any ideas about how to adapt.

As the parents and grandparents watched the young people struggle, they felt a deep frustration. They'd always been hard-working, responsible, church-going people. They'd kept their part of life's bargain, at home and on the job. What, they wondered, has happened to society? Who has allowed these changes that are taking their family from prosperity to near poverty?

As it happened, the good blue collar jobs never came back. The employment situation in 2005 wasn't better for people with no education beyond high school than it was in 1985.[14]*m*

The current generation has embraced the need for education and is doing much better, but it takes a long time to bring about significant change – not least because education-focused employers aren't prominent in the area. As a result, people who have suffered like the generations described above continue to comprise a significant part of the electorate – and the jury pool – in Lucas County.

The anger and frustration in the blue collar community that built over some twenty years were sure to have an impact on Lucas County politics and they did, weakening Democrats and strengthening Republicans.

Political Warfare: Republicans become more aggressive –The national push to grab blue collar votes

Traditionally, the Republican Party in Ohio had a moderate political outlook. Largely based on farmers and small business, the GOP represented traditional balance in society – in contrast to the Democrats who were associated with the radical changes coming from the labor movement.

But the Republicans' adoption of the Southern Strategy, from about the 1960s, changed the party. By acquiring a large number of traditionally Democratic religious conservatives who felt threatened by growing social change, the Republicans became more hard-edged. Subsequently, the party marketed itself to blue-collar workers with a message that focused on the virtues of traditional society and, especially during the Vietnam period, on patriotism.

But the Republicans didn't make major progress until two things happened: 1) abortion became a key issue for the Catholic Church and affected heavily Catholic areas like Lucas County; and 2) the part of the economy that employed unskilled workers began to weaken.

Although abortion was and is a key factor, one that helped elect Reagan in 1980, it was the economy that became the principal wedge. The Democrats didn't have answers to economic change, while the Republicans claimed they did. In retrospect, it's highly debatable that the Republicans had better answers than the Democrats, but their energetic and confident assertion that they knew exactly what to do made an enormous difference. Tom Noe, a very confident and energetic person, was well placed to have a key role.

NOE ENTERS THE FRAY

The best way to describe Tom Noe's early life is to let him tell it[15].

I was born on July 19,1954 at Wood County hospital in Bowling Green, Ohio. My father, Lawrence "Larry" Noe, was the composing room foreman for the Bowling Green Sentinel Tribune. He was a union printer for over 45 years at the Bowling Green paper and the

Swanton enterprise. He was my best friend and mentor and he passed away on May 12th, 1997 from lung issues stemming from 45 years of lead fumes intake and he smoked until about age 50. My mom, Doretta "Dottie" Noe was a homemaker until I was 11 and then a secretary for a seed corn company in BG. Her original boss was Bill Korn (I'm not making this up) and he lived next door to us. We moved from Summit Street to Klotz Rd. in Bowling Green when I was 4 (1958) and my sister sold the house when my mom passed away on July 16, 2011. I hit the parent lottery with them. I didn't know how little money my dad made working 6 days a week at the paper. Mom went to work when my sister was getting college age so they could help her get thru BGSU [Bowling Green State University].

Growing up in a college town was amazing. There was no class structure in BG. The richest of the rich and the poorest of the poor got along great. I attended grade school at St. Aloysius school and graduated from BG high school in 1972. I was a good student but my conduct grades were always a challenge!!! I owe Sister Mary Martin, my 2nd, 7th, and 8th grade teacher for all the successes I have had over the years. She encouraged my love of math and never held any of us back. I got my first paper route (for the BG Sentinel) in 3rd grade and then worked in the mail room there when I turned 15.

Noe went to the local public high school and from there went to Bowling Green, the local university. Always a good student, he found college an unexpected challenge:

My time at BGSU (as an accounting pre-law major) was short lived. Because of my ACT math score (very high) I was put into a sophomore level calculus class. We had no calculus in high school so I thought I was in a foreign language class!! I tell my kids (all college graduates) that I had a 4.0 in college... I got a 1.9 my first quarter and a 2.1 my second quarter (my math says that adds up to a 4.0!!!).

On Easter Sunday of 1973 I told my parents that I was going to take some time off from college and be a coin dealer full time. My dad was for it and my mom was not happy, to say the least. I promised her I would go back if the coins didn't work out! It was my advisor, Dr. O'Brien that helped me make a decision. I was making more money a year working a couple of days a week at a Toledo coin shop and setting up at local coin shows with my dad (that's how I got my dad started in the industry) than if I had graduated and become an accountant at one of the big 8 (at that time) firms. I should have asked Dr. O'Brien for advice on how to explain this to my Mom! She wasn't happy and I had to promise her I'd go back when I could.

My interest in coins began when I was 8 years old. Paul Schmitt (he ran the St. Al's credit union) took me and my dad to the Black Swamp coin show at BGSU. With my love of history, I was hooked that day. When I got my paper route, the circulation manager, Fermont R. Fluhart (that is his real name) would let me go through all the change the carriers brought him every Saturday morning after he went thru them for his collection!! I delivered papers to the banks and utility companies and they would let me buy anything worthwhile that they ran in to. When I was 16, I bought my first car, a Toyota Corolla, for $1498 brand new. That enabled me to quit at the newspaper and work part time for Ed Clemente at Ed's coin shop at the Woodville Mall in east Toledo. He had a teletype machine that was broadcast to hundreds of dealers and I was able to meet a lot of the national dealers that way. After dropping out of college I moved to Greenville, SC to work for William Hodges Rare Coin Co. After I made that decision, I proposed to my high school sweetheart, Liz Reynolds, and we were married on October 26th,1973 and she joined me in Greenville. ... Less than 6 months after she got there, Bill sold his company to a big dealer in New York city, Metropolitan Rare Coins, and I was part of the package deal!! We lived on Long Island and I commuted an hour + by train into Manhattan. We both hated it there and in July of 1974 I took a job at New England Rare Coins in Framingham, Mass.

Noe says he really learned the business for the first time in New England and loved the company. His success there netted him an excellent job offer in Miami. Noe also did well financially while in Florida, but didn't like it there, so he and his wife decided to move back to Northwest Ohio in 1981. He started a coin business, Numismatic Investments with his retired father. And that's when he got involved in politics, though he remembers a much earlier connection.

During the 1968 presidential campaign, I was the paper boy for the congressional offices of Congressman Delbert Latta's office in downtown BG. His longtime secretary, Ginny Fries was a neighbor of ours when I was born. I would volunteer to pass out things for her and help her stuff envelopes, etc. She asked if I would like to see the next President of the United States. Richard Nixon was coming by train thru Deshler, Ohio on his way to Toledo and the congressman was riding the train with him. So Ginny took me to see and meet Nixon when the train stopped in Deshler. After Nixon won she sent me a postcard from the inauguration postmarked the day he was sworn in. I grew up in a "mixed" marriage! My mom was Protestant Republican from little Delta, Ohio. My dad was a union Democrat, Catholic, and from Swanton, Ohio. Swanton and Delta were 8 miles apart and the rivalry was like OSU and Michigan!! So....I was a Republican at age 14 because of Del Latta....

But a connection doesn't mean a commitment. Noe reports that his more active involvement in politics was something of an accident:

> When I moved to Toledo in 1981 I met Jim Brennan. Jim was my neighbor a few houses away. We were unpacking on a Sunday night and my mom and dad were at the house helping and watching [their daughter] Allison for us. The doorbell rang and my dad answered. There stood Jim Brennan to welcome me to the neighborhood. He thought my dad was the homeowner and proceeded to get my dad to sign up to help the GOP and register him to vote since he heard the new neighbor moved to Ohio from Florida (remember, my dad is diehard Democrat!!). Dad told him he had the wrong "Mr. Noe" and hollered for me to come to the door. This is 1981 and I was moving into a $300,000 house in Ottawa Hills (like Bexley [a wealthy Columbus suburb]). I'm 27 years old with long hair and beard!! He introduces himself to me and I invite him in and apologize for the mess in the house. There were boxes everywhere. I asked if he wanted a drink and he says, "you got any scotch?" I told him there was an open box on the bar that hadn't been unpacked and to help himself. Two hours later I had an almost empty bottle of scotch and I was signed up to vote and a member of the local GOP. ... That was the beginning of a wonderful relationship with Jim Brennan both personally and professionally. I slowly but surely got involved with the party as secretary and became chairman in 1992. I took Jim's place because he ran unsuccessfully for County Commissioner.

Noe's involvement in politics was paralleled by one in charitable causes.

> I agreed to chair the fundraising drive for my daughter's Catholic grade school soon after I returned to Ohio. This was kind of scary for me because I knew the leaders of these campaigns were looked upon to be the major givers to jump start the campaign. After discussing this with my wife we agreed to pledge $45,000 over 5 years. This was a lot of money to us but we both believed strongly in a good Catholic education for our girls. I was reminded of the sacrifice my parents made in 1960, when they donated $1,000 to St Aloysius Church to build the grade school I attended from grades 1-8. My mom was a stay-at-home mom and I'd be surprised if my dad made $5000 a year at that time. But he always told me to "give until it hurts" and God will always pay you back multiple times. I lived that lesson every day of my life.

EARLY POLITICS

When Noe started with the Republican Party in Lucas County, the Toledo area was structurally similar to many other places in the Midwest. The city was manufacturing-focused, the unions had a major role, and the Democrats dominated local politics. Republicans were stronger in the suburbs, but their real power in the region was in the smaller cities and towns outside of the urban county. Thus, northwest Ohio as a whole was a contested area between Democrats and Republicans, but the only urban county, Lucas, was almost uncontested.

Local offices, for example the mayor's office, county commissioners, judges, prosecutors, auditor, etc. were almost exclusively held by Democrats and most of the lower level positions on the ballot did not have serious Republican candidates. Noe had a major role in changing this.

Noe's focus as a Republican leader was threefold: 1) he raised money for the party; 2) he recruited credible candidates; and 3) he attacked the Democratic incumbents.

The Democrats felt the impact of a revived Republican party almost immediately, learning that serious effort was now required to elect candidates in most races. Contests that were once lopsided quickly became close.

Major change took a few years, but when it came it was significant. By 1994, Republicans had reversed the previous trend and held three of the four state House of Representatives seats that were anchored in the County. They had also made serious inroads into local offices such as judges, city council, and the municipal clerk of courts.

Although the change in local blue collar voting patterns was generally consistent with national trends, it was arguably more significant in Lucas County than in most places for the simple reason that it was the center of a swing region in a swing state. And Democrats could reasonably associate their change in fortunes with the name "Noe," because Tom Noe's second wife, Bernadette, became Lucas County Republican Chair in 1998. Between them, Tom and Bernadette were the key antagonists of Democrats for nearly two decades.

Tom Noe had been active in local and regional politics for five or six years when he decided to seek a sales tax exemption for rare coins. Part of the reason for this was to aid his normal retail business, which was hurt by the fact that about half of the states, including many in the region, didn't tax coin sales. But the principal reason was sales at "coin shows." Like similar expositions in other areas, coin shows are attended by both retail and wholesale customers. It's common for dealers to do business with each other at these shows – and it's a major barrier if such turnover sales are taxed. In partial recognition of this, the state allowed dealer to dealer sales to be exempt from taxes through the use of a "sale for resale" exemption. Although cumbersome, this worked well until a 1987 show in Cincinnati, when the state tax commissioner challenged the exemptions.

Problems with the exemptions caused problems for Noe who had been an exhibitor at the Cincinnati show, so he decided to seek legislation to allow for a true exemption. The process began naturally enough, with Noe seeking advice and connections from local Republicans and a prominent Democrat. They suggested he hire a major independent political consultant, someone with ties in both parties. Noe did, and also created a state group of coin dealers who helped him lobby – which for the most part meant making strategic campaign donations. The bill got bipartisan support and was about to be signed by the Governor when the tax commissioner intervened, urging a veto. Pressure from the Democrats, who controlled the House, prevented this and the bill was passed and signed into law. Noe recalls that he was then able to get some big coin shows to come back to Ohio, though he also observes that he actually wound up paying more sales tax because his business shifted heavily to collectibles (things like autographed sports and political memorabilia) which were still taxed.

Noe's lobbying for a sales tax exemption was a textbook case of reasonable political involvement; you might disagree with the outcome but you can't say it's illegitimate since quite a few states –including three of Ohio's neighbors — had this kind of exemption. Even so, the buzz saw awaited.

The stereotype of politics in a state like Ohio has always been one of big city union bosses sitting around a table in a smoke-filled room and making decisions about what public resources would go where – a new highway for that area, a new bridge for another. Sometimes, in the stereotype, decisions would be made based on personal financial gain – i.e., corruption.

The stereotype certainly applied to some of Ohio's cities at some times in the past. But a different version has also applied in a similar way for Republicans in their various fiefdoms: they also had party bosses, and corruption was by no means uncommon. In the area of dubious achievements, the Republican version of the party boss system gave America William McKinley and Warren Harding.

Times have changed, and the role of bosses in Ohio is now feeble if it exists at all. But a level of corruption continues to exist in a subset of the lobbying industry: the independent consultant system.

Modern political campaigns need large sums of money, principally for purchasing advertising in electronic media, but also for consulting, polling, and computer systems. Limits on how much an individual donor can give makes fundraising difficult. Grassroots efforts help, but usually aren't enough.

Independent political consultants can help fill the gap. This system works as follows.

Someone needs something from the state, for example legislation for a tax exemption, or changes in law to make a for-profit entity eligible for state funding, or special allocations to a community, etc. The range of possibilities is vast.

An illustration, a composite of several real-life examples, concerns a businessman who was angry when a group of his employees left and started a new company – a sort of co-op where they were all independent contractors. The angry businessman went to an independent political consultant who took a large fee up front with more to come, then in turn went to a legislator known to be in need of financing and asked for his help. A price was agreed on and the consultant organized the specified flow of funds to the legislator's campaign. The consultant himself gave some money directly to the legislator, and also got the businessman, his wife, and senior managers to give some, etc. Gifts to other legislators, especially those in the leadership, were also needed and arranged.

When the checks were cashed, the legislator, with the help of the consultant, drafted a law that would regulate out of existence co-ops of the specific kind that annoyed the businessman. The draft law was then promptly filed for consideration. The co-ops were in deep trouble.

So, what happened? You'd like to think that the co-op people went to their local legislator, told the story and then the outraged legislator moved to oppose the proposed law. That only happens in fairy tales. In the real world, the little people, just like the businessman, have to "pay to play" in politics. In this case, the co-op got advice from someone who knew the system and they then hired their own consultant, who mirrored the process but from the other side. The result in this case was stalemate, though of course actual outcomes range widely. No matter the result, though, the consultants make money and the legislators get donations.

The most successful of the independent political consultants can become powerful people in the state. They give a lot of money to campaigns and are known as people who can make things happen. Technically, what they do is entirely legal. Practically, it's a gross distortion of an open political process and surely opens the door for deals that are more directly corrupt. When Noe decided to seek a sales tax exemption for his (and others') business, this is the world he entered.

It's important to emphasize that problems with the activities of some consultants shouldn't be taken to denigrate the larger role of lobbyists. Lobbying firms serve an essential role in government, primarily by managing effective communications among busy people. Many of the best people working in this field add value by developing the ability to provide accurate and succinct summaries of complex issues. Communications-oriented lobbying is unquestionably legitimate. Rather, it's the sophisticated manipulation of campaign finance laws by some consultants that is a concern.

ROLE OF THE BLADE

Toledo's only major newspaper, *The Blade*, was a major player in Coingate. The *Blade* is an example of the family-owned newspaper that once comprised the core of American news, but has now become scarce. The parent company, Block Communications, was founded by Paul Block, an immigrant from Germany, in the early 1900s. At one time Block controlled many newspapers on the East Coast and into the Midwest, but lost all except the *Blade* and the Pittsburgh *Post-Gazette* during the depression. Originally known as the *Toledo Blade*, it dropped the "Toledo" in 1960.

Block Communications, now run by the twin grandsons of Paul Block, owns television and cable systems as well as the newspapers.[16] Allan Block is chairman of the company, while his brother John (often called John Robinson) runs the two newspapers.[17] John Robinson lived in Toledo during the Coingate period, but it's reported that he has since moved to Pittsburgh. Even so, all agree he still keeps a very close eye on Toledo.

Like most of its traditional newspaper brethren, the *Blade* has always thought of itself as a guardian and protector of local interests, arguing for effective government in local affairs and pushing at the state level for at least proportionate public investment in the region. Most people in the region think of the paper as an extension of the Democratic Party (testimony from jury selection certainly bears this out – see below), and in fact it typically supports Democrats in state and national elections. But the *Blade* often supports Republicans in local contests and sometimes in national ones.[18]*m*

The *Blade* was deeply concerned with the change in the economy in the last quarter of the 20th Century and regularly noted the effect this had on Toledo and the region. One consequence of this was that, after 1990 when Republicans had almost complete control in Columbus, the *Blade* became more supportive of electing Republican legislators from the region: they would provide the region with much needed voices in the statehouse.

One highly visible case of regional advocacy by the *Blade* resulted in the creation of the Medical College of Ohio at Toledo in 1964. Paul Block (the twins' father) was much criticized in Columbus for his heavy push to secure this huge new public investment for his home town. The state's higher education planners thought creating a new medical school and putting it on the periphery of the state was the worst kind of parochialism. But a review of the records shows that Block was well aware of the fact – now widely accepted – that the presence of teaching hospitals improves the overall quality of health care in a surrounding region. That's both because the hospitals associated with the medical schools work at the state of the art, and because the other hospitals move to compete. In retrospect, Block's drive to create the new medical school (now a part of the University of Toledo) can be seen as a very positive move for the region.

The *Blade*, led by John Robinson personally, also became a strong advocate of support for what it called "the Other Ohio." The idea was that state funding was going primarily to the politically dominant "three C's" of Cincinnati, Cleveland, and Columbus, leaving little for the rest of the state.

Block was particularly critical of Columbus, which was growing in population and economic prowess even as other cities in Ohio declined. Here's a quote from Block in an interview with his own paper: "The worst of the 3Cs is Columbus. Columbus is just a greedy ravenous kind of monster, sucking, living off the taxes of the rest of the state."[19]

The reason for Columbus' growth was that its economy was based on banking, insurance, state government, and higher education rather than heavy industry. Block wanted to change the pattern by moving investment in state government and higher education elsewhere in the state, notably to Toledo.

Beginning in the 1980s and continuing for decades, Block campaigned to break up Ohio State and distribute its programs to universities around Ohio. The logic here was problematic, since it's well demonstrated that scale matters in research-focused institutions. Also, his invidious comparisons of the quality of Ohio State vs. the nearby University of Michigan, while certainly true in the 1980s and into the 1990s, are no longer valid. Ohio State's strong leadership from about 1980 has finally put it in the same academic league as its fierce rival in sports.

On the other hand, one can argue that Block's call to break up the increasing aggregation of government investment in the state capital was insightful, even prescient.

It wasn't much noticed at the time, but Reagan's policy of revenue sharing seriously disadvantaged places like Toledo. When the federal government handled things like workforce programs directly, it had regional offices that had no particular need to be in state capitals. But revenue sharing shifted the flow of monies to the states, which quickly expanded bureaucracies in their capitals. Columbus was getting additional public investment just as Toledo, which needed it more, was getting less.

Block's calls were derided as pork barrel politics, but there was actually some remarkable foresight and vision there, and it's unfortunate that states aren't moving toward more decentralization of agency headquarters. The idea that everyone has to be in the same place for meetings, then drive out to the regions to interact with the population, is deeply flawed. Certainly, the advent of computer and networking technology, together with the rising cost of energy, has made it more efficient to decentralize government.

The Blade and Investigative Journalism

In addition to its status as guardian of the region's interests, the *Blade* has also had an active role in investigative journalism. The paper won a Pulitzer prize in 2004 for a story on how the Army had covered up atrocities committed by an elite unit during the Vietnam War. Adding an edge to the achievement, the *Blade* beat out newspapers in much larger cities with far greater resources. Papers like the *New York Times* and the *Washington Post* are the typical winners in this most important category of Pulitzer awards, so when a smaller paper like the *Blade* wins the recognition that is special. John Robinson Block evoked his father in a celebration: "My father always said The *Blade* is a good newspaper every day it's published."[20] The *Blade's* sister paper, the *Pittsburgh Post-Gazette*, has also won a number of Pulitzers.[21]*m*

The Elections of 2004

Although America is returning to a much earlier pattern of extreme partisan hostility, few elections have been as bitterly fought as that of 2004 – the year of the Swift Boat fraud. Republicans were desperate to keep Bush in office, while Democrats, outraged by the Iraq War, were desperate to get rid of him.

Ohio, as has often been the case, was one of the few key states in 2004. And Toledo, especially after Republican gains in the area, was a key battleground. Tom Noe was very active in fundraising (including some illegal activities – see below) but his wife Bernadette was more visible because she was at the time both chair of the Lucas County Republican Party and of the Lucas County Board of Elections. The Board of Elections' role in 2004 was the source of intense controversy.

A *Detroit Free Press* story included the following:

> Well before election day, Lucas County's Democratic headquarters was broken into. Key voter data went missing.
>
> On November 2, inner city voting machines mysteriously broke down en masse. Polls opened late. The Toledo Blade has reported that the sole machine at the Birmingham polling site in east Toledo broke down around 7 a.m. By order of Secretary of State Kenneth Blackwell, no paper ballots were available for backup.
>
> At one school polling station the voting machines were locked in the office of the principal, who called in sick. The Gesu School in West Toledo temporarily ran out of ballots. There were huge lines, missing ballots and technical anomalies associated with the leased Diebold

Optical-Scan voting tabulators. Lucas County BOE Director Paula Hicks-Hudson admitted that the Diebold machines had jammed during the previous week's testing, but the BOE did not bother to fix them for the election.

Sworn statements at public hearings in Toledo and Columbus confirmed that scores of citizens were disenfranchised because they had to go to work. According to the Toledo Blade, at the Birmingham polling site in east Toledo, the sole machine broke down around 7am. When Ohio Rep. Peter Ujvagi tried to cast his ballot an hour later, a poll worker told him to place his ballot in "a secure slot under the machine" so it could be scanned in later, after Ujvagi had left. [22]

In April of 2005, the Secretary of State issued a report criticizing the Board of Elections and asking all members to resign. Many, but not all, of the allegations were similar to those in the *Detroit Free Press* article.[23] The charges are certainly serious, but it's interesting that none of the many articles on the Board of Elections gives any prominence to the fact that, by law, half of the board's members were Democrats.

The electoral challenges that came to a boil in 2005 reflected not only the bitterness of Democrats, but also a kind of "buyer's remorse" on the part of independents and even quite a few Republicans who saw the hostilities in Iraq continuing unabated, and with no end in sight. After a quick spike at the New Year of 2005, Bush's approval ratings started a plunge that took him from a high of around 60% to below 40% — all in one year.[24]

Even before the nation started four more years under George W. Bush, the relationship between the *Blade* and Tom Noe had become personal and hostile. Many observers say that Bernadette Noe was an important part of this. They describe the ex-Democratic activist (she changed sides in the mid-1990s after marrying Noe) as more aggressive toward political opponents and prone to directly criticizing the *Blade* on talk radio.

But a particular election incident focused on Tom. The *Blade*, which had endorsed John Kerry and been very critical of Bush, had strongly supported a visit by the financier George Soros to the University of Toledo campus just before the election. Because Soros was there principally to speak in support of Kerry, Tom Noe was outspoken in opposition, arguing that the *Blade* and others had forced the University to take a partisan stand right before an election.

The *Blade* fired back a week later:

> We would expect Mr. Noe to recognize that the open exchange of controversial ideas is what a university is supposed to be about.

But we would expect too much.

Frankly, we put more stock in a man who has written eight books on economics and measures his international influence in the billions of dollars than a man who deals primarily in nickels and dimes.[25]

The gloves were off as the *Blade* joined those seeking revenge, and Tom Noe moved up to become the prime target. On April 3, of 2005 the *Blade* proclaimed, in a series of stories threaded with suggestions of political favoritism, that the Ohio Bureau of Worker's Compensation (OBWC) had invested in a rare coin fund managed by Noe.

Part II- Coingate Erupts

The OBWC investment with Noe was public – approved in an open meeting – and operated quietly and apparently successfully for some seven years until the *Blade* article in April of 2005. The year that followed, however, was one of intense and bitter political struggle in which rare coins played a leading part.

NOE AND THE DEAL

To understand what happened with Noe and what came to be known as the "coin funds," it's necessary to go back to the inception to understand both how the investment with OBWC came about and also the nature of the deal that was reached.

In the mid-1980s through about 1990, several national businesses launched mutual fund-like investments in rare coins. Three funds were set up as limited partnerships with Merrill Lynch, and another was in a limited partnership with Kidder-Peabody. The Merrill Lynch-affiliated funds were liquidated after the initiator, Bruce McNall, went bankrupt.[26] The other appears to have done reasonably well.

Noe thought the idea of a mutual fund for coins was a good one, but felt that the initial efforts were flawed because the managers took their expenses and fees up front. In other words, the funds weren't particularly interesting to investors because the managers weren't sharing in the risk. Noe decided to pitch an alternative, in which the managers (the people who would buy and sell the coins) would take no expenses or fees but instead earn a share of the profits.

Noe had a lawyer draw up a draft plan and, beginning in the early 1990s, started to pitch it to everyone he could think of. His Vice President at Vintage Coins and Collectibles (hereafter VCC), Tim LaPointe, testified that this was one of Noe's preoccupations when LaPointe joined the business in 1991.[27]

Noe had little success with the idea until 1997, when he happened to meet Terrence Gasper, then the head of investments for the OBWC. According to Noe, he met the OBWC official when a friend asked him to recommend someone to help Gasper's daughter with a singing audition.

The OBWC is an interesting entity. As the name suggests, it was set up to provide a fund to support workers who were injured or disabled on the job. Employers are mandated by law to contribute a certain amount per month for each worker, and the OBWC, like any insurance company, invests the money. The OBWC also has a large staff to review claims and to administer payments.

The OBWC had always been a source of partisan tension in Ohio. The Democrats, who largely represented blue collar workers, were ardent champions. The Republicans, representing in large part employers, were hostile. In particular, Republicans claimed that OBWC fees to employers were too high because of fraud and abuse in injury and disability claims, and that these too-high fees were the "silent killer of jobs in Ohio." When Republicans were out of power they generally favored privatization of the investment (most states use private insurance companies for this purpose), but once back in office the appeal of managing the money was too strong and the OBWC remained a state entity even as power moved back and forth in Columbus.

As head of investments, Terrence Gasper sat on top of a giant pile of money – around $17B in 2005. Final oversight was in the hands of the Bureau's Administrator, appointed by the Governor, and there was also an advisory board with bipartisan membership whose recommendations were influential but non-binding.

Somewhere in the late 1990s, Gasper convinced the OBWC that it would be good to have a program that offered alternatives to the standard stock and bond investments that OBWC placed with the major national trading companies. The idea, which came to be known as the "Emerging Managers" program, also included a special bias toward Ohio-based firms.

Gasper encouraged Noe to apply for the Emerging Managers fund and, when the RFP came out, Noe quickly complied. Because he had already been working on the idea of such a fund, Noe had the key legal work already mostly completed. Following the guidelines, he applied for the maximum amount available, $25 million.

Noe's Ohio Coin Fund investment proposal was recommended by the advisory board and approved by the OBWC's Administrator. The entire amount was transferred to Noe's business account at Vintage Coins and Cards (VCC) in late March of 1998.

Two aspects of Noe's deal proved to be controversial: 1) did he make the connection with Gasper because of political ties to the Republicans who then controlled OBWC? And 2) how did he get such a one-sided contract through the OBWC's legal system?

The idea that Noe got his coin deal because of political connections is a central theme in Coingate, primarily because of Ohio's newspapers, especially the *Blade*.

Noe's story is that he learned of the Emerging Managers program by accident, through a personal connection. He doesn't deny, however, that his visibility in politics would have given him a kind of credibility that someone without his ties might not have had.

The newspapers speculated, albeit mostly indirectly, about the possible role of Paul Mifsud, the Chief of Staff to the former Governor George Voinovich, who left office in 1999 after eight years.[28]m

Mifsud was a focal point for two reasons. First, he was an important Republican operative and known to be close to Gasper, who was later convicted of soliciting bribes. Second, Mifsud was himself later convicted of taking a bribe and investigated for a time as being involved in a larger bribery scheme.

If there's more to the story than what Noe has said, we don't know and likely won't. Noe's point that a political unknown might not have been successful is well taken. On the other hand, the process wasn't by any means a secret: the RFP Noe responded to was a public one, his proposal was a public document, and the investment was recommended in a public meeting.

It's also important that the original coin fund's *Prospectus*, the document used to respond to the RFP and which was then embedded in the contract, is outspoken and assertive about the risks of investing in coins and the fact that such an investment is not for those concerned with liquidity. The *Prospectus* contains more text about risk than it does about opportunity. Certainly, this isn't the language of a con job.

The contract Noe and the OBWC signed for the Capital Coin Fund (later Capital Coin Fund I and followed by Capital Coin Fund II – CCF I and CCF II) proved to be controversial all by itself. Critics described the terms as being so favorable to Noe that they must have been part of a political *quid pro quo*. Noe agrees that the contract was a good deal for him, but argues that most of the controversial terms were related to the peculiar nature of the coin business as well as to the vulnerability he could experience if changing winds in Columbus caused the state to suddenly pull out of the deal.[29]

The contract described two categories of participants: managers and investors. The managers were Noe with his business, VCC, and a man named Frank Greenberg, whose business is called Delaware Valley Rare Coins (located in Pennsylvania). The investors included Noe and Greenberg as well as the OBWC, but the ratios were wildly disparate: Noe and Greenberg put in $50,000 each and OBWC $25 million.

After an initial startup period, profits were to be distributed 20% to the managers and 80% to the investors. Managers charged no fees and were compensated only from the profits. They could take only very limited expenses, primarily legal fees.

It's important to understand that the coin fund was constructed in almost identical fashion to a hedge fund (HF). In a HF, an investor buys in for a certain share of profits in a fund that operates for a certain period of time. The investor does not own the stocks or other financial instruments the HF buys, and often cannot withdraw any part of his share until the end of the term. The investor is only entitled to a proportion of the final profit (or loss). The HF's managers may or may not distribute profits before the end of the fund's term – this is at their discretion. The HF's managers must, of course, supply appropriate accounting documentation to prove that interim and final profit distributions are correct. All these typical provisions of HFs were the same in the coin funds. Despite the *Blade's* rhetoric, the state never owned even one coin.

The most contentious parts of the CCF contract(s) were: 1) the ability of the managers to invest in items other than rare coins; 2) the ability of the managers to take advances on profits and also to take loans from the fund; 3) the ability of the managers to self-deal – in this case meaning to buy and sell coins from and to their own businesses; 4) the fact that the accounting information provided to the investor – the OBWC — didn't have to include specific information about the inventory; and 5) the fact that the OBWC couldn't quickly and easily withdraw its investment. Relevant sections of the contracts are included in Appendix A of this book and are available on the book's website at: https://drive.google.com/open?id=0B9Sf_NQ6t8KJWURaNUpqQzZZcGs

Noe's explanation for these provisions is straightforward.

The managers needed to be able to invest in items other than rare coins because history showed that the coin market experiences slow periods – it was better to have the coin fund monies invested somewhere in these circumstances than to leave the money sitting in the bank.

Loans and advances were essential because much of the coin fund's business would be to act as a banker for dealers – to help them with upfront cash to buy coins at an opportune time, hold and then sell later. Such a process would leave profit for both the dealer and the bank.

The self-dealing provision was an extension of the coin-fund-as-bank concept and was essential, in Noe's view, for him and Greenberg to be able to maintain their existing businesses and customers. In other words, if the coin fund could help other dealers buy coins for their regular customers, why not also for the managers? Since the coin fund was a transient investment, it was very important to Noe and Greenberg to be able to retain over the long term the core customers who provided a key part of their business.

Finally, there was a part of the contract that was important only by omission: the audited annual financial statements that the managers were required to provide to OBWC did not specify that information on inventory be provided. Indeed, it was understood that this would *not* be made available.

The explanation for this is simple: any document received by the state is a public document and, if competitors were able to learn not only what coins the coin fund held, but also how much had been paid for them, it would be difficult if not impossible for the coin fund to sell at a profit. We'll see that, although politicians and public officials initially derided this argument for keeping the inventory secret, they came to strongly support it when the coin funds were taken over by the State of Ohio.

The provisions making it difficult for the OBWC to withdraw funds quickly and easily were based on the long-term nature of the fund. Noe and his partners expected for their investments to appreciate over a number of years, not in a month or so as people often expect with stocks. As a result, they wanted contractual insurance to keep OBWC from suddenly deciding to withdraw its funds and leave the partners with a loss based on fire sale prices.

The initial Capital Coin Fund appeared to do well for the first few years, reporting profits of just under $8 million by 2005. There were some internal concerns at the OBWC about controls and the appropriateness of some of the investments, but these were largely dismissed by higher OBWC management.

One important change, however, was that after a 2000-2001 OBWC review Noe was required to submit an inventory. In deference to his concerns about competitors, the documents were kept in an official's desk drawer and designated as "trade secrets" in order to escape discovery through a public records request.

On the basis of the reported profits, the OBWC decided to invest another $25 million in 2001. Although the records of the investment were all public, only a handful of people knew about it until the *Blade* launched its investigation in 2005.

Overall, the arrangement with OBWC seemed like a good deal for Noe. In fact, though, his big problem began with what almost everyone would consider a stroke of good fortune: the OBWC offered him far more money than he'd been planning for.

Again, Noe had been thinking for a number of years about how to construct an investment plan that would seem reasonable to investors, and his idea of a fund in which the managers don't take fees or expenses up front but instead take a share of the profits was not just logical, it was emotionally compelling. If the manager takes a risk and doesn't profit unless you do, it only makes sense that he has a very strong incentive to do well. The approach would obviously appeal to investors who were willing to go into this area.

The problem was that Noe's plan didn't scale well. At a fund level of $5 million or maybe $10 million, the idea made a lot of sense. Noe and his partner would do essentially what they had been doing for a number of years, just at a somewhat higher level. And, even if trading slumped a bit, it wouldn't be that difficult to make a profit since the fund wouldn't be that big a share of the total market.

Noe did what almost everyone would do when offered a larger amount of money to manage — he took it. If we think we're good at what we do, we generally think we can do more.

But changing from $5-10 million to $25 million turned out to be a huge difference.

First, it was much harder to fold the cost of the fund's operations into the existing business. To keep things going, there would have to be additional expenses for personnel and systems– expenses that couldn't be reimbursed until a year or so in the future when the business showed a profit.

Second, the pressure to keep funds invested in a way that would return significant profits was now much greater and much harder to satisfy. With a $5 million fund, Noe would have found enough action in the coin market to generate profits even in slow times. That would probably also have been true at $10 million. But with the need to get a good return on $25 million, Noe was stressed. As it happened, in the initial period there just wasn't enough movement in the coin market. If Noe didn't want to look like a slug in his annual reports to OBWC, he had to take risks. This explains accepting some loosely connected people as partners as well as his hastily considered investments in real estate (though these turned out well).

Scale matters. If Noe had stuck to his original plan, he would almost certainly have been fine. But, if you multiply the expected amount of the investment by five, the shape of the challenge changes significantly. It's an interesting example of perspective. From the point of view of the OBWC, $25 million was a very small amount, not enough to get much staff or advisory board attention. But from Noe's perspective, this same amount represented not just a huge opportunity but also a giant challenge – a challenge that required him to make adjustments he'd never planned for.

An outsider might ask why it is that trading in the coin market could be expected to generate significant profit – don't people who collect things just buy and hold? Why is there enough turnover to keep profits coming in?

The answer is that most people who invest in objects like rare coins do so at least in part with the idea that they're hedging the economy. They believe they are buying into a resource that, no matter the ups and downs of the daily economy, will certainly grow in value over time because there is a limited supply. These people don't buy primarily or even at all in order to hold and admire coins. In fact, the most valuable coins are kept in secure containers and can't easily be handled without serious risk of lost value.

Because they are very interested in and attuned to markets, investors of this kind don't simply buy and hold. Just as they would do with a stock, when they see a coin appreciate substantially they often decide that selling presents an opportunity to make a profit and reinvest. In other words, just as some true collectors admire the items they purchase and want to hold them, others gain satisfaction from the process of buying and selling.

Of course, for some people the two factors combine to impact behavior. They are traders who also enjoy the pleasure of collecting. Or perhaps the weight is the other way around. In any case, the fact is that the market for rare coins includes both existing and new investors and, as a result, has consistently offered the possibility of profit for those who trade as well as for the brokers who assist in trading.

For skeptics who think the whole idea of investing in rare coins is silly, remember that there has been a market for many categories of rare things as far back as we have recorded history. Markets in areas such as art are driven as much or more from scarcity as from intrinsic value. The same is true for gold, the value of which is driven far more by the fact that it's rare and has a finite supply than because of its use to fabricate things, whether electronic or decorative. Finally, scarcity is also a major factor with stocks. The market for shares of businesses is for the most part driven by company performance, but these days it is also significantly inflated by the fact that people (including retirement and insurance funds) have a large amount of money to invest and there aren't many places to put it. Indeed, when you deride the coin market as a legitimate area for investment, remember that much trading in the stock market is driven by traders' perceptions of others' perceptions about the economy rather than by any objective change in value.

THE BLADE ATTACK ON NOE

The Blade's first story on what became known as Coingate, published on April 3, 2005, was the result of a careful investigation.[30] The paper's reporters had looked at documents at the OBWC, had read a critical audit paper written by one of the staffers named Keith Elliott, and had interviewed numerous people, including Tom Noe.

The very long lead article wasn't a simple attack. For example, the extensive coverage of Noe's political background can't be seen as unfair in light of a reasonable concern that a very unusual investment might have been made possible by politics. There are favorable quotes about the investment from officials at the OBWC and on other aspects. There are some minor cheap shots, too. For example, out of the 50 states, the Blade used quotes only from state officials in Idaho and Vermont. And, not surprisingly, budget experts in both of these tiny states trashed the idea of investing in coins or similar.

This initial article covered a range of topics. One was the concerns of an OBWC internal auditor, Keith Elliott, who questioned a number of things: whether the managers of the fund should be allowed to buy and sell from their businesses to the funds (the "self-dealing" described in the contract); whether the mortgages held by the funds were adequately supported by the value of the real estate; and whether it was appropriate for the funds to pay advances to partners for coin deals that had not yet occurred. Elliott was also worried by the fact that the OBWC did not have access to the actual inventory of coins held by the funds.

Most of Elliott's concerns were dismissed by the OBWC management because they were consistent with the contract – for example the self-dealing was explicitly allowed and investments and loans could be made "whether or not secured."[31] However, as mentioned above and reported by the Blade, the Bureau did later modify the agreement to require that Noe provide an audited inventory, albeit one held separately in an executive's desk and, because labelled a "trade secret," not considered a public record.

The Blade also chronicled the fact that some coins had been stolen and some lost in the mail, and that one coin fund associate had lost money, causing the fund to write off about $800,000. A lengthy follow-up related Noe's problems with a partner in Colorado, the one who had had some coins lost in the mail, and with whom he was now engaged in an unspecified legal conflict.

Finally, the Blade article went into some detail about Noe's investments in a Toledo-area real estate business led by a man named John Ulmer. The story did report Noe's reason – that the coin market was slow and that he wanted to get some return on the CCF dollars while waiting to invest in coins. However, the story went on to cite local criticisms of the developer, who was portrayed as someone who exploited low-income families. Ultimately, likely primarily because of the Blade's attention, Ulmer was investigated and went to prison for investment fraud[32]m (see below).

The Blade's reporting, by focusing on its discovery of the investment, gave the impression that Noe's deal was secret. In fact, as mentioned previously, the meeting at which the CCF was created was a public one, and as the program continued, the OBWC even issued press releases about the overall "emerging managers" effort.[33] Had anyone been interested, Noe's deal could easily have been known back in 1998.

Still, no one could call this initial Blade story a hatchet job. Noe was quoted on key aspects and given space to explain what he was doing.

The real concern about this initial article, and increasingly with the ones that followed, was the *Blade*'s subtle misrepresentation of the investment. An ordinary person reading this article and especially the follow ups would think that the State of Ohio was buying and possessing coins. The article repeatedly refers to Ohio's investment in rare coins – "Since the state first ventured into rare coins." And, of course, the title of the article was "Ohio Agency Sinks Millions Into Rare Coins."

In fact, the state was buying into a fund that bought coins. The contract, which the *Blade* must have had access to since they had other materials such as audits, clearly describes an operation much like a hedge or a venture fund. As noted earlier, when you invest in this type of fund, you don't own the stocks and you don't have any management role – you just get a share of the profits after expenses.

If you look at the coin funds as hedge or mutual funds, which is the only way they should be considered, the question of which coins were where at which time is not really relevant. Losses with specific investors are relevant, but are taken in the context of the overall profit/loss at the end of a reporting period. Investors in these types of funds don't care if the managers made a few bad choices if they're offset by good ones. For example, later in the summer, when the OBWC dropped some low-performing investment funds managed by Ohio banks, neither the *Blade* nor any other paper looked at the banks' individual stock holdings and questioned the individual purchases, not to mention the compensation and personal life of the individual managers.

The *Blade*'s initial story, by beginning to direct attention to "missing coins!", set the paper's tone for the whole Coingate affair. The issue could have been "maybe bad investment?" and it could have also been "maybe political influence in getting a contract?" but instead, it was moving toward "stolen coins!!" And that appeal to popular emotion set into motion a chain of events in which no one in the public eye, even those who must have understood the flaws in the logic, was willing to stand up and offer a more balanced perspective.

THE SEARCH WARRANT

"…there were a series of agreements in that the State decided each day, sometimes twice or three times a day, that the agreement it had reached for an inspection protocol was no longer satisfactory to it, they wanted more, sooner, faster."[34]

The introduction to this book briefly describes the events surrounding the search warrant, and characterizes the process as an important violation of American values. This section will provide more information to support that argument and also illustrate the key role that executing a simple warrant can play in destroying fundamental fairness.

It's necessary to go back through the major events just prior to approval of the warrant to fully understand the issues.

A Quick Recap of the Background

The first week of April of 2005, which included the initial *Blade* story on the 3rd, had been a bad time for Tom Noe. But things got worse throughout the rest of April and into May. Here are the key events (for overall media coverage of the period see below):

- April 8- Newspapers reported that the Ohio Inspector General had opened an investigation into Noe and the coin funds.

- April 22- Another long *Blade* article described an incident of theft at Noe's Colorado affiliate and mentioned that a former partner, Mark Chrans, had a felony record and had lost some $800,000 in bad coin deals.

- April 23- Noe was publicly warned by the Ohio ethics agency about a potential violation because he invested in a start-up company run by professors at the University of Toledo. Noe was perceived to have a conflict because the Board of Regents, of which he was a member, had an oversight role with the university. In fact, Noe was concerned about this and wrote to the Ethics Commission in early December of 2004 asking for an advisory opinion. In his letter, Noe pointed out that the business had no legal relationship with the university. The Ethics Commission didn't respond until late April of 2005, in the heat of the *Blade* attacks on Noe, when it sent a letter stating that there was a conflict. In fact, from the point of view of someone more knowledgeable about the issues than the Ethics Commission, it seems very doubtful that Regents oversight did extend to this area.[35] Also important, Noe did mention his coin fund businesses on his State of Ohio ethics disclosure forms.[36] Despite the background, and the important fact that Noe was never charged with an ethics violation, the public impression was highly negative and Noe resigned from the Board of Regents.

- April 27- The FBI announced that Noe was being investigated for possible violations of campaign contribution law. A few days later, the Bureau raided Noe's residence and took some materials away.

- May 5- The OBWC announced that its investments in the coin funds would be dissolved; negotiations with Noe's lawyers began in the context of a civil action filed by the state in Judge Cain's court in Columbus.

- May 15- A long *Blade* article said that Noe had been in deep financial trouble in the 1990s and suggested that political connections could have been the reason for the OBWC investment.[37]

— May 22- The *Blade* went in-depth on Mark Chrans, the former Coin Fund associate who lost money. The article focused on the fact that Chrans had a previous felony conviction (Noe said he didn't know that). The article ended by quoting a challenge from a Democratic politician running for the office of Attorney General: "We need to shut down whatever is left of this."[38] The incumbent Attorney General's spokesperson responded that he was "evaluating several options but no decision had been made."

— Monday, May 23

• Defense lawyers and lawyers for the state met in the morning in the Columbus chambers of Judge Cain who was overseeing the civil case – the OBWC vs. Noe. Defense lawyers accepted the State's request for an inventory/ inspection of the assets belonging to the coin funds, and agreed to begin that process with visits to the affiliate sites in Delaware, Colorado, Florida, and California. The site in Ohio, in Maumee, was to be done last because an inventory for the assets held there was not yet available. Defense lawyers emphasized that a delay in Maumee was essential because the lack of an updated inventory meant that it might not be clear whether particular coins held there belonged to the Coin Funds or to someone else. It was common, they pointed out, for other dealers to send coins to colleagues for inspection. Defense lawyers also continued to express concern that the valuation of the Funds could be affected if detailed records, including purchase prices, became public documents and could then be accessed by competitors.

• Later in the afternoon, lawyers for the state told the defense that they had changed their minds and that inspection at Maumee needed to begin immediately. No specific reason was given, but the suggestion that the decision was made by the Attorney General was never challenged. In light of the *Blade*'s article the previous day suggesting that the incumbent Attorney General was failing to move on Coingate, this speculation is entirely reasonable. Defense lawyers responded that they would act as soon as possible, but that the lack of an inventory and the fact that lawyers from their firm had already been sent around the country meant that Maumee definitely couldn't start the next day. They suggested that the inspection begin with collectibles that were held by the coin funds. The state's lawyers agreed, although in the meantime OBWC employees appeared in Maumee and asked to see coins. Noe's staff did not allow the inspection, citing the agreement in Columbus.

- Tuesday, May 24

    • Inspections began in Maumee and around the country (the sites were in Colorado, Delaware, Florida, and Pennsylvania).

    • Despite having been told that coins wouldn't be provided that day, OBWC personnel at the Maumee site again asked to see coins. Staff at Noe's business again responded that, as mentioned in the court discussions in Columbus, an inventory was not available. The OBWC personnel then proceeded to work on collectibles.

    • OBWC personnel, in cooperation with the Ohio Highway Patrol, continued to maintain around the clock surveillance on the Maumee site.

- Wednesday, May 25

    • Inspections at the four sites across the country were completed without difficulty.

    • OBWC personnel at the Maumee site again asked to see coins and were again told that an inventory was not available. They continued to work on the non-coin collectibles. Later that day, an agreement was reached among lawyers in Columbus that would allow access to the coins the next day.

- Thursday, May 26

    • After midnight, the surveillance team in Maumee observed people removing boxes from the building that housed Noe's business. In their report, they said that they were worried that important records and/or coins, all of which were considered state property, were being removed.

    • Early that morning, a team that had been working for about two weeks and included representatives of the Lucas County Prosecutor, the Auditor of State, the Ohio Inspector General, the OBWC, and the Highway Patrol made a final decision to seek a search warrant. They described the information from the surveillance that morning as the trigger, though the continued unavailability of coins in Maumee was also mentioned as a key factor.

    • Before the warrant was completed and presented to the magistrate, the State Task Force knew that an inventory had been made available by Noe's lawyers to the team of inspectors at the Maumee site and that inspection of coins there had begun.

- Just prior to the presentation of the warrant, the State Task Force learned of attorney William Wilkinson's comments during a meeting that day in Columbus about a "shortfall" in the valuation of the Coin Funds. A verbal description was given to the magistrate before he signed the document.

- Later that afternoon, the warrant was executed, with Ohio Highway Patrol staff arriving to seize materials — thereby preventing other Ohio investigative staff from completing their assignment to inventory coins.

It's important to understand that executing a search warrant was not just a slightly more forceful version of sending inspectors and auditors to the front door. This search warrant authorized the state to seize and remove relevant materials and records from the premises. That meant not just coins and collectibles but also paper and electronic files – in other words all of the computers. No business can operate in such circumstances, so a search warrant effectively meant closing VCC and laying off its staff for some period of time. Reopening after such an event isn't easy, even ignoring the damage to a business' reputation that follows a televised raid by law enforcement.

In fact, once the state possessed the records and materials, the onus was on Noe to prove that they should be returned. All the state had to say was that it needed the seized items for an investigation and it was able to keep them unless and until Noe's lawyers could convince a judge to order their return; something that isn't easy to do, especially if the judge is in Toledo and working under the harsh glare of the *Blade*. Effectively in this case, executing a search warrant was forcing a bankruptcy – something that would likely have been true even if the coin inventory had been intact or if there had been a good and immediately available reason for why it wasn't.

The Defense Challenge to the Warrant and the Prosecution's Response

Detailed information about the process leading up to the search warrant is available because the defense team formally challenged the warrant's validity. The challenge didn't occur at the time, but in a pretrial motion over a year later, in July of 2006. The motion was aimed at making information obtained in the warrant inadmissible in the trial. Various briefs were filed, and these were followed by two days of testimony in late July of 2006.

The Defense Case

The defense's arguments to suppress search-related evidence relied on six core arguments:

1) The warrant contained no allegations that Noe violated Ohio law and no evidence in support of that;

2) The scope of materials seized far exceeded the mandate of the warrant;

3) Material and "recklessly misleading" statements of fact were made in the warrant and in the process of securing it;

4) Important facts that would have made the warrant invalid or inappropriate (such as Noe's complete cooperation with the inventory and with the state's lawyers in the civil action in Columbus) were excluded;

5) Some of the information included was years old and not relevant to the issues at hand; and

6) Information was given to the judge outside the warrant that was inappropriate and inaccurate.

Overall, the defense appeared to make an effective argument that the warrant was deeply flawed and intentionally misleading. It's notable that the defense brief demonstrates two outright falsehoods in the warrant: 1) that the Coin Funds were not permitted to purchase collectibles (the contract did allow this and discussions and agreements between Noe and the OBWC about collectibles were in fact well documented); and 2) that a contempt hearing for non-cooperation had been initiated against Noe in the civil court in Columbus (simply not true).[39]

The prosecution's response relied primarily on technical, legal issues, though it did allege two key things: 1) Noe did deny entry to his Maumee business location prior to the State's request for the search warrant; and 2) defense attorney Wilkinson's assertion of a "shortfall" in the Coin Funds was valid evidence of theft (the "shortfall" remark was made on the morning of May 26, the day the warrant was presented to the magistrate). Beyond these points, the prosecution's brief simply ignored many of the allegations in the motion to suppress, and specifically failed to respond to the two egregious falsehoods cited above.

Testimony

Testimony on the defense motion took two days in late July of 2006.

The defense pushed hard on several of the fronts presented in their motion, especially on the argument that the warrant contained no allegations of legal violations in Ohio. In response, neither the prosecution's brief nor their witnesses offered much in the way of support for this aspect of their warrant.[40]*m* The OBWC's chief investigator did suggest that they had discovered new evidence of problems in Colorado during a visit just prior to the issuance of the warrant. But, when pressed, the investigator couldn't substantiate that the information really was new because he had neglected to review all the information Noe had previously provided to OBWC on the Colorado situation.

Another example of the state's failure to check its own records as part of an investigation emerged during the trial, when the head of the OIG, Tom Charles, testified that some six weeks into the investigation he hadn't personally read any of the OBWC files. It also became clear from the same testimony that, if Charles' senior staff had the files, they'd neglected to apprise the people in the field of their content. Thus-

> Q [Wilkinson for the defense]. Okay. Well, as we've established earlier, there were collectibles that were part of the Coin Fund assets; isn't that correct?
>
> A. [Tom Charles] Yes.
>
> Q. Okay. But your inspectors on the ground didn't know that at the time?
>
> A. No.
>
> Q. All right. So they might have thought they were getting the runaround when in fact they were seeing things that belonged to the Coin Fund; isn't that true?
>
> A. You could assume that, yes.[41]

Lacking evidence that the warrant actually did allege a violation of Ohio law, the prosecutors simply asserted that the State Task Force acted in good faith, sincerely believing that there was some such violation, and that this belief was all that was required for a warrant.

Similarly, the prosecution offered little to offset the defense contention that the warrant failed to mention Noe's cooperation, for example the fact that he was the one who had alerted the OBWC to the Colorado situation. Also, the warrant failed to note that Noe had been fully cooperating with the civil court in Columbus — including agreeing to inventories at the four sites in other states and accepting an inventory in Maumee, with just a few days of delay for very good reasons.

The prosecution didn't challenge the defense on the importance of these points. Instead, they merely asserted that leaving out these facts was not misleading.

Continuing to ignore the substance of the defense's charges, the prosecution's response skimmed over the negotiations on access to Maumee and failed to mention the fact that access was ongoing at the other four locations. Instead, the prosecutors defended their "denied entry" assertion in the warrant by simply mentioning a technicality — that the contract required Noe to make his books available "for inspection and audit" during normal business hours. In addition, the prosecutors said that "Noe had no legitimate reason" to prohibit the OWBC from inspecting assets on demand — passively denying the legitimacy of Noe's expressed concerns about the availability of attorneys, the lack of final inventory and the problems it might present, and the danger of trade secrets becoming public. Normal fairness would have recognized all of these points as "legitimate reasons."

On the issue of attorney Wilkinson's "shortfall" comment, the defense pointed out that a "shortfall" in a financial account is by no means an indication of criminal activity and that characterizing it as such was inappropriate and had the goal of misleading the magistrate. The prosecution simply disagreed, while again emphasizing that their understanding of Wilkinson's comments – whether accurate or not — constituted reasonable cause to support a warrant.

The warrant's conclusion that the surveillance of Noe's business revealed criminal activity was also supported in a very passive way by the prosecution. Again, as with the other issues, prosecutors avoided specific and active support for the actions and decisions of those conducting the surveillance. Once more, they essentially confined themselves to arguing that the conclusions they advanced met the minimum legal standard for a warrant.

Apparently because they knew that the weight of precedent was on their side, the prosecution's overall defense of the search warrant was, in a word, relaxed. For the most part prosecutors offered only vague defenses of the assertions in the warrant and instead relied on larger arguments about having probable cause. And, as noted earlier, the prosecution completely ignored the two flat out falsehoods in the warrant.

Despite employing a largely passive strategy, the prosecution did make some important and revealing assertions, both about the nature of the coin funds and about whether a warrant was needed at all.

With respect to the nature of the funds, one of the more interesting technical arguments made by prosecutors was contained in their response to the question of whether the warrant alleged any criminal activities in Ohio (vs. in Colorado). The prosecutors' brief on this point emphasized that all but one of the Coin Fund affiliates, including the one in Colorado, were incorporated in Ohio with Noe as their "statutory agent," and therefore that criminal activity regarding them was appropriately a violation of Ohio law.

The prosecutors' emphasis on the affiliates being Ohio companies is of interest for their case as a whole, since they later worked hard to push the non-Ohio entities out of the picture. Including the affiliates in the charges against Noe would have made it difficult to avoid looking at the state's overall investment in the coin funds, including whether there was a profit for the funds as a whole. But prosecutors did not want the jury to consider Noe's activity from this larger perspective. Instead, they wanted jurors to see it only as a series of transactions that took place in Noe's main office in Maumee. Unfortunately for Noe, the defense lawyers were never able to take advantage of the fact that the prosecution contradicted its Ohio-only strategy in defending the search warrant.

In addition to the above, the prosecutors made two key legal points on whether they should be able to retain and use the seized evidence at trial.

First, they said that even if the court found violations in the warrant, the materials should still be available for use. This is because case law allows evidence to be used except where there are egregious – usually meaning deliberate — violations of the warrant process.

Second, the prosecutors argued that they would have been able to secure the documents anyway through other means.

As with essentially all of the technical responses from the prosecutors, these points were well taken from the point of view of law. However, the final argument, that documents could have been secured by other means, raised an important contradiction:. Why get a search warrant if you know you can get the materials through another approach? This point, together with the question of why a search warrant was executed after the site had already been opened to investigators, will be addressed in the conclusion to this section.

Overall, the defense team destroyed the prosecution's witnesses in the search warrant hearings. The attack was tactful, and sometimes reads as if it were kind of folksy, but it was still devastating.

Prosecution witnesses acknowledged that there had been an agreement to review the out of state sites before moving on to the Maumee location and that they had changed their minds shortly afterwards, insisting on seeing the Maumee coins right away. They did not challenge the assertion that suddenly changing their minds caused a huge logistical problem for the defense lawyers since defense attorneys were out at the various sites around the country. The prosecution also didn't actively challenge statements by defense witnesses that the change of plan occurred because the Attorney General, an aspiring candidate for Governor who was under pressure by the *Blade*, "wanted to see a coin."

The witnesses also acknowledged that Noe's lawyers had presented good arguments for a few days delay in Maumee. One logical reason for delay was that they [the defense] didn't have an updated inventory and were concerned, since the site had coins with multiple owners other than Noe and VCC, that the investigators would mistakenly attribute to the coin funds items belonging to someone else. And, although the state's official position at this point was to disagree, the witnesses also acknowledged that the defense attorneys were continuing to express concern about the danger to the coin funds overall valuation if the details of the inventory were made public.

These active and passive admissions by the prosecution removed the foundations of the search warrant's fundamental argument: that Noe and his attorneys weren't cooperating. The hearings demonstrated that they clearly were. Given how important this cooperation was in light of the warrant's assertions to the contrary, it should have been important news. But the *Blade* ignored it.

The Role of the Blade

The *Blade's* belief that something was wrong – stolen coins! – with Noe's OBWC investment was the major reason for the search warrant. Did the paper have justification for its pressure?

The *Blade* first reported on Mark Chrans' loss of $850,000 on April 22.[42] That's certainly significant in absolute terms, but much less so in the context of $50,000,000. This is just over 1.5%, not all that much when you consider that profits were being made in other areas of the fund .

The *Blade* also gave the strong impression in the same April 22 article that a lot of money was lost with Noe's Colorado affiliate, but a careful reading of the story shows that supporting evidence wasn't there. And subsequently reported information –available to the *Blade* at the time if it had asked — shows that the coins were insured and there was no loss. Also available for the asking at the time of the April 22 article was the fact that Noe had seized $900,000 in profits owed to the Colorado company because of concerns over business practices (see below). That very large interim profit helps put the Chrans loss in perspective.

If one strips away the rhetoric, it's clear that the *Blade's* pre-search warrant argument that the funds were likely to lose money was speculation and not based on any solid evidence. When all was said and done the impression of chronic loss it strove to create wasn't at all accurate – and that includes the idea that Noe "stole millions."

While the *Blade* was seeing things that weren't there prior to the search warrant, it napped through the defense's challenge to the validity of the warrant a year later.

The *Blade's* coverage of the defense's critically important search warrant challenge can be summarized in this exchange between Noe's attorney William Wilkinson and Henry Hudson, then of the Ohio Highway Patrol and the person who signed the request for a warrant and gave it to the magistrate:

Wilkinson- As you sit here today, you've learned things that happened that aren't accurate in your search warrant; isn't that correct?

Hudson- Yes.

What's significant in this exchange is that neither the quote nor the overall line of argument that the search warrant was largely phony was reported in the *Blade*. Before and after this hearing, *Blade* stories on Coingate emphasized pithy, colorful quotes, the kind of short bursts of information that convey a lot of information quickly. But not in this case; perhaps because the information might be favorable to Tom Noe.

The *Blade*'s approach to Noe had actually shifted before the search warrant was issued, with its May 22 article on Mark Chrans.

As had been mentioned in an earlier, April 22 *Blade* article, Chrans was an affiliate of Noe's who lost a substantial amount of money in the early years of the funds. His mistaken investments caused Noe to write off about $850,000. Even though Noe had reported the loss and the circumstances to the OBWC, and even though the core of the story had been reported a month earlier, the *Blade* still felt compelled to send a reporter to California to interview the erstwhile partner.

The May 22 article contained no substantive new information about Chrans' legal history or about the losses. But the *Blade* wanted a good story, and its readers got that. The article provided personal details, including not just on Chrans' past felony conviction, but also on his family background, the place he was living, and his interest in yoga. The purpose of the article seemed to be clear: associate Noe with odd and perhaps shady characters. This set the stage for connecting the situation to politics by closing the article with an inflammatory quote from a key Democratic politician mocking the inaction of the Republican Attorney General.

The *Blade*'s in-depth and personal focus on Chrans, a colorful but peripheral figure, contrasts sharply with its distinct lack of interest in the demonstrably fraudulent nature of the search warrant.

For example, it was clear from the hearings that the language of the warrant led the magistrate, as it would have done any reader, to believe that Noe was complicit in various coin-related crimes in Colorado. The problems in that state were serious (though not nearly as bad as reported from the fiscal point of view), but the warrant's language neglected to mention that it was Noe who had reported them. This is like suggesting that a witness who reports a crime must be guilty of something because he was around and saw it happen. This twisting of facts was no small matter – and a whole lot more important than Mark Chrans' interest in yoga. Why didn't the *Blade* mention it?

And why didn't the *Blade*, so good at attacking perceived weaknesses in defense arguments, notice that the response of the prosecutors to the glaring weaknesses of the search warrant was technical and legalistic rather than substantive and responsive to the key concerns? Why not mention the two direct falsehoods in the warrant?

Indeed, why didn't the *Blade* tell its readers that, in his ruling on the warrant, Judge Osowik described one of its assertions as "recklessly" false?[43] (The warrant said that there was a contempt citation on Noe in Columbus, but there was none).[44]

The history of *Blade* reporting on Coingate, from the May 22 Chrans article to the end of the trial and beyond, shows a consistent pattern: when there was evidence that appeared to be harmful to Noe, the language was colorful and pungent. When the evidence ran the opposite way, the *Blade* adopted a diffident, detached view, just mentioning the facts and sometimes not all of them.

A reader with some analytical skills could easily discern that, beginning in late May of 2005, the *Blade* was striving to give the impression of being neutral and unbiased while actually pitching a strong point of view – Noe is guilty of…something. The purpose of the ongoing legal process was to find out exactly what.

Unfortunately, we know that the American public as a whole is sorely lacking in the kind of analytical abilities needed to separate pretend neutrality from active bias. And, as we'll see later, the people of Lucas County, Ohio proved to be no different in this regard than the larger American populace.

Conclusion on the Search Warrant

There wasn't real drama in the hearings on the search warrant, at least in the sense of wondering about the outcome: judges rarely throw out evidence from a search warrant. Generally, there have to be clearly defined constitutional issues before evidence is disallowed. For example, a judge can severely criticize the actions of police and prosecutors while still allowing evidence to be used in court.

But the problem with the Coingate search warrant wasn't really about the evidence. Instead the core issue was whether the warrant was actually needed.

Was the objective to seize and secure materials that weren't otherwise obtainable or that might disappear absent quick action? That seems hard to believe. First the highway patrol and other officials didn't interfere when they saw boxes being removed from Noe's business in what they considered to be a clandestine and likely illegal action. Second, there is the state's own assertion in court that it could have obtained the needed evidence by other means than through a search warrant. Remember, although it did turn out that records had been tampered with, the fact is that, at the time the warrant was issued, the authorities had no reasonable evidence for believing this to be true.

Or, was the purpose of the raid to give the public, and especially the *Blade*, the impression that there was movement in dealing with Coingate? Given the political situation of those overseeing the state's side of things, and given their sensitivity to media criticism, this seems the only possible explanation.

Criticism of the search warrant shouldn't be taken to mean that the evidence seized should have been denied to the state. The authorities had a right to the records of the coin funds and, to allow a complete audit, logically also to copies of Vintage and Noe's accounting. Access to the inventory had already been agreed. The problem isn't the fact of this access, it's how it was secured. A handover of the inventory was in process, and the various government agencies had no valid reason to believe that they wouldn't get everything they wanted by simply asking for it. They pursued the search warrant because they wanted visible action (including a photo-op) to get the *Blade* off their backs. The action was legally acceptable (though at the margins), but morally wrong. The moral flaw goes beyond the motivation. The manner of getting access to records and inventory had as an entirely unnecessary consequence forcing a company out of business and causing many people to lose their jobs.

Another way of understanding the consequences of the search warrant is to consider what would have happened in the case of someone who had no role in politics and was of no interest to the media – just a businessman who had a contract to invest some OBWC funds. We'll call this person Non-Political Noe .

Just like the real one, Non-Political Noe (through his lawyers) would have agreed to provide immediate access to the inventory at all sites except, for the same reasons, would also have asked for the short delay in Maumee.

But now there's a difference. Without the *Blade* pressuring the authorities, the state's Inspector General wouldn't have issued a press release announcing an investigation. And the process wouldn't have been personally overseen by the state's Attorney General. Why would the state's top law enforcement officer be involved in what was to that point a simple civil dispute? People would have seen it as absurd if he'd intervened and there would have been suspicions he was harboring some kind of personal grudge.

Instead, the process would have been left with a civil court judge, and he or she would have found the explanations given by Non-Political Noe to be quite reasonable and allowed the little bit of extra time. One reason that a civil court judge would have been amenable to delay is that he or she would have likely taken the time to read the contract and, unlike the state investigators, would have known that the OBWC was actually seeing assets belonging to the coin fund when its investigators reviewed collectibles.

It would have been amazing if, in the case of Non-Political Noe and the corresponding absence of pressure from the *Blade*, the OBWC had argued against a request for a delay of a single day and pushed instead for a search warrant. The civil court judge would have quickly rejected this idea as unnecessary, noting that the materials could easily be secured by other means. Further, the civil judge might well have held the authorities in contempt when he realized that they knew but had failed to tell him that the activity the search warrant was designed to ensure had already begun when the warrant was presented to him.

Back in the real world, it's clear that the primary purpose of the search warrant was to make government officials look good to the media – even the Inspector General was there for a photo-op packing boxes — and they used considerable public resources to achieve their goal.[45] But the *Blade*, which would normally be scathing about such frivolous behavior by government, was quiet in this case. Apparently, wasting public resources is acceptable if the purpose is to please the *Blade*.

The outcome of the search warrant was twofold.

First, by focusing on coins rather than on the totality of assets, the public officials, both at the state level and in Lucas County, bought into the *Blade*'s narrative of the state of Ohio as coin collector rather than fund investor.

In a normal business conflict of this kind, the story would have been one of an investor questioning the value of assets held by a partner. This is the kind of boring thing that few readers pay attention to – even when politics is involved – a point that's illustrated by another OBWC case, that of MDL[46]*m*, where a huge amount of money ($215 million) was actually lost, but which got far less attention because of its dry and technical nature.

But the *Blade*'s decision to focus on the coins made the affair more tangible and therefore more emotionally charged. Most important, it deflected attention from the overall value of the investment and instead helped the prosecutors focus their charges solely on individual coin transactions, a decision which ensured that future jurors looking at Noe and the coin funds would be seeing the trees and not the forest.

Second, the publicity surrounding the search warrant was enormously harmful to the public's view of Noe. The term "denied entry" was employed over and over again to suggest that Noe was urgently trying to remove coins that belonged to the State. The many references to the Colorado episode cemented the idea of Noe being involved in theft and fraud, while news stories ignored the important fact that Noe had reported the problems and that he too was a victim (a loss to the state meant a loss of profits for Noe). Because of its access to the OBWC records, the *Blade* knew that Noe had solved the Colorado situation in a way that involved no loss to the coin funds.

Ultimately, defense attorney William Wilkinson's description of a "shortfall" in the funds —discussed next — was a bigger media issue. Even so, careful analysis shows that the search warrant fiasco had an important impact on both prosecution strategy and public opinion.

A Turning Point: Noe's lawyers stumble

What did Wilkinson mean when he referred to a "shortfall" in the presence of a group of state attorneys?

Noe believes that his lawyer was referring to the decline in overall valuation in the context of a forced sale. In a meeting the day before, Wilkinson had asked what the loss to the valuation of the funds would be if Noe was forced to sell quickly? If he had to liquidate in a fire sale? Noe says he replied that the loss in overall valuation in such a situation would be in the range of $10 to $15 million.

So, we know that risk to the coin funds' overall value was in Wilkinson's mind just before he made his statement.

On the other hand, all the attorneys in the room say they were focused on the inventory then in process, so it's reasonable to assume they would have been thinking of that. And, none of them says that Wilkinson used the word "valuation," a term that could have redirected their thinking (an affidavit from one of the state lawyers present can be found with this reference[47m]).

We do know that Wilkinson could have had the inventory in Maumee as well as the overall valuation of the funds in mind. He had just the day before received the hastily-completed Maumee inventory and agreed to have it turned over to the state and used in the overall assessment of the coin funds. It's possible that he had found the time to do a careful review, and in the process noticed the large difference between the 2004 and 2005 Maumee inventory numbers and the fact that these did not appear to have been justified with documented transactions. It's possible. But, given all that was going on at the time, it seems improbable that he would have had time to do such a careful review.

Even if Wilkinson had become aware of the inventory problems in Maumee, it's unclear why he would have wanted to prepare the public for bad news in this awkward way. That's especially true because, in the short period of time available, Wilkinson couldn't have known for sure that there wasn't in fact a good explanation for the status of the Maumee inventory. It isn't common for lawyers to attribute bad behavior to their clients without first looking for an explanation; indeed, it's most typical for the explanation to precede the acknowledgment.

Waiting a week or more for the investigators to announce preliminary conclusions from their inventory analysis would have offered Wilkinson more opportunity to provide context– important since the defense attorney had had almost no time to discuss the case with his client.

The idea that Wilkinson was referring to the Maumee coin inventory is enhanced by the suggestion of some of the state lawyers that the defense attorney, when asked to clarify what he meant by a shortfall, had said that "it" was "gone, missing." Of course, whether the "it" referred to inventory or valuation isn't clear.

Interestingly, no one reported that Wilkinson had said that *coins* were missing.

Some fifteen months later, in the context of a defense motion to prevent the prosecution from bringing up the shortfall statement in the trial, Wilkinson did say, though not directly, that his "shortfall" statement referred to future lost value in liquidation. However, it was the prosecutors, in their reply, who offered the clearest and most succinct version of Wilkinson's position:

> Noe argues that the aforementioned statements [an affidavit summarizing the conversation is attached to the document] do not concern Noe's theft, money laundering, or other offenses regarding the BWC investment money but instead are statements of opinion or forecasts of future developments regarding the liquidation of the coin funds.[48]

The prosecutors went on to affirm that, while Wilkinson's argument was a possible interpretation, there are others that could be made — including the prosecution's own interpretation that the statement was in effect an admission of theft. Then, remarkably, the prosecution made a very surprising suggestion: let the jury decide.

> Because the statements are, at a minimum, ambiguous (capable of more than one interpretation), it should be for the jury to place its interpretation on the Wilkinson statements.

Ignoring the prosecution's decision to explain the meaning of the word "ambiguous" to the judge, this shows a significant turnabout by the prosecutors. When the issue was the overall valuation of the coin funds, the prosecution was adamantly opposed to allowing the jury to have any role.

From the defense's point of view, a trade of positions would have been reasonable: they'd have been happy to concede admission of Wilkinson's statement (because, as we'll see, the jurors almost certainly already knew about it) in return for being able to present information on valuation which, thanks to state policy, was most definitely a mystery to the jurors and the public as a whole.

Moving back to May of 2005, what Wilkinson meant to say was almost irrelevant. If he meant to refer to valuation, he should have clarified immediately. But he didn't, and as a result the various players in the state suddenly switched or solidified their positions. Democrats, who had long been following the *Blade* in suggesting theft, now treated it as a fact.

Republicans, who had moved toward being critical of Noe during the prior weeks and especially after the FBI announced it was investigating him for campaign violations, also now accepted theft as the only conclusion. It's unlikely there was any kind of collusion on this point; there's no suggestion of a meeting where senior people came to a formal decision. Rather, everyone with experience would appreciate that the Republican strategy should now become one of getting Noe off the table as quickly as possible because a major election was coming up in just sixteen months. If that meant asserting he was guilty before knowing the facts, then so be it.

The *Blade*, which had been suggesting theft for some weeks, now also treated it as a fact. In addition, the newspaper's emphasis on the state as coin collector hardened, and there was no serious discussion of the OBWC investment as a whole – other than coins — after this point. From Wilkinson's statement forward, the *Blade* focused on missing or stolen coins and largely ignored other aspects.

But the most significant outcome of the Wilkinson statement was its impact on the state investigative group. Up to this point, the state had a diverse and not especially well coordinated team looking at Noe. The state's Office of Inspector General was reviewing issues from the perspective of the OBWC, including Noe's funds but also others. Lucas County prosecutors were involved but apparently primarily only because the search warrant was served in their jurisdiction. Prosecutors in the state capital of Columbus were taking part because of the civil case there and because of possible crimes in their county (Franklin). The Auditor of State had begun a special audit of the Coin Funds. Federal agents were involved but not in a leadership role – puzzling since another OBWC investment was treated as a federal case. The Attorney General appeared to be investigating everything and coordinating overall.

But after the Wilkinson statement, the focus of the investigation changed to a newly constructed entity called the State Task Force.

THE STATE TASK FORCE

Coming off of the Keystone Cops effort that produced the search warrant, the various law enforcement parties involved in Coingate created a formal team, known as the Joint Task Force of State and Federal Agencies Investigating the Bureau of Workers' Compensation Coin Funds' Investments. Thankfully, the group created no acronym and was simply known as the "State Task Force."

Members of the task force were: the Lucas County Prosecutor; the Franklin County Prosecutor (the state capital is in Franklin County); the Ohio Inspector General; the Ohio Highway Patrol; the Ohio Ethics Commission; the Bureau of Workers' Compensation; the US Attorney's Offices of the Northern and Southern Districts of Ohio; the Ohio Attorney General; and the FBI.

The membership lists suggests a heavy-duty law enforcement focus and that's accurate. But politics was still very much a factor.

As an example of the political pressure connected to the State Task Force, consider again that Jim Petro, the current Attorney General, was running for Governor and had faced criticism from both sides for lack of faster action on Noe. Of all those under political pressure, Petro was taking the most heat.

Also, another of the other key members, Franklin County Prosecutor Ron O'Brien, was a candidate for the Republican nomination to replace Petro as Attorney General. At the time the State Task Force was doing its work, O'Brien was being strongly criticized by rival candidates on both sides for going light on fellow Republicans suspected of ethical violations and corruption.[49] As with so many others in the prosecutorial structure, he had a strong incentive to take a tough stand on Noe.

And then, of course, there was Prosecutor Bates, an elected Democrat with partisan and personal ties to active opponents of Noe.

One of the first post-search warrant actions by task force members was the decision on May 27 to hire Development Specialists Inc. (DSI), headquartered in Chicago, to liquidate the assets of the Coin Funds. The choice of DSI was made by retired Judge William T. Bodoh, a lawyer with a Cincinnati firm who was himself appointed to oversee the OBWC civil case by the Attorney General. It is not known how DSI was chosen; there does not appear to have been any kind of bidding process. The rationale for liquidating the funds immediately was given as Attorney Wilkinson's statement about a "shortfall."

In other activities, the state's financial oversight group, the Controlling Board, approved a special $750,000 appropriation to support the OIG's investigation. Curiously, the OIG, which regularly draws attention to the amounts expended on other government efforts, neglected to mention this addition to its budget in its various reports.

The most important action in this period, however, was the decision to hire an accounting firm, Crowe Chizek of Chicago, to do a special audit of the books of the coin funds and related entities, including of Noe and his various business entities. It later emerged that this contract was for about $500,000; that amount may have been supplemented later – the records aren't clear.

As with the hiring of DSI, there appear to have been no competitive bids for the Crowe Chizek hire and no contract is available on the public record. It's curious that, as politicians and government officials were decrying OBWC's secret contracts (which were actually open), they appear to have been busy creating mostly covert contracts of their own.

As we'll see shortly, the State Task Force wasn't just a group that launched contracts, it was the organization that turned a broader investigation into one aimed exclusively at Noe. There was no visible breach of legal or ethical standards in the process, but if there was a conspiracy in Coingate, it would be found in the State Task Force.

ETHICS IN THE HEADLINES

The roughly seven month period — from the seizure of Noe's business and the closing of the Coin Funds in late May of 2005 until Noe was indicted in February of 2006 — was a busy time for the various state actors and for the newspapers.

The big Noe-related headlines in the summer and fall of 2005 were around the ethical problems of Governor Taft and his staff. Relentless investigations by the *Blade* and also by Ohio's major newspapers revealed that Taft had failed to list on his ethics report gifts of various kinds, especially golf outings. One golfing event, in Toledo, had been paid for by Noe.

The Governor's problems were fodder for the press and for Democrats, but when one steps back from them it's easy to see that, absent the fierce political environment, they didn't amount to much. There's no indication that Taft wanted or needed gifts. Instead, the various ethics problems clearly represented sloppy record keeping by his aides rather than any deliberate attempt to seek personal gain or violate laws.

But there was other Noe-related news during this period that revealed some very negative practices. Noe's habit of inviting senior public officials to expensive dinners at Morton's restaurant in Columbus was heavily publicized by the *Blade* and others as "Noe's Supper Club." Only one of the persons attending these events, which lasted over a long period of time, reported the meals on her ethics form, as clearly required by law. The omissions are perhaps not surprising since the average cost per person was over $150. And it wasn't just the meals: one former senior Taft aide, while he did report his family's visit to Noe's Florida home, nevertheless faced ethics charges because he substantially understated the value of his stay.

Even more serious, Noe offered loans to several of Taft's former staff who, as members of boards and commissions, were required to file ethics charges but failed to do so.

Technically, Noe did nothing wrong with the meals and loans and was not charged. However, he was certainly aware of the ethics laws and would certainly have known that all these gifts (of meals) and loans were required to be publicly listed and that the recipients were unlikely to do that because it would have drawn immediate and very negative press attention — the ethics forms were not merely public but carefully scrutinized. Certainly, if the press had known about the loans as well as the OBWC funds, connections would have been made, with the conclusion being that Noe was cultivating the former but still well-connected senior officials in the hope of protecting his deal.

The ethics investigations also revealed that Noe had used some individuals, including at least one former aide of the Governor, as "conduits" who were charged with illegally sending money from Noe to various state politicians, including some Supreme Court judges. Noe took these actions, which predated the similar federal case (see below) with the clear intention of violating the law.

Given what we know of Noe's focus in the preceding years, it's most likely that his principal motive for offering loans and gifts to senior people in the administration was to maintain influence in politics.[50]*m* But the objective of protecting his deal with the OBWC can't have been far from his mind, and he should have realized that former and current aides, while not exactly innocent victims, were compromised by his actions.

Laundering campaign donations through conduits was explicitly illegal for Noe as well as those who helped; and in these cases Noe clearly encouraged others, for the most part less established in their careers and therefore more vulnerable, to assist him in illegal activity.

A common explanation for Noe's complicit violation of ethics and campaign finance rules is that he wasn't unique, that secretly funneling money as well as offering gifts and not reporting them was the prevailing culture in Columbus. For this reason alone, the *Blade*'s aggressive pursuit of Coingate performed an important public service, one that led to more assertive enforcement of campaign finance and ethics laws in subsequent years.

THE FEDERAL CASE

Tom Noe was indicted in October of 2005 with three felony counts of illegal campaign donations. Although he didn't plead guilty right away, there was never any real doubt about what happened: Noe gave about $2,000 each to 24 people so that they could make donations in their own names to the Bush campaign. Noe had already donated the maximum amount, so the indirect gifts were illegal.

Since many of the various parties quickly admitted the illegal donations, resolution was just a matter of time. As it happened, Noe waited to plead guilty until May of 2006 and was quickly convicted. He was sentenced to 27 months in federal prison on September 12, shortly before his state trial began. Some of the various "conduits" also faced ethics charges and were fined. At least one blamed Bernadette Noe:

> "Ms. Shultz told investigators that she agreed to take Tom Noe's money to attend the fund-raiser only after Bernadette Noe put "extreme pressure" on her to attend. Ms. Noe never was charged with a crime."[51]

Tom Noe has been openly contrite about these actions,[52] acknowledging that his poor judgment harmed friends. He has also suggested that he had bad legal advice on whether the particular mechanism he used (tickets to a fundraiser) was actually legal. It's certainly possible he received poor advice, but Noe really should have known that any attempt to get around the campaign finance laws was risky, offering the danger of harsh public criticism if not legal vulnerability.

Friends of Noe have commented that this kind of evasion of campaign law goes on all the time and that Noe's sentence here was unusually severe. Neither of these defenses has much weight, though. The fact that prosecutors don't catch everyone isn't an excuse to punish no one. And, the scale of Noe's effort, his attempt to disrupt the investigation by asking people to claim that he had given them loans, and his slowness to finally accept guilt probably provides the rationale for the sentence. As with the ethics violations, Noe's actions demonstrate the poor choices of someone who was eager to remain a key political player in his home state.

The Story Behind the Story

Most observers say that Noe's problems in Toledo started because of a conflict between Bernadette Noe and one of the "conduits" for the Bush event, longtime Noe family political protégé, Joe Kidd:

> "Less than six months after the October, 2003, Bush fund-raiser in

Columbus, Joe Kidd faced another difficult choice.

Ms. Noe had accused him of taking a $2,000 cash bribe from a consultant for Diebold, the voting-machine manufacturer he had secured for the county, and Lucas County prosecutors wanted to talk to him.

As he weighed whether to tell prosecutors everything, some of his closest friends discouraged him from talking. They knew what this could mean - for Tom and the party.

What happened next changed many lives. Instead of defending himself against Ms. Noe's accusation, Mr. Kidd made one of his own: Tom and Bernadette Noe had arranged for him to become an illegal campaign conduit - to President Bush."[53]

Kidd acted as soon as he learned of Bernadette's accusations against him.

Joe Kidd was a Republican. Paula Ross was a Democrat. But when she arrived at Mr. Kidd's office at the Lucas County Board of Elections one day in January, 2004, she wasn't there for a partisan scrap.

As director of the elections board, Mr. Kidd had a better relationship with Ms. Ross than her fellow board member, Republican Bernadette Noe.

Mr. Kidd recalls Ms. Ross walking into his office and asking...How is it going?' I said, 'Fine.' She said, 'I think you better sit down.'

Ms. Ross then told him that Ms. Noe had gone to Lucas County prosecutors and accused him of soliciting or accepting money from a consultant for Diebold, the voting-machine manufacturer.

Mr. Kidd said he soon learned that prosecutors had been told he had received a $2,000 cash bribe from a Diebold consultant.

He said he was shocked, because he knew it wasn't true.

Ms. Ross advised Mr. Kidd to get an attorney.

"She said she's serious, she's taking you out," Ms. Ross told him.

"Bernadette ought to be careful about making allegations of wrongdoing because there are plenty of fingers that point right back at her," Mr. Kidd said he replied...[54]

Later, Mr. Kidd met with Tom Noe and asked him to ask his wife to "call off the dogs." Noe said he couldn't, Mr. Kidd recalled...

"'What do you want me to do? I can't control her,'" Mr. Kidd recalled Noe as saying in a recent interview with The Blade, the first he's granted since the Noe scandal broke last year.[55]

Kidd went on to speak to Lucas County prosecutors about his role as a fundraising "conduit" for the Bush campaign. After a hiatus of some months while the Lucas County staff investigated the charges against Kidd, his case was turned over to the FBI. Kidd told them everything. Most observers believe that news of the federal investigation is what caused the *Blade* to develop the Coingate story.

Mr. Kidd later turned up in the news when he and another Republican activist felt that they were hurt because the outline of a book they were planning to write about the Tom Noe/ Coingate story was published by a newspaper.

> Two Republican insiders working on an account of the Ohio investment scandal involving Tom Noe are suing the Toledo Free Press for publishing sections of their book proposal.

> Joe Kidd and Jon Stainbrook accused the weekly tabloid of illegally obtaining their outline of Bush League and publishing a June 7, 2006, story that damaged possible earnings from publication of the book...

> "They stole our property, published its secrets, and greatly diminished the value of our story," Mr. Stainbrook said. "Essentially, overnight the Toledo Free Press robbed us of 2 1/2 years of hard work."[56]

An uninvolved author might feel that they were far too optimistic about the financial value of this kind of story.

POLITICAL CONSENSUS: GET NOE/ DUMP NOE

Noe's many problems, and especially the federal case, made him a lightning rod for criticism from both sides.

The Democrats increasingly saw Coingate as a powerful gift. Given the national environment, they already had high hopes of securing the Governorship. But they now also saw a possibility they had not expected to have for a long time: control of both houses of state government. The Republicans, in power during both the last two post-census periods, had gerrymandered legislative districts with high precision. It would take an electoral landslide, not a mere majority, for the Democrats to gain control of the legislature. All of a sudden, though, Coingate seemed to make that possible.

Republicans saw the same message from the opposite perspective. They feared losses not just in 2006 but also in 2008 – including the Presidency. Their obvious goal for Coingate became one of limiting damage, and the best way to do that would be to move Noe from the stage as quickly as possible.

The origins of the Republican decision to dump Noe can be seen in the agreement of GOP officials to the search warrant. The first factor in Republican acceptance of this dramatic step would have been the announcement of the federal investigation. Given the number of people Noe involved as "conduits," and given the fact that the investigation had been in process for quite a few months, Republican leaders would certainly have known that Noe was going to be charged and found guilty —it was just a matter of time. But such violations of campaign law aren't unusual and don't resonate much with the public, so the initial leadership reaction was likely to have been one of accepting Noe's slow disappearance from the political scene.

But, with the earth beneath Noe loosened by the feds, the thing that finally unleashed a landslide was the previously mentioned *Blade* Mark Chrans story on May 22. There had been no specific allegations of criminal action on Noe's part prior to that point, and the story contained no significant new information about losses to the coin fund or about Chrans' legal history. Rather, by pursuing a story with the simple goal of titillating its readers, the *Blade* gave the impression it wasn't going to give up on its pursuit of Noe until he was destroyed. In addition, by also asking a prominent Democrat for a quote about Republican inaction, the *Blade* signaled it was committed to using the affair to provoke a partisan conflagration, one that Republicans were certain to lose because they were in office. Thus, speed was essential in removing Noe from the limelight, and it was therefore possible to approve even such a legally bizarre action as a search warrant without any evidence of criminal activity or of non-compliance in a civil suit.

Unfortunately for the Republicans, legal processes don't move immediately from allegation to indictment to the courtroom. Any experienced observer could see that Noe's trial was likely to take place close to the November, 2006 elections. Given this, the only possible choice was to disassociate the party from Noe.

The Republican rejection of Noe happened quickly, and took the most radical possible form.

Governor Taft- "Mr. Noe has clearly deceived and betrayed many people at organizations and has irresponsibly managed the state's moneys," Mr. Taft said at a Statehouse news conference. "If he is guilty of criminal conduct, he should receive the most severe punishment possible under law."[57]

State Party Chair Bob Bennett- "*When* he's found guilty, he should face the strongest possible punishment" [emphasis supplied].[58] "Noe lied to nearly everyone. He stole money meant for injured workers and he broke the law. It is as simple as that. The criminal is responsible for his crime and if people want to shift blame for Noe's criminal actions, they are doing it for partisan political purposes, Mr. Bennett said. Tom Noe is a crook. He should go to jail."[59]

Attorney General Petro was an especially important player, since he was running for the Republican party's nomination for Governor and expected to have a tough fight. Petro, likely pressed hard by his campaign staff, was outspoken on Noe, launching what critics called an "investigation-by-press-release." Petro told the press, among other things, that "There was an absolute theft of funds going on," and that "There is a pattern of corruption, and the profits reported by Mr. Noe were fictitious." He also flatly stated that "the coin funds never turned any profit for the state."[60]

From the perspective of fairness to Noe, all this was a disaster. Every visible office holder was pronouncing Noe not just guilty, but as an exemplar of all that was wrong in politics.[61]m And the *Blade* was very much a part of this.

THE BLADE FROM SEARCH WARRANT TO INDICTMENT

The *Blade* published a great many Coingate-related stories in the period from the search warrant to the indictment, i.e., from about June 1 of 2005 to February of 2006. On one side, the Coingate episode led the *Blade* to launch an outstanding series on political corruption. Many of the other stories were only tangentially related to Noe and many were procedural or technical. However, two substantive stories and one editorial stand out as revealing the *Blade*'s point of view.

The "Sell the Coins at Cost" Editorial

In one of The *Blade*'s odder pronouncements, it opined in May of 2005 that the Attorney General should release all coin fund records, including the inventory of all coins held and what the coin funds paid for them.

The paper began its opinion piece logically, if rather darkly: "Frankly, while we and all Ohioans hope that liquidation of the coin inventory will recover the state's investment, there is a strong likelihood that it will not."[62] As noted earlier, this was before the raid on Noe's business and no justification of any kind was offered for the "strong likelihood."

From there, though, logic seems to be eclipsed by anger:

> To shield the process [of liquidation] is a shameful violation of the public trust, and it could put the state in the position of snookering coin collectors. The value of a coin is what a buyer is willing to pay for it. If maximizing the state's return depends on potential buyers' misperceptions about just what the state holds, that is abhorrent government behavior.

Coins could be sold, the *Blade* continued, at "artificially high prices if the process is not totally transparent" and the victims would be "ordinary collectors."

Of course, no company in this kind of business – including art, antiques, jewelry, or a host of other similar vendors – releases the price at which it purchased items when it puts them up for sale. And, needless to say, ordinary retailers don't post the prices they paid to suppliers or wholesalers. Thus, the *Blade* is arguing that the State of Ohio should adopt a sales strategy that puts itself at a significant disadvantage vs. others doing the same thing. Why?

To illustrate the reality of what actually happened with the funds, sales appear to have been primarily at auctions and to dealers. In the case of the auctions, Ohio was like everyone else in not listing the price paid. And, because dealer transactions often occur when the purchasing dealer has already identified a buyer, they can be lucrative: one relatively small transaction with a dealer netted $128,000 in profit.[63]

This editorial certainly seemed to suggest that the paper's leadership was eager to see the coin funds return as little money as possible – the better to justify charges against Noe?

Colorado and Stolen Coins

The mini-saga in Colorado, mentioned earlier, is a little complex. It began in October of 2003 when Noe's partner there, Michael Storeim, reported that two valuable coins owned by the coin funds and sent to a service for grading were missing from the return envelope. It was a big deal because the coins were estimated to be worth $300,000. Storeim reported the incident to local law enforcement and Noe reported it to the OBWC.

After some time, Colorado authorities closed their investigation without making charges, but the affair caused Noe to be suspicious of Storeim. Eventually, he came to believe that his Colorado partner was skimming profits through an Internet-based scheme and that he may have stolen an additional number of coins. Noe hired forensic accountants to investigate.[64]

Because Noe's preliminary conclusion was that Storeim was guilty, he took two actions: 1) he had colleagues go to the Colorado store and seize items owned by the coin funds; and 2) he withheld some $900,000 that the coin funds owed to Storeim as profit distributions. These actions were also reported to the OBWC. Together, Noe's decision to retain profits owed to Storeim more than compensated for any loss to the funds from the $300,000 pair of coins (which were covered by insurance in any case), the possibly stolen coins, or the Internet skimming scheme. This was the status when the State of Ohio took over the coin funds (and many of Noe's assets) in May of 2005.

Once it had information about the situation in Colorado, the *Blade* quickly resurrected its favorite "stolen coins" story line, publishing a batch of stories during the summer of 2005.

One theme from the *Blade's* coverage was that, "Mr. Noe did not report the theft to Ohio authorities or to police."[65] And, in another article: "In the wake of the theft from an Express Mail package which never was reported to police by Mr. Noe...."[66] Altogether, the "did not report" claim was repeated many times during the summer of 2005.

That Noe didn't report the theft was technically true, but certainly appears to have been deliberately misleading: Why would Noe report to the police something he knew had already been reported to them?

Another *Blade* theme was that wine, cigars, and other items found in Storeim's house "might have" been purchased with coin fund monies — "A half million dollars of Ohio's coin money might have been poured into 3,500 bottles of wine stored in a cellar at the suburban Denver home of a former employee of Tom Noe, Colorado authorities say."[67] The *Blade* article that started the skein of "wine and cigars" headlines didn't initially provide much to support the "might have," but eventually said that some items had been purchased on a credit card belonging to the coin fund affiliate. Some two months later, August 5, it still "wasn't clear" if the purchases had been reimbursed and there was even continuing uncertainty that one of the cited purchases was on the Ohio-related account at all.[68] A year later, Colorado authorities were still "studying" the bookkeeping to see if Ohio money was involved in wine purchases.

A third issue was whether Storeim had taken a number of less valuable coins owned by the Ohio funds –121 is the number most frequently cited. The *Blade* also repeatedly cited Noe for not reporting this theft to the police. But there was a good reason he hadn't done that – Noe's assistant, Tim LaPointe, wasn't the best inventory manager in the world and while Noe was still in charge there had been some doubt as to where the coins were. As it happened, Noe was right not to report a theft because the coins were later found among VCC's assets. The *Blade* reported this, but for those who missed the story, the negative impact on Noe's image remained.

In summary, the *Blade* described Noe as failing his responsibility to report thefts to the police and for negligence in overseeing the accounts of an affiliate. But the first charge wasn't true. And if the second one couldn't be unraveled by the Colorado law enforcement in a year, it's hard to blame Noe, who in any case got all the money back and more.

When judges of the Sixth District Court of Appeals later noted that, "it may be argued that the news media was not entirely unbiased with regard to the prosecution of appellant,"[69] the Colorado stories could have been "Exhibit A" — of a list that would have run to "Z" and beyond.

The Cayman Islands Affair
As mentioned earlier, the Lucas County Prosecutor's office avoided the

investigation-by-press-release strategy of the Attorney General and the Sheriff's Office in Colorado. There were, however, two important situations in which Mrs. Bates decided to talk to the press. The first of these was of very questionable appropriateness and must have served to feed the strong anti-Noe bias fostered by the *Blade*.

Sometime in early November of 2005, the *Blade* received an anonymous communication containing letters dated in 2003 in which a banker in the Cayman Islands –a notorious haven for tax evaders — thanks someone for referring Tom Noe to him. The clear implication in the letters is that Noe has money in this offshore bank.

The *Blade* had a potentially major story with this communication, but faced a challenge: you can't publish stories about anonymous communications without some kind of external verification. If you do, you not only open yourself up to lawsuits, you effectively advertise that, by publishing first and investigating later, you are a willing pawn in any dispute or vendetta that comes along.

Since the *Blade* had a limited ability to verify the situation in the Cayman Islands – accounts there are secret after all – it found another way to justify publication: it asked the Lucas County Prosecutor for comment.

The expected response from Mrs. Bates would have been a firm "no comment." It seems logical that by saying anything else the Prosecutor would be providing free and difficult-to-retract publicity for the sender of an anonymous letter together with highly prejudicial and jury-biasing information for a potential defendant.

Despite the obvious dangers, Mrs. Bates did choose to comment, thereby likely enabling the *Blade* story.

The *Blade* quoted Mrs. Bates as saying, "We're going to thoroughly investigate every aspect of the letters," then going on to add, "We're looking for the money. Where's the money? We should try to account for every nickel." Bates also said that the matter of a possible Noe account in the Cayman Islands had been referred to the US Attorney's office."[70]

The US Attorney's office, acting ethically, refused any comment in response to the *Blade's* inquiries.

Bates did say the letters might be forged, and the *Blade* did find some contradicting information about their legitimacy. But these were pebbles dropped into a stream of text about how notorious the islands were as a center of tax evasion, including a role in providing assistance for drug kingpins and terrorists.

In an apparent attempt to support the idea that Noe might be culpable, the *Blade* emphasized the fact that Noe had travelled to the Bahamas recently. The Bahamas and the Cayman Islands are different places and not all that close, but this appeared to be irrelevant to the *Blade*.

In fact, Noe had no account in the Cayman Islands and investigation of the verifiable information in the anonymous letters showed them to be fake. The *Blade*, which according to sources ran the initial story "above the fold" in its printed edition, is reported to have issued the retraction deep inside the paper (the location can't be independently verified since the electronic edition doesn't show position in the paper and the retraction does not appear in searches, either via the *Blade* site or from Google.)

Coverage of the Valuation Press Conference

On December 23, of 2005, Noe's attorneys organized a press conference in Columbus that was designed to demonstrate that the coin funds had made a profit for the state.

The Blade story on the event first allowed its readers a very quick statement from defense lawyer Wilkinson:

"Our purpose in coming here today was to try to help the public understand the actual results from operations of the coin funds, so no one would be misled by the inaccurate characterization of the coin fund as a failed one," Mr. Wilkinson said.[71]

That's all Wilkinson got to say in the article before the prosecutor and others weighed in:

> Lucas County Prosecutor Julia Bates dismissed the news conference as an attempt to sway the public, prospective jurors, and newspaper publishers.
>
> "They're sending spin out into the world," said Ms. Bates, whose office is criminally investigating Mr. Noe and possible wrongdoing associated with the coin funds.
>
> Even if the coin funds have increased in value, it doesn't necessarily mean a crime wasn't committed, she said.
>
> Ms. Bates said Mr. Noe's attorneys could be attempting to influence public opinion to weaken calls for vigorous prosecution. But it won't have any affect [sic] on her investigation, which has been ongoing since August, when a special grand jury began hearing evidence in Lucas County, she said.
>
> Attorney General Jim Petro in May filed a lawsuit against Mr. Noe in an effort to recover money believed to be missing from the coin funds. Mr. Petro has presented evidence to the court that Mr. Noe stole $4 million from the coin funds. Mark Anthony, a spokesman for Mr.

Petro, noted yesterday that Mr. Noe and his attorneys did not answer questions about the coin funds' shortfall and the alleged theft.

"They could not, and still cannot, account for $13 million in the coin-fund assets, and we brought compelling evidence of at least a $4 million in conversion," Mr. Anthony said.

Mr. Anthony also said the numbers presented by Mr. Noe and his attorneys were "hypothetical."

"Hypothetical numbers always make sense in a hypothetical world," Mr. Anthony said.[72]

Finally returning to the press conference, The *Blade* reported Wilkinson as saying:

Mr. Noe and his attorney said they used information from public reports, Development Specialists Inc., which is the firm that the state hired to liquidate the rare-coin investment, and other "third" parties to reach their estimate of $61.8 million.

The estimated figure includes:

$7.9 million in alleged profits already distributed to the bureau.

$16.775 million, which has already been liquidated.

$100,000 in outstanding stock.

$4.08 million in outstanding loans.

$33 million in coin inventory.

Once that was reported, another challenge followed:

Retired Judge William Bodoh, who was appointed to oversee the liquidation of the coin funds, said the projections presented at the news conference do not seem to line up with the actual numbers from coin-fund records.

"We are in the midst of liquidating the funds and this does not appear to reflect liquidation," said Mr. Bodoh, who plans to study the information presented by Mr. Noe.[73]

One interesting aspect of this story is Prosecutor Bates' willingness to speak out. Until this point and with the important exception of the Cayman Islands affair, Bates and her colleagues on the State Task Force, in sharp contrast to their loquacious colleagues in Colorado, had shown an admirable reluctance to speak to the press. But the valuation press conference was one of only two important exceptions (together with coverage of the fake Cayman Islands letters). The reason for the attack on Noe's press conference seems obvious: if the funds were seen to have made a profit, it would be much harder to secure a criminal indictment for theft, not to mention a conviction.

Overall, the *Blade's* article on the press conference avoids any kind of thoughtful analysis, instead substituting an unmistakable thread of sarcasm: Noe's claims are absurd, every responsible person says so. Note also that the *Blade* inserts "alleged" in front of previous profit distributions in the list of funds returned. In fact, the validity of this distribution was never challenged in the many legal processes.

There's an interesting contrast to the *Blade* story in an article published by another media outlet, the *Business Journal* in Columbus.[74]

The *Business Journal* coverage of the press conference reported the skepticism of Bodoh and others, but was balanced and gave much more space to Wilkinson, quoting him to the effect that it was grossly inaccurate to characterize the coin funds as "excessively risky, a failed investment." The MDL loss of $215 million was a failed investment, the lawyer said, not the coin funds which had made a profit.

The *Blade* also missed an interesting comment from Wilkinson, "If my statement earlier about a possible $12 million to $13 million shortfall has confused anyone about the results of operations then I'm sorry about that." A puzzlingly enigmatic statement and food for thought – but apparently not for *Blade* readers who didn't see it.

In fact, the value of the coin funds was an extremely important issue about which a lot was already known. In internal documents, DSI was predicting almost a full $50 million recovery within a month of the state seizing the funds.[75]*m* And some information was actually already published.[76] But the *Blade* had almost from the start expressed skepticism that the coin funds would return the amount invested – despite providing no foundation for this belief – and the article on Noe's press conference seems designed to reinforce the paper's existing point of view.

Although coverage of the press conference illustrates the attitude of the *Blade*, it also represents the first step in what seems to have been a fatal error on the part of Noe's attorneys. Instead of using available data, such as records of purchase prices and whatever information the state possessed, they suggested they were trying to estimate the value *after* Noe lost control in May of 2005. This set them up for the prosecution's charge that the value of the funds "post-Noe" was irrelevant. More on this critical point later.

The *Blade* ran an editorial on the Noe press conference ("No News, Much Spin." December. 26, 2005.)[77]

The editorial reengaged with the *Blade's* previous theme that the coin funds had lost money and derided the argument that the funds would return a significant profit:

But this was spin-doctoring, nothing more, and it was labeled as such not only by Lucas County Prosecutor Julia Bates but by the Chicago-based consultant in charge of liquidating the assets of the now defunct coin funds venture.

William Brandt put it bluntly. When the liquidation is complete, he said, "I think you'll find a significant portion of that return isn't there."

We believe he is absolutely right. The citizens of Ohio should never lose sight of one thing: Even if some of the coins purchased with $50 million in public funds managed to increase in value, that is a function of the marketplace in rare coins. It does not mean that a substantial portion of the taxpayers' millions is not missing, and it does not mean that a crime was not committed.

One of Mr. Noe's attorneys, Bill Wilkinson, acknowledged several months ago that as much as $13 million of the state's money could not be accounted for.

If that money was indeed misappropriated for Mr. Noe's personal use, that's a felony. If a portion of the investment managed to turn a profit, it does not obscure that fact, and no amount of spin by Mr. Noe's legal team can make it OK.

In fact, we have to wonder if the admission earlier this year that between $11 million and $13 million was missing was an attempt to, in effect, inoculate the public against more devastating disclosures - and much larger losses - down the road.

We anticipate that when this long and complicated mess is finally sorted out, the money Mr. Noe will claim to have earned for the state will come nowhere near what he was given to invest. What Ohioans have a right to expect is their $50 million in principal back, plus whatever realized gain has been achieved. Tough to imagine they'll get it.

Reportedly Mr. Noe has not been especially forthcoming or cooperative with authorities as they work their way through the legal complexities of the matter. If that is so, and he's ultimately convicted, he will be entitled to no expectation of leniency.

In the meantime we hope the next time Tom Noe schedules a news conference, he brings some news. It's going to take a lot more than an aggressive "spin" cycle to clean up the dirty laundry of Coingate.

The *Blade's* seemingly deliberate misunderstanding of the purpose of the funds is again on display. The paper argues that Noe shouldn't be given credit for coins that rose in value, even though buying particular coins with the expectation that their value would increase was the whole point of the investment.

Interestingly, in news articles, the *Blade* referred to Wilkinson's comment as a "valuation shortfall" but used "missing" in the editorial, which of course implies theft.[78]

As it happened, the *Blade* was wrong and the funds did return a significant profit; a point it didn't fully acknowledge until 2015.[79]

The *Blade* editorial was another step in building a public narrative that the coin funds had lost money for the state and its injured workers. We'll see that the Lucas County prosecutors picked up on this theme but with a special spin: presenting a story of major loss to the public while at the same time refusing to consider in any specific way the overall value of the funds.

Delays in Reporting?

The summer and fall of 2005 saw the publication of several stories alleging that news of Noe's federal investigation, and perhaps also the story of his OBWC investment, could have been reported earlier by the *Blade*.

In fact, the Lucas County Prosecutor, Julia Bates, had received allegations about the federal crimes back in March of 2004. She waited until September to turn them over to federal authorities because her office was investigating a related allegation and had to clear that first (this is the Kidd investigation mentioned above).

On October 16, 2005, the *Blade*'s Ombudsman published an article on the actions of a former reporter for the paper, Fritz Wenzel. The story was in response to an article in the national political paper, *Salon*, which argued that Wenzel knew about Noe's illegal campaign donations long before they were public – many months before the election --and chose not to publish a story about them because he (Wenzel) was a Republican and didn't want to hurt Bush's chances for reelection.

In response, the *Blade*'s Ombudsman made the point that the paper would have had no reason to protect Bush and, although there was some concern on the part of editors that Wenzel was partisan, the evidence in his actual work product was at best slim. The article then went on to say that it took *Blade* reporters time to investigate Coingate and earlier knowledge wouldn't necessarily have been sufficiently complete to allow publication before the election.[80]

Although the *Blade*'s position was that the paper didn't have knowledge of either the federal investigation or the OBWC investment before the 2004 election, in late 2005 John Robinson Block spoke almost wistfully to a Salon.com reporter about what might have been, saying that if Coingate had been known before the election "most Republicans I know agree that Kerry would have won Ohio and won the presidency."[81]

Taken in their specifics, the various allegations about a conspiracy to suppress knowledge of Noe's campaign finance violations, or possibly even the OBWC investment, fail to convince. In particular, there's no reason to believe that those in law enforcement and at the *Blade* who held knowledge of Noe's federal crimes had reason to protect him – to the contrary, in fact.[82]*m* But taken as a whole, the stories provide more evidence of the political anger that pervaded Ohio and especially Lucas County.

The Blade on Corruption and Political Donations

The *Blade*'s Coingate series sent it on a parallel journey to look at the role of campaign contributions on actual or potential corruption.

Starting with Noe's desire to be a Bush "Pioneer" (someone responsible for at least $100,000 in donations), a series of articles in 2005 and into 2006 looked at the actions of Pioneers and Rangers (responsible for $200,000+) across the country. The *Blade* managed to get interviews with quite a few of Bush's major donors, questioning them on how their businesses were affected by their giving. These were excellent, important stories and are every bit as relevant today as they were then. They also illustrate an important commitment to investigative journalism by a smaller paper.

AUDIT AND INDICTMENT

As mentioned earlier, the Auditor of State commissioned a special audit of the Coin Funds and of Noe and his businesses in June of 2005. The special audit became the basis for the indictment, which was issued on February 23 of 2006.

Indictment

The indictment document is itself of little interest. It specifies 53 counts: one felony of the first degree, one of the second, four of the third, and five of the fourth. There are also eleven counts of money laundering and eight of tampering with records (all third-degree felonies). Finally, there are twenty-two counts of forgery, all fifth-degree felonies. Most of us hope to never know what all these degrees of felony mean, and for those few who do, this is not the place to seek enlightenment.

In fact, there's really no knowledge to be gained from the indictment; to get any understanding of the charges you have to read the Bill of Particulars, which was issued on April 18, nearly two months later. In passing, one wonders: Should prosecutors issue an indictment without knowing the particulars? And, if they do have the particulars, why not put them in the indictment?

It's time to move on to the special audit – the document on which the crimes cited in the indictment are all based.

Background on the Audit

The auditing firm chosen by the State, Crowe Chizek, LLC (hereafter "Crowe") worked from the early summer of 2005 through to the winter of that year. Many references during the trial and elsewhere emphasize that Crowe's auditors worked directly with the State Task Force and were able to call on its members for investigative help and, when needed, for subpoenas.

Crowe was hired to perform the following tasks:

• Participate in the identification and accounting of coin fund assets which, in addition to rare coins, may include collectibles, accounts receivable, agreements relating to real property, and other contracts. Further investigate discrepancies noted.

• Review transactions and agreements relating to CCF. Transactions reviewed may include, but not be limited to, OBWC capital contributions, asset purchases and sales, and payments for administrative fees. Determine whether discrepancies exist relating to these transactions and agreements.

• Identify any discrepancy between the value of the CCF's assets and the approximately $55.4 million principal investment made by the OBWC.[83]

At the same time, the Auditor of State hired the well-known auction house, Sotheby's, with a charge to "Inventory, catalogue [sic] and appraise CCF coins and memorabilia." Sotheby's report was included in the release, but not given much attention; this firm's report will be discussed in later sections.

The special audit (it wasn't an actual audit in traditional terms) is technical and repetitive – not an easy read. But the document advances some key themes that are at the foundation both of the state's legal case and of its deeply intertwined public relations strategy.

Unsupported Inventory Purchases

The central findings from the special audit were that the books showed a large number of Unsupported Inventory Purchases (UIPs) in which Noe, legitimately using his authority as manager of the coin funds, sold coins from his main personal company, VCC, to one of the coin funds. Crowe determined that, in cases amounting to some $12 million dollars, the internal VCC documents did not show that VCC actually possessed the coin it said it had sold to the coin fund. In other words, the transaction was fake because VCC sold the coin fund a coin that didn't exist in its own inventory and therefore couldn't become a physical part of the coin fund's inventory.

For each of these transactions, Crowe determined that the state was entitled to "recovery," i.e., that Noe had misappropriated public funds and that the state was entitled to get the money back from him. Crowe cited only civil law in this regard; it was the State's discretion to make the charges criminal (while also pursuing recovery in the civil courts).

Crowe was not able to show that all of the UIPs were actually fake. Although the audit pointed out that Noe's record-keeping was not good, the special audit nevertheless relied on VCC records to determine that a transaction was actually unsupported. Crowe acknowledged, albeit very indirectly, that some of the transactions might in fact have been legal because of errors in the records. However, the firm stated that, even if Crowe erroneously cited something as a UIP, the finding for recovery would still be valid because state law requires accurate records.

Despite the flaws in Crowe's methodology, it seems unlikely that it was off by a huge margin in the dollar amount of the undocumented purchases. Crowe had access not only to the various accounting documents, it also knew which coins and other items were actually found in the various inventories. And, we also know from later events that Noe was in fact using the mechanism of fake coin sales to borrow money from the coin funds.

"Use of Cash" Analysis

Crowe's report also spends a great deal of time on what it calls a "Use of Cash" analysis.

The "use of cash" analysis works like this:

Start with a situation in which the VCC accounts are in deficit and a deposit from a presumably fraudulent "unsupported inventory purchase" arrives from the coin fund. Let's say the deposit if for $100,000.

The combination of a deposit arriving as the result of presumed fraud, together with the fact that the VCC account is in deficit, triggers for the Crowe accountants a state of fraud in the VCC account. As a result, Crowe says that the next $100,000 of checks written by VCC are presumed to have been paid for by illegally obtained monies.

This seems entirely reasonable until you consider another scenario:

The same as above except that an unquestionably legitimate $100,000 deposit from a VCC sale to a non-coin fund customer is added to the VCC account — right after the allegedly fraudulent one and before any checks are written.

An ordinary person would presume that the untainted deposit would cancel out the presumably fraudulent one and no subsequent checks would be assumed to come from illegal funds. But that isn't the case with Crowe's "use of cash" analysis – Crowe's accounting ignores the deposit and *still* says that all the next $100,000 of checks written by VCC used stolen money. Just for reference, and to understand how odd this approach is, if the untainted deposit arrives one second before that from a coin fund, there's no problem; if it arrives one second later, there's fraud in the air.

The "use of cash" issue will be discussed in more depth in the section on the trial. For the moment, note that Crowe's approach of ignoring deposits was strongly challenged by the defense in the trial and that the author has been unable to find evidence that the practice of ignoring deposits to track payments is a standard industry practice..

But the most important question about the "use of cash" analysis is: why was it needed at all?

The "use of cash" approach to understanding coin fund accounting wasn't needed for the theft allegations, since those were based on the "unsupported inventory purchase" charges. And, it doesn't appear to have been needed for the money laundering charges, either.

As with so many things in the state's approach to Noe, it appears the explanation can be found in very well-calibrated PR. The "use of cash" strategy allowed the prosecution to call witnesses who would go through an endless number of checks in order to offer dramatic examples of what it purported to be public money – paying for personal expenses such as landscaping in Florida. This process had the effect of capturing the public's attention and aligning it with the prosecution. We'll see later that it also had a profound impact on the jury.

Other Issues- Collectibles

Crowe's report also said that the state should recover the value of the collectibles in Noe's inventory. Crowe argued that, even though the collectibles were in the possession of the state and their value had increased since purchase, funds expended on them should be recovered since purchasing them was illegal under the OBWC contract with Noe. The assertion that the contract didn't allow the purchase of these items relied on selective quoting of the contract — in fact, they *were* permitted and the OBWC knew about them. Indeed, the argument that the state had the right to seek financial compensation for things it had never lost (and indeed had profited on) turned out to be a bridge too far. The prosecutors, who doubtless encouraged the approach initially, appear to have changed their minds and decided not to use this argument in the indictment. One reason could be that the prosecutors were themselves initially confused about whether collectibles were allowed and only later came to understand both the language in the contract and the fact that OBWC had formally agreed to collectibles and other non-coin acquisitions.

Other Issues- Improperly Allocated Profits

Crowe's analysis of the books also showed several occasions where Noe distributed profits to himself and to his partners but did not do so in the proper proportion to the OBWC. These analyses, which amount to $709,829, appear to be correct but also seem not to have been mentioned in the criminal trial.

Other Issues- No Reference to Loans

Crowe went to great lengths to discuss the aspect of the contract that mentions the requirement for Noe to keep and maintain accurate records. Various passages referring to this were cited over and over. However, the special audit is silent on the fact that Noe was allowed to take loans and advances from the funds.

THE STATE TASK FORCE SHAPES THE CHARGES

As noted earlier, the Auditor of State's charge to Crowe Chizek called on the Chicago firm to:

- Participate in the identification and accounting of coin fund assets which, in addition to rare coins, may include collectibles, accounts receivable, agreements relating to real property, and other contracts. Further investigate discrepancies noted.
- Review transactions and agreements relating to CCF. Transactions reviewed may include, but not be limited to, OBWC capital contributions, asset purchases and sales, and payments for administrative fees. Determine whether discrepancies exist relating to these transactions and agreements.
- Identify any discrepancy between the value of the CCF's assets and the approximately $55.4 million principal investment made by the OBWC.

In the circumstances, this charge was reasonable in both scope and specificity. What's remarkable, is that the Crowe report ignored almost all of it.

Specifically, looking at the first bullet, the special audit reported on some coin-related transactions but not all or even most of them, incorrectly described the legal status of collectibles, and did not at all look at accounts receivable, real property, and other contracts.

With respect to the second bullet, the special audit described only a slice of asset purchases and sales and ignored payments for administrative fees.

The third bullet, requiring the accountant to look at "any discrepancy between the value of the CCF's assets and the principal investment made by the OBWC," was entirely ignored in the report.

You would think that a client who requested an audit with careful and specific language would be angry when it received such a small part of what it asked for. But that wasn't the case here. Indeed, the client was delighted because, quietly and behind the scenes, the scope of the audit had been sliced down to an investigation that focused on a single thing – supporting a criminal case against Tom Noe.

How did a truncated audit support the case against Noe? Wouldn't a full audit, including the findings against him, been feasible? These are reasonable questions, but the fact is a full audit would have hurt the case against Noe and it seems certain that's why it wasn't done. And it also explains why the Auditor of State refused to release the special audit's working papers, which might have revealed instructions on how the original charge should be narrowed and limited.[84]

Ignoring the full range of assets was central to ignoring the "discrepancy between the value of the CCF's assets and the approximately $55.4 million principal investment made by the OBWC." That's because, if you gather information on everything, the individual totals can be added up into a grand total. And having a grand total could show a profit and showing a profit would make a criminal case much more difficult. A jury would certainly wonder how there could be theft in the presence of profit. As we'll see, the prosecution could have made such an argument (most effectively in civil court), but strongly preferred not to have to do so. Keeping the overall value of the OBWC investment secret was highly desirable from the perspective of a criminal indictment and subsequent conviction.

As it happens, the careful shaping of the audit served other purposes as well.

Not including any of the out-of-state entities helped to prevent the case from becoming a federal one (as happened with nearly all of the other OBWC criminal cases). If the goal is criminal indictment and conviction, the federal route is much more problematic than one based in Lucas County. Federal attorneys and judges aren't subject to local elections and are therefore much less likely to be vulnerable to the pressure of a local newspaper like the *Blade*. To illustrate, where a local judge would have likely faced a storm of criticism and subsequent electoral retribution if he'd decided to approve a change of venue, a federal judge wouldn't have been concerned at all.

It isn't accurate to say that people in the federal system would have been completely shielded from Lucas County and Ohio politics, but it would be fair to say that by comparison they were mostly isolated. Likely another factor in the decision to avoid federal court was that state courts allow television coverage while federal courts do not. Many of the key players were interested in publicizing the Noe case.

An interesting side effect of the decision to exclude out of state entities such as Noe's affiliates in other states, is the apparent inconsistency in treatment of coin transactions. The Crowe audit does mention, very briefly, concerns about transactions in some of the affiliates.[85]m

For example, buried on page 43 of the audit (near the end) is this:

CCFI Inventory Purchases from DVRC of $2,700,000

We have not been able to substantiate transactions characterized within the CCFI accounting records as DVRC inventory purchases totaling $2,700,000. The first inventory purchase transaction was recorded as occurring on March 31, 1998 (the day BWC funded CCFI) in the amount of $1,500,000.[86]

This section of the audit was entirely ignored in the trial, until the last day. The state's final witness, on November 3, was Deneen Day, a special investigator for the OBWC. Ms. Day spent what must have been many hours going through coin fund and VCC accounts with the prosecutors. She showed in the process an exhaustive knowledge of the accounts, creditors, and payees – all-in-all a detailed and comprehensive knowledge of the OBWC coin fund investigation. However, her testimony revealed this on cross examination from defense attorney William Wilkinson:

Q- And were you aware that there was an advance of $1.5 million — did you come to learn in the course of your investigation that there was an advance that was made to Mr. Greenberg for $1.5 million very early in the coin fund operation?
A- I don't know for a fact or recall that it was an advance to him. Might have been something but I don't recall right now.
Q- I mean, you don't know if there were any coins purchased with that $1.5 million, do you?
A- All I know is that it's recorded as coin inventory.
Q- It's recorded as coin inventory, but you don't know if any coins were purchased, do you?
A- I don't.
Q- Haven't you also investigated Mr. Greenberg concerning his dealings with the coin funds?
A- No, he's not been investigated by me.[87]m

Unlike every one of the "unsupported inventory purchases" made by one of Noe's entities, available evidence strongly suggests there was no "use of cash" analysis for this transaction with Greenberg. In fact, there was no further comment on this in the audit and it wasn't mentioned in the indictment or in any other documentation that could be found in research for this book. There is a reference to recovery of accounts receivable from DVRC in the table summarizing assets provided by the liquidator, DSI, but there is no explanation of what it represents.

The state of the available records makes it impossible to trace these particular financial exchanges from beginning to end, but it appears that no legal action of any kind was taken against Greenberg and his company and that payments (or repayments) to OBWC were secured through negotiations.[88] Based on what is known, these negotiated settlements appear to have been entirely appropriate and reasonable — very much in contrast to what happened with Tom Noe.

There's a similar and even less documented issue with the affiliate in Colorado. Various statements describe the coin inventory there as being from a third to a half "off" of what it should have been. And there's indication that the manager of that affiliate paid a debt to the coin funds. But the available documents suggest there was no criminal investigation at all – just a negotiated settlement.

Although neither the Auditor of State nor the Attorney General retained documents about the Coingate investigation (see below), the files of the Governor's legal liaison to the OBWC retained in the State Archives contain some tantalizing information.

The most intriguing scrap from the attorney, Karen Huey, is a handwritten note on a spreadsheet provided by the liquidator, DSI. The document is undated but it is close to others from the summer of 2005.

Next to the listing of $13,500 shown for Noe's Maumee location, Ms. Huey wrote: "- 12 13m that is missing is a valuation issue not a theft issue"[89]

This fascinating note suggests that the idea that Noe stole money was not accepted by all of the various players early on.

Several other notes suggest that the investigative teams were interested in manipulating the audit. A July 7, 2005 memo from Mike Grodhaus, an Assistant Attorney General, contains a worrisome statement: "The IG is very concerned – and rightly so – that whatever numbers DSI comes up with match what AOS comes up with. If they don't then "the State" is going to look foolish. We are very hopeful that the AOS will take us up on this offer."[90]

As it happened, this problem seems to have been solved by keeping DSI's work secret.

In fact, even though the initial view appears to have been that there was no theft by Noe and that he was a simple debtor like the coin fund affiliates, there was ultimately no negotiation of a financial settlement with Noe, and no decision to leave the issue with the civil court in Columbus. Instead, sometime during the meetings of the State Task Force, the decision was made to charge Noe not just with felony theft and its substantial penalties, but also with Ohio's version of the RICO statute, which carries a minimum ten-year sentence.

As a final point on the State Task Force, consider that the various state actors were at this time regularly attacking Noe for "misleading" the OBWC about what he was doing with some of their funds. As we'll see, that's a fair criticism – Noe certainly did some misleading things.

On the other hand, the state authorities, who possessed full knowledge of the value of the coin funds' assets, actively misled the public about what they knew. They would have had to provide the information about overall value in a range, but that was an established approach. For example, the OBWC's Terrence Gasper was charged by authorities with generating a "loss to the state" of $20 million to $50 million."[91]

Noe's misleading actions were designed to hide loans that he was entitled to take but didn't want to disclose because he was concerned they would draw criticism. The state's misleading actions were designed to put Noe in prison for at least ten years and likely longer. It's fair to ask, which was the more serious violation?

WOULD "NON-POLITICAL TOM NOE" HAVE BEEN CRIMINALLY INDICTED?

This section has already alluded to an alternate version of Tom Noe, Non-Political Noe, and concluded that, absent the pressure of the *Blade*, there's almost no chance the authorities would have sought a search warrant for his business and none whatever that a judge would have agreed to one.

This is a good time to stop the narrative and consider the full story of Non-Political Noe to this point and how it would have differed from his real-world analog.

Remember that Non-Political Noe is a prosperous Toledo-area businessman, visible in charitable circles but politically inactive (as is his family) and essentially unknown to the media. He's made the same deal with the OBWC and also made the same "unsupported inventory purchases."

The alternate scenario begins when a new administrator takes over at the OBWC in January of 2005 and, on learning of the coin fund contracts in early April, decides the investments are undesirable and orders his staff to close them down as soon as practicable. Lawyers would then have met lawyers and, in light of the contract provisions, it would have been agreed that the funds would be wound up in something like 18-24 months. Remember, a new administration in Columbus changing its mind and forcing a damaging fire sale is the kind of scenario Noe was concerned about when negotiating the initial contract. It's the reason he put buffers in the contract preventing immediate termination. In fact, the deliberate approach to liquidation specified in the contract was originally agreed on in April-May of 2005 and would have been used if media pressure – entirely related to Tom Noe the high profile political person — hadn't forced the raid on his business.

Back in the alternate scenario, Non-Political Noe has 18-24 months to sell assets, some of which are highly liquid, like stock, and some of which require more time, like coins and collectibles. As specified, Non-Political Noe has also used coin sales-purchases ("unsupported inventory purchases") as a vehicle to take advances on profits. But in this case he has time to use funds from sales of his more liquid assets to balance the accounts from which he's taken the advances. As a result, the books he presents to OBWC on closing appear completely clear – the advances aren't visible. And, he's able to present the OBWC with a significant profit on its original investment – likely about $13 million, including the earlier profit distribution.

OBWC auditors, in reviewing the closing books, at first don't see any problem. Since Noe put cash equal to the then current value of the missing coins into the accounts from which he'd taken advances, everything looks OK.

However, they could have looked deeper and discovered the internal transfers Noe needed to make in order to cover the advances he'd taken but documented inappropriately as coin sales from VCC to OBWC.

Understand, though, that "could have looked deeper" doesn't mean "would have" – there's evidence that, even in a time of intense scrutiny, OBWC did not do this kind of retrospective and detailed analysis with other investments such as those the Bureau had made with Ohio banks. For example, a *Blade* article in July of 2005 reported on OBWC's termination of its investment in a fund run by Allegiant, a subsidiary of National City Bank. The fund lost around $70 million.

When asked how the losses at Allegiant occurred, a Bureau spokesman "said he was unaware of the investment strategy or the individual stocks acquired and sold by Allegiant."[92] *The Blade*, apparently asked no follow-up questions, or if so didn't publish them. And there were no further stories. In our alternate scenario, in which Tom Noe is a political unknown, it seems certain the *Blade* would have shown the same lack of curiosity about his

OBWC investment.

However, back to the scenario. Assuming that the OBWC auditors did scrutinize the books, and did discover the "unsupported inventory purchases," it's almost beyond the realm of possibility that, in a situation with no external media and political pressure, they would have asked for a criminal investigation. "Yes," the executives would say to each other, "some of the documents were falsified. But yes the money has been replaced. So why make a big, expensive deal out of it?"

Even in the very unlikely case that the OBWC would have pressed a prosecutor to file criminal charges, the highly probable response from that office in a non-political environment would have been "this isn't for us – take it to civil court." And, of course, there would have been no entity in the legal system to challenge the prosecutor's decision – we'll see later that the range of discretion available to prosecutors *for the same activity* goes from "don't bother us" all the way to "hit 'em with RICO." And if the person being considered for prosecution isn't a high profile politician, no one in the media and therefore in the community would pay any attention to where in this huge range the prosecutor's decision fell.

However, let's assume that for some reason the OBWC was determined to get criminal charges filed. In such a case, it would likely have had to use political connections (e.g., through the Governor's Office) to get the prosecutor's attention. But, even under political pressure, the prosecutor would have agreed to nothing more than to file a charge of tampering with records. Theft and allied offenses would have been ignored as far too difficult to prove: the jury would have seen the overall profit and said, "where's the theft?"

Would anyone have suggested a bunch of felony theft charges for a politically invisible Noe? With RICO thrown in and an (effective) no parole sentence of eighteen years? Definitely not. Joseph Deters of Hamilton County in Ohio (Cincinnati), a real-world prosecutor for some 25 years, observed of Noe "I have murderers and rapists who do less time than this…We'd probably have put him in diversion in Hamilton County."[93]

There is another possibility, one that will be discussed in more depth later: what if the Bureau had decided to parse the case in the same way as Prosecutor Bates and the State Task Force, and argue that profits from other parts of the coin funds couldn't be used to cover the profit advances taken in coins? That's certainly a possible path. However, as will be explained in more detail at the end of Part III, it's still not a criminal one because the sole issue would be debt, not theft. If taken to civil court it would have led to an interesting debate that might or might not have left Noe owing a significant sum to the OBWC. But, again, such an interpretation wouldn't have resulted in Non-Political Noe spending a single day in jail.

On a separate tangent, what would have happened if the prosecutor in Toledo had said something like, "I can't investigate this case. My husband has had a business conflict with Mr. Noe?" Well, in such a situation the case would have been transferred – likely to the state capital where it could have been in any event. The media wouldn't have covered it and no one would have thought anything more about it — except someone might have praised the prosecutor for avoiding the "appearance of impropriety."

Or, on another separate tangent, what would have happened if the judge assigned to Non-Political Noe knew – or had just learned that Noe had filed an ethics complaint against him? This judge would have swiftly recused himself and everyone would have understood — ethics are very important to all professionals and no one can easily dismiss from their mind this kind of charge against them. Another "appearance of impropriety" issue.

Back in the real world, the one in which the *Blade* was alleging that Noe had stolen vast amounts of money and in consequence fearful politicians from both parties were lining up to attack him, none of these things happened. In the quiet shelter of the State Task Force, the civil path was dropped in favor of a criminal approach and subsequently no one was willing to recuse her or himself. In the real world, Tom Noe found himself a passenger on a train heading straight to criminal court.

It's interesting that, although we know when Noe's journey through the criminal justice system began, we don't know much about how the destination was determined. Given that an array of state and federal agencies participated in shaping the criminal case against Tom Noe, one would expect there would be records of how decisions were made. But that's not the case.

In fact, no records of any kind concerning the decision on changing the audit to focus on Noe can be found.

In early 2017, the author sent Freedom of Information requests (usually called FOIAs) to three Ohio agencies: the Attorney General, the Auditor of State, and the Inspector General. The requests, based on a significant amount of reading to that date, were crafted to be both broad and specific. For example, they sought "all correspondence" on key subjects and with key parties. Also, each request pointed out that, because the final Inspector General report wasn't issued until 2014, records in all agencies involved should have been considered active to that date and should still be available even if there was a retention schedule of five years.

The requests to the Auditor of State and Attorney General yielded nothing: not a single page about the state's Coingate activities was made available.

The Auditor of State and the Attorney General cited the time period and records retention laws. The Inspector General was more helpful, even offering some suggestions for querying other agencies, and eventually provided documents related to its investigations, but none connected to the State Task Force and the crucial Crowe Chizek "special audit."

Interestingly, the Inspector General's office said that they had simply republished DSI's data on valuation and not looked at the underlying data. This is an *investigative* agency?

Is there a conspiracy to keep what happened in Coingate secret from the public?

The answer is likely no if the question relates to the current agencies and their leaders. It's improbable that anyone working at any of these places now has any interest in these events or any reason to cover anything up.

The same can't be said for previous leaders. They had many reasons for destroying records.

All three agencies participated in the State Task Force in 2005-2006 and all three would have known that correspondence, for example with the accounting firm Crowe, and with the liquidating firm DSI, could have proved embarrassing if made public. For example, it seems certain that there would have been written communications telling Crowe how to change the scope of the audit from the original broad charge —one that was formally stated and provided in writing — to the much narrower focus on Noe and coins in Maumee. Written statements would have been necessary because businesses like Crowe don't abandon agreed upon contract terms on the basis of a phone call or a hallway conversation. As we know, the *Columbus Dispatch* asked for records at the time and was told that information wasn't available because the Auditor considered communications with outside firms to be secret.

Information about Coingate went from secret to non-existent.

Coingate occurred entirely in the digital era. The cost of storing records in a time of compressed digital data and multi-terabyte drives is so low it's hard to calculate for an event that involved merely thousands of pages – you have to get to millions of pages before cost becomes an issue[94]*m*. In fact, it's *deleting* records that is expensive. Deciding what can go and when requires significant personnel time.

Coingate was an important episode in Ohio history. This was certainly known at the time, and Ohio has laws on the preservation of historical records. The spirit of these laws is that citizens should know what happened in the past.

If the leaders at these three agencies were proud of their role in Coingate, if they believed as their press releases at the time stated, that the experience offered an important lesson in law and government, wouldn't they have spent a few dollars to keep a coherent set of records in one easy to find place on a backup drive?

We know that the cost of storage and access is negligible, and we know that it's more expensive to delete than to keep. But now we also know that in Ohio, if something is embarrassing or incriminating, it goes down the state's version of George Orwell's "memory hole."

FAST TRACK TO TRIAL

Ohio's legal structure is based on a typical county-based system. The County Prosecutor and Court of Common Pleas and District Appeals Court judges are all elective offices. The law allows the elections to be partisan but doesn't require it. However, in most counties, including Toledo's Lucas County, partisan ballots have been the norm for a long time.

Profile of Julia R. Bates

Mrs. Bates, still the Prosecutor in 2017, is a graduate of the University of Toledo School of Law who worked her way up in the prosecutor's office over twenty years, finally running for and winning the top job in 1996. Ms. Bates is a Democrat, but is not seen as actively partisan beyond the necessity of running for office.

By any measure, Bates had a number of conflicts with respect to Noe's case. Notably, her husband, James, was at the time of the trial the administrative judge in the Court of Common Pleas. This meant that, to the extent that the trial judge had a boss, it would have been the Prosecutor's husband. Family relations also offered other connections – Mrs. Bates' step-daughter and son-in-law were both *Blade* reporters.[95]

Bates did not participate personally in the trial, at least in the sense of appearing in the courtroom. The lead prosecutor in Noe's case was a deputy, John Weglian, who was assisted by Jeff Lingo, Kevin Pituch, Lora Manon, Larry Kiroff, and David Buchman (an Assistant Prosecutor from Franklin County).

Although Mrs. Bates' profile in Coingate was low, she was arguably the single most important person in the entire case. Despite the presence of the State Task Force, the final decision on what charges to file must have been hers. As we'll see later in the text, prosecutors have extremely wide discretion about what charges to file, and there is no real oversight or system accountability for their decisions. Thus, Mrs. Bates can be seen as responsible for charging Noe under Ohio's version of the RICO statute, deciding that he and his assistant comprised a criminal enterprise and that Noe should face a ten-year minimum sentence under that count alone. (More on Prosecutor Bates' conflicts later.)

Profile of Judge Thomas J. Osowik

The Lucas County website doesn't provide much information about Judge Osowik – like Prosecutor Bates he's a graduate of the University of Toledo School of Law and has worked in the region for many years. During Coingate he ran for a seat on the Sixth District Court of Appeals and was elected (his endorsement by the *Blade* is discussed below). By all accounts, Osowik is a well-respected judge who had acquitted himself well in an immediately previous trial that included intense publicity. He is and was seen as non-partisan, though Noe challenged that in the effort for recusal described below.

The Defense

Noe had some difficulty finding a lawyer for his case. Normally, someone in his position would select a local criminal attorney. There were several in the community with outstanding reputations, but they were not available because they had been engaged by people investigated in Noe's federal case.

Lacking a local connection, Noe chose William Wilkinson, a partner with one of Cleveland's major national law firms, Thompson Hine (TH). The firm actually had some prior experience with rare coin litigation, and Wilkinson, who worked out of the Columbus office, was a very successful lawyer with expertise in civil financial litigation – he wasn't a criminal attorney in the usual sense.

Wilkinson, who comes across in the transcripts as an amiable and sometimes folksy personality, was in fact under great personal stress during the trial. It turned out later that his marriage of almost 40 years was breaking up in bitter conflict at exactly the same time: he and his wife separated in December of 2006, just a month after the trial ended.[96]

Wilkinson's co-counsel, John Mitchell, based in Cleveland, also had an extensive background in financial matters but supplemented that with considerable criminal expertise. At times, Wilkinson and Mitchell were assisted by Judson Sheaf and Craig Calcaterra of TH.

MAJOR PRETRIAL MOTIONS

The Noe case was somewhat unusual in that there were a number of very important issues to be resolved before the trial began. The first of these came from the defense: a request to disqualify local judges and instead bring in a visiting judge. Subsequent to that the defense filed a request to move the entire trial out of Lucas County to a place in Ohio outside the *Blade*'s circulation area (change of venue). The prosecution also had a major motion: a request to disqualify Noe's attorneys because one of them, Wilkinson, was likely to be called as a prosecution witness. Since Judge Osowik had already been selected as trial judge, he had a key role in the initial decision process.

Disqualification of Lucas County Judges

The defense began its effort on March 1 of 2006, shortly after the indictment and audit were released. The first stage was an affidavit[97] requesting that all judges in the Lucas County Court of Common Pleas be disqualified from serving on Noe's case. This disqualification would specifically exclude Judge Osowik, who had recently been given the case in a random assignment system.

According to the *Blade*, the defense's 27-page brief caused quite a stir in the Toledo area:

> To hear Tom Noe tell it, his efforts to awaken a moribund local Republican Party led to watershed gains by the GOP in Lucas County and had a profound effect on the party's takeover of statewide offices.[98]

The brief, obviously written by Noe's lawyers in an "as told to" format, does make interesting reading – and certainly helps to explain Lucas County Democrats' hostility to both Tom and Bernadette Noe. In addition to describing Noe's more energetic and much more successful efforts than in the past to get Republicans on the ballot and get them elected, the brief mentions both of the Noes' efforts to exploit factional divisions in the Democratic Party.

In an interview with the author, Noe said he didn't recall the national or state Republican parties offering any kind of training sessions to help local leaders be more aggressive in taking on Democrats. That might be, but the tactics sound very similar to those used from about 1985 forward as Lee Atwater and his acolytes moved the Republicans toward a harder edge. The Republicans had long argued that they held moral leadership in America, and now they were using that self-belief to rationalize ever fiercer attacks on Democrats.

An especially important part of the defense's disqualification brief was a section that argued that Tom Noe had been involved in filing an ethics charge against Judge Osowik, who had been accused of using a public database to help the Democratic Party. As it happened, the Supreme Court at the time the complaint was filed considered the complaint too insubstantial for investigation and never pursued it. More important for the case at hand, Noe himself didn't file the complaint, but assisted another Republican.

The indirect nature of Noe's role helped Judge Osowik make a credible statement that he didn't recall Noe filing any complaints against him – indeed, he argued he didn't recall the complaint at all.

Judge Osowik went on to say that he could be fair.

Although the defense brief was filed in Lucas County, it was directed to the Ohio Supreme Court, which is charged with considering requests to disqualify local judges and replace them with a visiting judge.

Chief Justice Moyer of the Ohio Supreme Court reacted swiftly to Noe's brief, responding with a ruling on March 8.[99]

Noting that "we elect judges in Ohio," Moyer observed that:

> The fact that the defendant may have opposed the judge's bid for elected office is insufficient to warrant disqualification, absent some evidence of actual bias. The same is true of the defendant's role in the filing of a grievance against the judge in the 1990s.[100]

Moyer went on to dismiss the specifics of the brief:

> The defendant's use of the term "political enemy" to describe Judge Osowik and other judges in Lucas County perhaps reflects the defendant's own views about the judges, but it tells us nothing about Judge Osowik's views of the defendant. The judge's response to the affidavit *does* provide information about the judge's views, and that response conveys no hostile feeling or spirit of ill will… The information in the judge's response in fact suggests that he is dedicated to providing equal justice under law to all persons and that he takes seriously his responsibility to be fair and to give the appearance of being fair."[101]

Here's a summary of the Supreme Court ruling: "No matter the circumstances, if the judge says he isn't biased, he isn't. It's too much trouble to go beyond that." The idea that the Supreme Court was itself free of political bias in this matter is unwarranted and will be discussed later. [102]m

And, of course, there's this important point about Osowik's knowledge of Noe: if we accept, as we should, the judge's statement that he didn't know Noe had been involved in an ethics charge against him, we also have to accept that, by virtue of reading the defense's complaint, Osowik *did know* about this before the trial began. As will be shown in the discussion on bias and psychology (Part VI), an attack on one's ethics is not something that most people, especially in professions that depend on ethics, can realistically ignore.

The *Blade's* initial story about the defense brief reveals how far the newspaper had gone toward outright advocacy against Noe. The overall tone of the article, as shown in the quote given above, was sarcastic. A typical reader would conclude from the initial text that Noe, because he is a bad and egotistical person, greatly exaggerates his own importance. This impression from the *Blade* was bolstered at the end of the original article by drawing attention to some fairly minor errors in the brief.

What was missing from the *Blade* coverage, in what by now had become a firm pattern, was any sense of perspective. One can snipe at individual examples, but the truth is that the Republican Party had become much stronger in Lucas County in the last twenty years, and this change had coincided directly with the appearance of Tom Noe and his far more energetic — and combative — leadership. In such an environment, would Democratic officeholders, once comfortable and even secure in their jobs, become resentful? Put another way, were they immune to normal human biases?

The *Blade* article interviewed a number of politicians, but solicited no comment from a scholar in law or political science about the fundamental issue of whether a legal proceeding can be fair in light of the sustained and bitter political conflict that Noe's lawyers described – the *Blade* didn't challenge the fact of this conflict.

At least in recent history, the *Blade* has focused on colorful stories and employed colorful language –typical of print media as they compete with their electronic siblings. But thoughtful and balanced commentary was by no means absent in either its news stories or its editorials. Noe was an exception, though. It seemed a decision on his proper fate had already been made by the management; the courts were now in the execution phase.

Given all this, it's ironic that certainly the best argument for disqualification of Judge Osowik as well as other judges in Lucas County came from an unlikely source: the *Blade*.

A *Blade* editorial in the summer of 2006, blasted Ohio's Republican Party chair, Bob Bennett, for suggesting that Judge Osowik's decision to delay Noe's trial into the fall was political. Bennett thought that Osowik, a Democrat, was agreeing to a delay request from Noe's attorneys so that the trial would be held closer to the November election and therefore be more harmful to Republicans.

The *Blade* disagreed.

> But the delay cuts two ways, both for Judge Osowik and for Noe.

> If the judge were to be perceived by voters as giving Noe an unfair deal in the courtroom, voters might withhold their support for him at the polls.[103]

The "him" referred to here is Osowik, who was running for election as a judge of the Court of Appeals.

The "unfair" means an action that would be positive for Noe.

In other words, the *Blade* agreed that Judge Osowik would likely make decisions based on his own political situation.

The paper was also saying that the public had a strongly negative view of Noe – the reason they might "withhold their support for him [Osowik] at the polls."

Given that the *Blade* should be considered very knowledgeable about both local politics and public opinion, the paper offers a powerful argument for the idea that the decisions of local judges are affected by local politics and – by extension – that the jury pool would be affected as well.

In another context, the *Blade* also strongly supported the idea that prosecution of political cases should come from outside Lucas County:

> "...employment of a prosecutor from outside the county should help ensure that the investigation will move forward expeditiously and without fear or favor of local political considerations."[104]

Strongly stated, except that this opinion doesn't refer to Noe, but to four of the "conduits" for the Bush campaign who, because they were or had been office holders, faced Ohio ethics charges in addition to the federal violation.

The outside prosecutor in the conduit case was from Scioto County, whose main town, Portsmouth, is 233 miles from Toledo; but the *Blade* appears not to have objected to the expense of his travel.[105]

In summary, the *Blade's* position is that: 1) an outside prosecutor is needed when it's necessary to avoid "fear or favor of local political considerations;" 2) the electorate and therefore the jury pool in Lucas County was very hostile to Noe; and 3) one could reasonably expect Judge Osowik's legal decisions in Noe's case to be influenced by his upcoming race for a position on the Court of Appeals.

Speaking abstractly, the *Blade* wanted a fair trial for Noe; but in practice, a trial wouldn't be fair unless it resulted in convictions on the key charges.

Request for Change of Venue

The defense continued its work with another critical motion: one to get a change of venue – to move the trial somewhere else in Ohio where the media coverage of Noe was less intense. As with the request to disqualify judges, this motion was based on a concern about bias. The defense argued that the population and hence the jury pool in Lucas County had been hopelessly biased by the pretrial publicity.

> The freedom of the press guaranteed by the United States Constitution sometimes yields prejudicial and sensationalistic journalism. This is a price society pays for the assurance of a press free of governmental interference. However, that same constitution also guarantees that the

defendant charged with the crime will receive a fair trial, free of the influence of the media. Accordingly, Thomas Noe is entitled to enter a courtroom filled with prospective jurors whose views have not been influenced by media coverage. That will not happen if his trial is conducted in Lucas County. Since April 2005, Thomas Noe has been the subject of an unceasing barrage of intensely negative and prejudicial media coverage. This assault, perpetrated in the Toledo *Blade* and other local media, includes the near daily publication and running of inflammatory statements and accusations against Mr. Noe. This overwhelmingly negative pre-trial publicity has poisoned any potential *venire* in this case by sending a prospective jury pool a clear message: Thomas Noe should be considered guilty before he can even be tried. As a result, Thomas Noe cannot receive a fair trial in Lucas County and, accordingly, requests a change of venue to another county.[106]

Later, in a hearing on the motion held on June 14, Wilkinson said "I've never seen a case in my career in the time I've been practicing law where the governor, the attorney general, two Justices of the Ohio Supreme Court, have all come down and said some prejudicial statements that indicated my client's guilt."[107] Wilkinson went on to say, "Even after the Pope died, Your Honor, Mr. Noe shared half the headline in the Toledo *Blade*."[108] And, in response to whether Noe was a public figure, the lawyer responded – "a large part of Mr. Noe's public persona has been developed through this story."[109]

The response of the prosecution was simple: the trial court has to make a good faith effort to seat a jury before it can consider a change of venue. And, echoing statements made earlier by Judge Osowik, prosecutors also stressed that, even if a potential juror had knowledge of the case and had perhaps formed an opinion, he or she could be expected to lay these thoughts aside and base a verdict solely on the evidence. Prosecutor Bates added, "I believe cases should be tried in the place where the activity occurred by citizens impacted by that activity."[110] Given that no one ever suggested that Lucas County was affected more by OBWC losses than other areas of the state, this comment seems very odd.

Judge Osowik said relatively little in the hearing, but did observe to Wilkinson that, if you consider what the Governor and others said, in theory you couldn't hold the trial anywhere in Ohio.[111]

The Defense's briefs on change of venue were excellent. Using the Westlaw system, they had access not just to newspapers but also to transcripts of television and radio broadcasts. Given what we know from psychology, the short statements about Noe in the latter were of great importance, for example, one Toledo television news brief on March 17 said of Noe "He was suppose [sic] to invest in rare coins."[112] And the same station on March 29: "Noe stole money he was supposed to of invested."[113] We'll see when we discuss the psychology of juries in Part VI that statements like these, which come and go rapidly, enter the recipients' minds in a way that makes evaluation difficult and are therefore often retained as fact.

Reading through the more than a thousand pages of publications and transcripts provided in the defense briefs also provides an interesting insight: there was almost no coverage of Coingate in Cincinnati and effectively none in Dayton, two Ohio cities a reasonably short distance away from Toledo on I-75. The *Blade's* later statement that there was no place in Ohio substantially unaffected by publicity seems simply not true.

Second-guessing the performance of lawyers in a trial is easy – there's always something to criticize. But there's not much wrong with what the defense did in arguing for a change of venue. Their core argument was strong and the data were overwhelming.

However, the defense's strong connection of the issue of pretrial publicity to the famous trial of Dr. Sam Shepard was probably not a good decision, since it allowed the prosecution to emphasize the many differences. In fact, although one important aspect of the Shepard case was different –the judge's statement that he thought Shepard was guilty – the larger atmosphere of nearly uncontested community-wide belief in guilt was very similar. However, for the defense to make this connection they would have had to draw attention to the psychological research then extant, something they chose not to do. This issue is covered in depth in Part VI.

Still, it's not clear that even the best exposition of research would have had any effect. Judge Osowik had clearly already decided, based on his own experience, that you can always find an unbiased jury. Period. To be fair, he may have been correct — based on his experience. Unfortunately, this situation was well outside that experience. Osowik denied the change of venue motion as simply "not well taken" on July 3.[114]

Prosecutors' Request to Disqualify Noe's Counsel

The prosecution had a bombshell pre-trial motion: a request to disqualify Noe's legal counsel. The rationale for this unusual strategy was twofold: 1) the prosecution argued that Thompson Hine attorneys had "impeded the execution of the Court order that was issued by Judge Cain [the civil court judge in Columbus] on [May] 24th." and 2) that the prosecution intended to call Wilkinson as their own witness to testify about what he meant by his statement about the $10-$13 million "shortfall." Prosecutor Weglian spoke without equivocation: "…the Thompson Hine lawyers are going to be called.[115]

Thompson Hine attorney Jud Sheaf was a particular focus of the first part of the motion since he had refused to allow the auditors access to the coins on the 25th because there was as yet no inventory. In fact, Noe's firm, VCC, had sent an inventory to the Thompson Hine office late on the 24th but the Thompson Hine office in Columbus had neglected to tell Sheaf.

Sheaf testified during the hearings and was justifiably angry. He agreed there had been a failure in communication from his office but demonstrated that he had consistently acted with the highest integrity in a very difficult situation. Indeed, the prosecution's attack on Sheaf was more than puzzling when you consider that errors of communication were both more numerous and more consequential on the state side.

In reply to the motion, Wilkinson pointed out that, although they had talked briefly by phone the week before, he had first met Noe on the 25th in the midst of a rapid-fire series of interactions with the courts. He defended his firm's actions by pointing out that the civil judge in Columbus, who was actually the supervising legal authority at the time, had offered no complaints about his firm's actions. Finally, he emphasized that comments like the one he made about a "shortfall" haven't been shown to be admissible in case law. The defense's summary was that "…the motion isn't supported by any Ohio law, any Ohio precedent, and it's not supported by any facts."[116] In addition, they noted the potential hardship to Noe, since Thompson Hine had already put in about 6,000 hours on the case and had a partner with experience in defending executives in the coin industry.[117]*m*

Judge Osowik eventually denied the prosecution's motion and neither Wilkinson nor any other Thompson Hine lawyer was called as a witness.[118]

RICO AND OTHER PRE-TRIAL ISSUES

In addition to the three major – and unusual – motions described above, the Pre-Trial period saw the filing of a number of other motions together with many discussions with the judge about procedures.

Discovery, Etc.

When Noe first contacted Wilkinson and reached an agreement on representation, Wilkinson didn't know that criminal charges were in the offing and therefore got Noe's agreement to have the law firm pick up all of Noe's records for copying. However, once the raid on VCC was complete, and it was clear criminal charges were likely, TH agreed to return all the records to the state. After the indictment, this led to a series of meetings with Judge Osowik in which the various lawyers and the judge provided lots of evidence that they didn't understand computers very well. Still, despite the endless "you failed to give me [fill in the blank]" verbiage captured in the transcripts, it

Garrison Walters

seems clear that the prosecution, which now held almost everything, was mostly playing fairly on discovery and was essentially making documents available to the defense as needed.

Bill of Particulars

On April 18, the prosecution issued a Bill of Particulars, a document that provides detail on the charges made in the indictment.[119] The defense then filed a fairly standard motion to require a more specific bill of particulars on April 28: "...Mr. Noe is left with nothing more than the general allegations contained in count one of the indictment with which to prepare his defense."[120]

The prosecution responded that the Bill of Particulars included all the specificity required by law. The judge agreed and said that the defense could use discovery to get anything it wanted.

Statute of Limitations, Consolidate Charges

The defense offered a motion to dismiss an array of charges based on the statute of limitations. The essence of this argument was that the concerns raised internally in the OBWC about various aspects of the initial coin fund amounted to state knowledge of the alleged crimes and that this in turn meant that the time for the state to act had passed in light of the statute. The prosecution responded that the internal discussions didn't amount to state discovery of the crimes listed in the indictment. The judge agreed with the prosecution, noting that the internal OBWC discussions did not concern actual alleged crime.

The defense also moved to consolidate a number of the counts because "[they were] committed in the defendant's same employment, capacity, or relationship, these counts must be tried as a single offense."[121] Consolidation was important because it would have the effect of reducing possible penalties. The prosecution's very odd response was that there were two victims and therefore (on a technical legal basis), consolidation was not appropriate. The two victims were the state and the other manager of CCF I, Frank Greenberg of Delaware Valley Rare Coins.

The judge's decision on this point was interesting. After noting that the prosecution was arguing that Greenberg was a victim because Noe's thefts deprived him of profit, Osowik wrote "The Court finds this declaration intriguing but unamusing and not convincing."[122] The judge then ridiculed the idea that Greenberg was legally a victim and agreed to consolidate eight counts, but left count one, the RICO charge, separate.

The idea of Greenberg and DVRC as victims raises some interesting questions that will be dealt with later.

Dismiss the RICO Charge

On June 12, 2006, the defense filed a motion to dismiss Count 1 (the RICO) charge, arguing that it was technically defective because it lacked essential specificity. The brief argued that the state must allege that the "enterprise was separate and distinct from the defendant."[123] Failing to do this was a "fatal defect."[124]

The prosecution, in a well-argued and well-written response from Assistant Prosecutor Kevin Pituch, challenged that this specificity was required, and cited extensively from case law on the federal RICO statute to show that wide latitude is given to the prosecution in the use of RICO, including in the definition of an enterprise and an individual's connection to it. Pituch's response cited a case in which the courts even agreed that the individual and the enterprise could be the same.

Judge Osowik swiftly and tersely dismissed the defense motion on July 3.[125]

On the surface, the defense appeared to lose badly on the RICO issue, choosing to file only a limited, technical challenge to the most powerful element of the prosecution's case. But the appearance is misleading. In fact, the RICO class of statutes, of which Ohio's was a part, offers such broad discretion to the prosecution that it's effectively impossible for the defense to challenge a RICO count directly – that is to say on the merits. In other words, as stated in the Prosecution's response cited above, the prosecution has almost complete freedom to define an enterprise. And a "pattern" can be just a few acts which can easily be broken out of a larger action. So, a technical motion, even one as feeble as that used here, is all that was available to the defense lawyers. The issue of RICO and prosecutorial discretion will be discussed in considerable depth in Part VI.

Summary of the Pre-Trial Issues

One important aspect of the pretrial motions and discussions was that the nature of the funds and the question of Noe's ability to borrow from them was never brought up. Nor were there discussions about the prosecution's decision to view the case at the micro level –just coins at the Maumee location rather than the enterprise as a whole. The defense did raise the issue of valuation, but got no support from the judge. It appeared that Wilkinson and Mitchell were expecting to be able to bring up the valuation issue toward the end of the trial – likely in the defense case.

PRESS COVERAGE OF THE PRE-TRIAL PERIOD

The *Blade* provided little coverage of the pre-trial court hearings, except as noted above. The other Ohio papers paid even less attention. The major press issue during this period was the campaign-driven "investigation-by-press-release" strategy of Attorney General Jim Petro. This finally ended when the judge presiding over the civil case in Columbus rebuked the AG for saying that Noe had been shown to be guilty.[126]

One striking omission in coverage was the *Blade's* treatment of the Auditor of State's report on February 22. Most of the *Blade's* story was on the Crowe audit, but there was mention that Sotheby's had valued the collectibles at $2-3 million (this came with an erroneous statement that Noe had not been allowed to purchase collectibles). But the *Blade* omitted any mention of Sotheby's estimate of the value of the coins and the fact that the coins and collectibles taken together were estimated to be worth about $21 to $27 million.[127]

This omission wasn't surprising. Rather, it was part of the *Blade's* radical change of philosophy on the overall valuation of the coin funds. We've seen that, early on, the *Blade* showed an acute interest in this topic, even predicting in an early editorial that the funds would lose a lot of money and repeating that point in the editorial that followed Noe's December, 2005 press conference. The management's interest waned, however, as the outlook for the funds improved. Thus, when *Coin World* published a front page article on October 16 of 2006 describing the considerable value returned at that point with a lot more apparently to come, the *Blade* was silent.[128] The newspaper that had the resources to send reporters to Florida to write about the details of Noe's daily life didn't bother to mention significant news that arrived directly in its office (*Blade* staff were familiar with *Coin World* at this point). This near complete disinterest in the value of the funds continued. When the state announced the expectation it would make a profit (the day after the trial), the *Blade* didn't even do its own story but picked up a short note from the AP. In fact, there was never an important article on valuation after 2005.[129]*m*

It's interesting that the *Blade*, likely sensing that the public wouldn't agree with the idea that this was a case for the RICO statute, rarely mentioned the term in connection with Noe. There were several references in the spring and summer in connection with legal proceedings, but all connections to the acronym appear to have stopped once jury selection and the trial approached. The prosecution also avoided use of the term, using it just once during jury selection and apparently never after that (though the *Blade* did use the word "racketeering" in a headline when the trial started).[130]

Even in announcing the guilty verdict, the *Blade* didn't use the term "RICO." Rather, it used "pattern of corruption."[131]

Although the *Blade* didn't use RICO in words, it tried to employ the same thought in photos. Consider the *Blade's* photo (on the left) from the May 20 change of venue hearing and the Columbus Dispatch's photo (on the right) used for its version of the same story.

Thomas W. Noe's attorneys contend the former coin dealer can't get a fair trial in Toledo on the 53 state charges he faces.

Noe

The *Blade*'s treatment of John Ulmer offers useful evidence in considering the issue of whether a "non-political Noe" would have been treated differently. Ulmer was introduced to the public in the early Coingate articles as someone with whom Noe had invested and, in passing, as someone who was not much liked by community activists as a result of his priorities. The *Blade*'s reference drew the attention of investigators who looked into Ulmer and discovered a massive fraud – essentially a Ponzi scheme.

Ulmer's case was by every important measure far worse than Noe's alleged worst – but the outcome was radically milder than what actually happened with Noe. Ulmer's loss was in excess of $15 million, and he and others were charged with RICO. Nevertheless, despite years of denying guilt, Ulmer got a much better plea bargain offer, accepting a ten-year term that was later reduced to less than six. Noe was reportedly offered a minimum 10-year sentence with no possible reduction. Ulmer ultimately got an offer of repayment as a way of reducing the sentence. This was very much by contrast to Noe's case because, as we'll see shortly, the prosecution argued that it would be inappropriate for Noe to use money from one account to repay what it said was taken from a different account. Also, Ulmer's release deal on the promise of repayment comes despite the fact that Ulmer appeared not to have any significant resources.

It's reasonable to wonder if Ulmer's case wasn't handled very differently by the Lucas County prosecutors because it got much less attention from the *Blade*. Despite the larger loss, deliberate fraud, and significant pain to a large number of victims right there in the Toledo area, Ulmer generated a small fraction of the *Blade* coverage given to Noe. A web survey of the roughly four years from the start of an investigation to the conviction, suggests the *Blade* published fewer than 30 stories on Ulmer, most of which were dispassionate and matter-of-fact.[132m] And no editorials. It's difficult to get an accurate count due to problems with the *Blade's* search engine, but coverage of Noe was on the order of twenty times greater, including numerous editorials in just the first 18 months. Certainly, the many dimensions of the Noe case would have justified somewhat greater coverage, but there were no Ulmer equivalents of tabloid-like *Blade* articles such as "Noes Sighted in Florida," or the visit of reporters to the Keys where they quizzed Noe's neighbors about the family's daily activities,[133] or the numerous hostile editorials that consistently suggested worse Noe misdeeds were yet to be discovered.

A PRE-TRIAL FAIRNESS SCORECARD

Judge Osowik was well within legal and ethical guidelines when he refused to recuse himself. The support of the state's Supreme Court affirms that. On the other hand, in his years in the courtroom the judge must have observed many people who had managed to convince themselves they were behaving appropriately, when they clearly weren't. Osowik should have taken advantage of that perspective to understand that he might not be fair even if he believed he was, and should have withdrawn and encouraged other Lucas County judges to do the same.

A just system has to begin with fairness. If the initial stages of the legal process are shaped in a biased way, the ability of the accused to secure justice is severely compromised. Correction is possible and it certainly does happen, but bringing improper charges causes our expensive and deliberate justice system to flow counter to fairness by shifting an enormous burden to the defendant. In this case of Coingate, given other biases and flaws in the system, the shift was sufficient to drive the outcome toward an unjust conclusion.

Prosecutors, having brought charges that were unreasonable and unfair, did their best to assert them in the legal process. In the pre-trial case of Tom Noe, the prosecutors were very skilled in retaining their initial strategy.

When faced with the need to defend a search warrant that was deliberately misleading and contained obvious falsehoods, prosecutors eschewed any defense on issues of substance and, knowing they would win, instead retreated into the technical confines of the law.

The spirit of the RICO concept is very much at variance with the way it was used against Tom Noe, but it was legal because lawmakers, expecting prosecutors to use their discretion wisely, structured laws in the RICO family with a great deal of flexibility. When viewed from the perspective of fairness, Noe's prosecutors abused their discretion while managing to stay well within the law (more on this in Part VI).

Confronting the obvious fact that a year and a half of negative publicity must have tainted the jury pool indirectly as well as in the direct formation of opinions, prosecutors avoided arguing the importance of publicity and instead relied on the mechanical procedures that are normally – but not necessarily – in effect. It's important to emphasize that, while the normal process is for the judge to attempt to seat an unbiased jury, the judge has the discretion to decide that this wouldn't be reasonably possible and grant a change of venue. And the prosecutors have the discretion to recommend such an outcome.

Finally, from the perspective of fairness, the attempt to disqualify Noe's counsel is discouraging. It's difficult to see what benefit calling Wilkinson to the stand would have had for the prosecution. The jury already knew from the press that a "shortfall" had been mentioned. Calling Wilkinson would only have given him a chance to explain, allowing him to go to the larger question of valuation. Since the prosecution would then have opened a door they wanted to keep tightly shut, it seems more than improbable that they actually intended to have the defense lawyer testify.

Sadly, the only reasonable explanation for the prosecution's request to disqualify Thompson Hine appears to have been to deny Noe expert counsel. This aspect of the prosecution's behavior is highly disturbing.

WHY NO PLEA DEAL?

There's not much information available on the discussions for a plea deal, which would have taken place sometime between the assignment of Judge Osowik and the start of the trial – likely concluding at least a month or so before the scheduled fall date. Noe is vague on the details, not surprising in the circumstances. What he does recall is that the prosecutors insisted that he plead guilty to theft and accept a minimum ten-year sentence. Noe didn't agree because he didn't believe he was guilty of theft.[134] Apparently, the prosecutor did not offer the opportunity to plead guilty to lesser charges –notably tampering with records and forgery. Noe would certainly have accepted the tampering charge, and probably the forgery if it was the only option. But he was adamant about not pleading to theft and obviously shocked at the prospect of serving a ten-year sentence in addition to the two years on the federal conviction.

Was the prosecutor acting properly when she offered such harsh terms? The consensus from legal observers is that she was on the far end, but in the ballpark. Of course, a bigger question is whether the charges were appropriate in the first place.

Would the *Blade* have attacked a more reasonable plea deal — for example one that dropped RICO and most theft charges and allowed for a year or so in prison? Based on the available evidence, the clear answer appears to be "yes," and that fact must have been understood by the prosecutors.

Part III- Trial

INTRODUCTION

Tom Noe's trial was not well suited for television drama. There was almost no information presented that hadn't already been published in the newspapers (at least in the *Blade*) and the witnesses were on the whole not interesting. Worse, the prosecutors' presentation of their case was anything but coherent – probably because witnesses were not available in the preferred sequence. In any case, there's no good way to tell the story of the trial by taking the testimony in order. As a result, instead of going blow by blow and day by day, this book will cover the important issues thematically. An exception will be the opening and closing arguments, which will have their proper place in sequence and will be covered in full.

PROSECUTOR WEGLIAN'S OPENING

Lead prosecutor John Weglian provided the opening arguments for his group. His remarks were sharply focused and succinct. Here are the key points, presented as bullet points because, at least from the transcript, they read more like that type of presentation than as a narrative:

- Noe desperately needed money when he negotiated the CCF I contract. He owed a bank about $650,000 and had claims from customers of about $200,000.
- When he got the money on March 31 of 1998, Noe immediately took $1,375,000 and put it to personal use, paying off his debts. To justify the transfer of funds, he claimed that CCF I was buying coins from VCC, but no documentation exists to prove that happened, and the evidence is that VCC didn't have the inventory to sell in any case.
- There are no itemized receipts for these supposed transactions. He didn't itemize the coins he claimed moved from VCC to CCF I. He kept two sets of books. The CCF I books show that coins were purchased, but the VCC books show "notes payable" (debt) to the CCF I.
- He can't claim to have borrowed the money because there are no records indicating loans. There are no IOUs or notes payable in the CCF I books. "If he thought for a moment he wasn't stealing, he would have signed a promissory note, and he would have agreed to pay reasonable interest on the note, and he would have informed the Bureau of the existence of the note. But there was

no note. There was no interest."[135] Weglian stressed that Noe didn't want to show borrowing because he knew OBWC auditors looking at the books would be alarmed and opposed.

- He stole by "never providing an itemized listing of any of the property that he claimed he bought from or sold to the Coin Funds out of Vintage..."[136]
- The Keith Elliott review pointed out serious problems in the Coin Fund.
- Elliott's concerns led to "an annual physical inspection of all the coins that were supposed to belong to the Coin Fund."[137] Noe strongly opposed this because he didn't want the Bureau to know there were no coins in the inventory.
- Tim LaPointe (Noe's vice president at VCC) came to them with an offer to cooperate. He knew he'd helped in the theft and "wanted to get a good seat on the bus" by showing up early and helping. Detail on what LaPointe was promised followed, with focus on the fact that LaPointe had no specific promise for a reduced sentence.
- Noe borrowed coins from other dealers in order to fake inventory, and dealers will testify to that.
- Showed the jury the Ohio theft statute:

    Ohio R.C. 2913.02 defines theft and states:

    (A) No person, with purpose to deprive the owner of property or services, shall knowingly obtain or exert control over either the property or services in any of the following ways:

    > (1) Without the consent of the owner or person authorized to give consent;

    > (2) Beyond the scope of the express or implied consent of the owner or person authorized to give consent;

    > (3) By deception[.]

    "Deprive" means to do any of the following:

    (1) Withhold property of another permanently, or for a period that appropriates a substantial portion of its value or use, or with purpose to restore it only upon payment of a reward or other consideration;

    (2) Dispose of property so as to make it unlikely that the owner will recover it[.] R.C. 2913.01 (C).

- Forgery is explained as "…writing checks out of Vintage's accounts to people he knew, forging their endorsements on the back of the check and depositing these checks into his personal account and claiming that those were coin purchases in Vintage's records."

Comments on the Prosecution's Opening

Weglian's opening made key points effectively. The focus on Noe's financial situation, which was to become a key theme in the trial, was crisp and reasonably detailed.

The subsequent emphasis on the lack of IOU's or similar documentation was obviously designed to offset the defense's argument that Noe was taking loans. But Weglian contradicted himself on this point and actually did so in successive paragraphs. After stating that Noe "never had an itemized inventory…"[138] the Assistant Prosecutor went on to say that "Noe provided Plante Moran [VCC's auditors] with the itemized list of the coins which he claimed the Coin Fund owned…"[139]

There's a fairness issue here: an itemized list of coins owned by the coin fund is obviously an "itemized inventory." Weglian seemed to want to confuse the jury on a technical point – there wasn't an inventory initially but that was changed and an inventory existed for the full period.

Anticipating that LaPointe's testimony would be important, and that the defense would attack his credibility because of his deal with the prosecution, Weglian went out of his way to show that there were no specifics to the deal; LaPointe was only promised a recommendation of leniency if he told the truth and it would be up to the judge to decide. This was likely an important point for the jury.

In the kind of partial truth that pervaded the prosecution, Weglian emphasized the prosecution's view that Noe's response to a closer audit (after Keith Elliott's concerns surfaced) was because he didn't want more scrutiny. But Weglian didn't mention at all Noe's key argument – that making his inventory records public would hurt his competitiveness. This is a deliberate attempt to mislead by not providing all of the relevant information.

Weglian's emphasis on Noe's apparent use of $786,000 from CCF II to make a profit payment for CCF I echoes the state's theme that the coin funds were a "Ponzi scheme." However, the point was not made honestly, since the prosecution failed to mention the other ~$8M in profit that had already been paid and that was not in dispute. By omitting this much larger amount, Weglian left the impression that there were no profits for CCF I, only funds paid back from CCF II. Also, of course, this careful parsing of the finances

127

fits into the prosecution's overall desire to only show a carefully selected part of what happened to the coin fund monies.[140]

Finally, Weglian was clear in describing what the theft statute meant, and clear that the money laundering and forgery charges were linked to theft. But he was vague to the point of vapid in describing how money laundering and forgery were actual crimes in the case at hand. Not surprisingly, Weglian glossed over the RICO charge (and didn't call it that).

If fairness requires a balanced explanation of facts, the prosecution's opening fell well short.

ATTORNEY WILLIAM WILKINSON'S OPENING

The main theme of Wilkinson's opening was "consent." Noe, he emphasized, had permission in a "binding legal agreement" to do the things he did. If he had consent to do something, it can't be a crime. Wilkinson followed this by stressing the difference between civil and criminal court. If someone thinks Noe owes them money, then that is dealt with in civil court. But criminal court is entirely different and is used only for crime – and there's no evidence at all that Noe committed the crime of theft.

Wilkinson covered some of the key points of the contract, mentioning that Noe described the investment as speculative, but pointing out that the OBWC went ahead because it wanted to diversify. And, he argued, diversification was a reasonable thing for them to do given that they had $16 billion[141]$m$ in their holdings. He also minimized the problems: "This [loans and advances, profit distributions being taken before the deal takes place] is known by the Bureau of worker's compensation in 1999 and in the year 2000, but there wasn't an investigation."[142] Indeed, he emphasized, after Elliott raised concerns the Bureau went ahead and invested another $25 million in 2001.

The contract, Wilkinson said, allowed Noe to "enter into any other business arrangements…"[143] and also, he had two years to repay if a distribution was improperly taken.[144] Wilkinson also threw in the puzzling argument that the clause that allowed Noe two years to repay even if a distribution was taken inappropriately was indeed a flaw in the contract and that it represented attorneys at OBWC falling down on the job. Even so, "Nobody is going to take the position that the contract allows theft, but if the contract gave consent, there can't be a theft."[145]

Wilkinson also showed the jury the language of the theft statute and repeated that it didn't apply to Noe. Like Weglian, he described the money laundering and forgery charges as connected to theft ("companions"), but in this case emphasized that, after discarding the theft, you simply had transactions between VCC and others that, while they might be odd, harmed no one. "If the money wasn't stolen, there is no money laundering."[146]

Wilkinson threw scorn on the Crowe Chizek report in advance by pointing out that it was common in the coin industry for there to be a gap between delivery of a coin and payment but that the Crowe auditor didn't know that. He went on to say that what Crowe did wasn't a real audit and doesn't "meet the standard you'd use in balancing your checkbook."[147]

In reference to LaPointe, Wilkinson said that the assistant will testify that Noe and he always intended to repay, and then again cited the two-year period for repayment given in the contract. He added that LaPointe had been very inconsistent in what he said in his pre-trial depositions and wasn't to be trusted because of his poor recollection and also because the prosecution had given him an incentive to damage Noe with their plea deal.

Wilkinson opened up a broader view by pointing out that, although there might be fewer coins in Maumee than they expected to find, "they found a lot of other assets."[148] He then went on to say, "When the new fund manager comes here to testify, you're going to hear evidence that the state isn't going to get back 35 million on this 50 million investment, or 40 million, or 45 million, 50 million. But there is a profit."

At this point, Weglian objected, "Your Honor, I'd like to object. Profitability or non- profitability in the coin fund is not the issue. The issue involved in this case is the theft of the assets of the coin fund." When Osowik turned to Wilkinson for response, the defense attorney simply said he was finished with that and the judge allowed him to continue.

Finally, with respect to the RICO charge, Wilkinson said "You're not going to hear any evidence about any racketeers or any mobsters or any mafia or any other criminal enterprise which is a required element of that count..."[149] Weglian again objected at this point and Wilkinson again said he was finished with that issue and Osowik again allowed him to continue.

Comments on the Defense's Opening

The most important omission in Wilkinson's remarks was any specific reference to the undocumented coin purchases. He addressed the issue somewhat indirectly by referring to "fewer coins than they expected to find" and emphasizing that Noe could take loans – though he also didn't mention why Noe didn't document the loans or, rather, why he documented them falsely. Thus, there was no answer to Weglian's telling point that Noe wanted to deceive OBWC auditors as to how much cash he was taking out of the funds. The jury can't have missed the lack of response to Weglian's extensive description of fake inventories and this was likely damaging. One wonders if it wouldn't have been wiser to admit to the tampering with records charges at the outset – as well as agreeing that Noe did need more cash for operations than he had expected when he submitted his proposal.

Wilkinson failed to point out the contradiction in Weglian's assertion that there was no itemization in the inventories when there clearly was. And, as a result, he failed to make the argument, described below, that in specifying coins with defined values to the inventory, Noe was effectively detailing his debt and attaching it to items that were likely to rise in value. In other words, if Noe said that a particular $30,000 coin was in inventory in 1998, then when the funds closed at the end of their eleven-year term or earlier, he would have to provide not just the $30,000 originally paid but whatever value the coin had at the time of sale. The amount Noe owed would almost certainly be more than that originally recorded since coins were rising in value (especially true once the recession began in 2007).

While there were some flaws in the defense's opening, it was strong overall. Wilkinson's emphasis on the contracts and the permission they gave was an important point, and his quick shot at the use of the RICO statute and preemptive strike on the Crowe audit were both well-done.

In arguing that you had to consider all assets, not just the coins, and that when you did so you'd see that the funds had shown a profit, Wilkinson put his hand on a critical door. Unfortunately, he was never allowed to open it.

Overall Summary on the Opening Presentations

Both sides were effective. The defense used more logic and was more direct in addressing issues (though certainly not completely so). But the prosecution did a superior job of connecting with the way ordinary people think.

Themes in the Trial

The key themes in the trial were: 1) "framing" testimony from investigations; 2) theft (various sub-categories); 3) forgery and money laundering; 4) the nature of the contract; and 5) valuation- the defense's inability to present the overall value of the coin funds.

Framing Testimony- Investigators

The term "framing testimony" is used here to mean information elicited from witnesses that is intended to set the stage for the jury. For example, many of the law enforcement and related witnesses provided testimony in response to riveting questions such as "So where was the file cabinet when you entered the room?" However, some aspects of the framing testimony were important. Among the first called were Tom Charles, head of the Office of the Inspector General, and Tom Wersell, a senior investigator for the OBWC who led his organization's investigation of the coin funds.

The direct examination of the two men was basically factual, but the defense got both to admit a number of embarrassing things, reinforcing the Keystone Cops image left by the search warrant episode. Charles, who issued a press release that he was starting an investigation on April 7 of 2005 (four days after the initial *Blade* stories), offered little evidence as to why he wanted to start looking – a point that was striking because the initial newspaper stories carried no specific allegations of crime. He did cite letters urging him to wade in from legislators – all of them Democrats. But letters from politicians asking for investigations of people from the other party are sent all the time and couldn't have been compelling. Because the Inspector General was unable to offer a good reason for the press release, an independent observer might well conclude from his testimony that Charles, the state's self-styled "public watchdog," was mainly just looking for publicity when he engaged with Noe and the OBWC.

Wersell, in charge of fraud investigations for the OBWC, admitted he hadn't read the files on the coin funds even seven weeks into the investigation. Thus, although problems with the Storeim business in Colorado (reported by the *Blade*) were given as a major reason for the investigation, Wersell didn't know that concerns in Colorado had long since been reported to OBWC.[150] Also, although he cited some of Noe's investments as a red flag, Wersell wasn't aware of the earlier Keith Elliott review of the contract and didn't know about the acquisition of collectibles even though they were approved and listed in the inventories.

> Q. All right. Now, in regards to Maumee and the collectibles, what if any preparations had you made to examine collectibles at Maumee?
>
> A. We didn't have any preparations.
>
> Q. Why was that?
>
> A. Cause we were unaware that there were collectibles.[151]

One wonders, did Ohio's "investigators" get *all* their information from reading the *Blade*?

Theft- The Accounting Testimony

The prosecution called a number of people to discuss accounting for the coin funds and for VCC. The first group included three staff who worked for Noe, followed by the outside auditor for his businesses, and finally the OBWC internal auditor, Keith Elliott, who had questioned the coin fund agreements in 1999.

The testimony of Sue Metzger on the 17th was striking because she told the prosecution that Noe had said that he used the coin funds "like an ATM." This was presented, indirectly, as a Noe "confession." When talking to the prosecution, Metzger described the remark as referring to the coin funds,[152] but in cross-examination she admitted that this was just her interpretation and that Noe hadn't actually referenced the coin funds as the source.[153]

An outraged defense pointed out to the judge that Ms. Metzger had not reported the ATM expression in her earlier interviews with investigators and that the defense had not received her much later deposition in which she actually did use it (they were not present as they should have been). Given these circumstances, the Metzger testimony was hardly credible (not even considering the likelihood that Noe, at that point knowing that he was in legal jeopardy, had actually made such a comment). But Judge Osowik allowed it to stand and the defense didn't have a good opportunity to challenge her. The impression on the jury must have been substantial.

The prosecution laid part of its foundation when one of the staff members, Jeanne Beck, agreed that she had a number of times recorded purchases by a coin fund from VCC and sent the checks to the business' outside accountant even though there was no invoice to go with it. While she said this did sometimes happen with non-coin fund transactions it was contrary to the usual practice.

On cross examination, Mitchell got her to admit that these transactions didn't necessarily represent theft.

> Q. From time to time when money flowed from the Coin Fund into Vintage's accounts, on certain occasions you were told those were loans; isn't that true?
>
> A. That's true.[154]

In another exchange, Assistant Prosecutor Lingo asked staff member Priscilla Livingstone:

> Q. All right. Based on what you knew about Mr. Noe, based on what you knew in regards to what the store was making, did the two seem to balance?
>
> A. No.[155]

But Wilkinson easily offset this in his cross-examination:

> Q. Would it be fair to say that the retail portion of Vintage's revenue was in the minority and most of the revenue came from wholesale, estates, appraisals, and such?
>
> A. Yes.[156]

Although the staff comments on accounting were important, the core testimony concerned the Crowe Chizek audit (discussed in some detail earlier).

As with the prosecution's overall case, the testimony of the Crowe auditor, Emlyn Neuman-Javornik wasn't really organized thematically. Since taking it as it was given –sequentially — leaves a logical jumble, the various exchanges will be reorganized here into four categories: 1) the Unsupported Inventory Purchases; 2) Application of checks ("use of cash"); 3) Allowability of Collectibles; and 4) Allowability of loans and advances.

The prosecutors' opening questions – framing questions so to speak – put considerable emphasis on the part of the contracts that required the managers (Noe and Greenberg) to "maintain complete and accurate records" and this point continued to be a theme in the Crowe testimony (and with others). In any case, though, the prosecution's questions quickly focused on "unsupported inventory purchases."

   – Crowe-Chizek and Unsupported Inventory Purchases

Prosecutor Weglian took Ms. Neuman-Javornik through coin purchases – when the coin funds were recorded as having bought coins from VCC (and other affiliates) – and asked each time whether Crowe could verify that the specified coin was in VCC stock and therefore available for sale. If not, as noted earlier, the transaction was considered illegal and was added to Crowe's "findings for recovery" — numbers that eventually became the foundation for the theft charges.

The methodology used by Crowe was that, if a coin was really available for sale it should be indicated in VCC's QuickBooks accounting system or, failing that, in other records kept by VCC. Put another way, if VCC was going to be able to sell a coin, there had to be evidence that it actually possessed it.

Crowe found many cases where the supporting documentation for a sale from VCC to a coin fund was not present, and each time that occurred the amount of the purchase transaction was added to the firm's finding for recovery. Ultimately, the number was about $12 million — $12,176,540 to be precise.

There were many flaws with the Crowe method. First, although early in the testimony (and in the audit) Crowe described VCC's record-keeping as poor, it nonetheless relied on those same records as definitive when calculating a finding. This is ironic because, when Crowe described an inventory item as missing from VCC's systems, they observed that VCC staff "often" or "frequently" kept such records in their systems. "Often" and "frequently" are not "always." It's entirely possible that on many occasions the items actually were in inventory and the transaction was valid but was nevertheless characterized as fraudulent simply because Crowe couldn't find the records on the VCC side. Not finding something, especially in a chaotic set of records that was not fully searched, is not the same as saying it doesn't exist.

Also, the Crowe report acknowledged that at the beginning VCC had paper records for many transactions and didn't have an electronic system for the coin inventory until some years after CCF I was in operation. This data problem was exacerbated in testimony when Wilkinson got Ms. Neuman-Javornik to admit that, while she and her colleagues looked across the electronic records for a long period of time to find corresponding information supporting a purchase, they only looked at the paper records for a matter of "days."[157] This is important because it relates to Wilkinson's point in the opening arguments that coin dealers often made cash transactions well before the item sold was actually delivered to the buyer.

There was some contradictory testimony on this point later. For example, an OBWC staff member stated they didn't find any hand-written invoices for the entire period. On the other hand, Wilkinson found a number of boxes of paper records, including invoices, that Ms. Neuman-Javornik admitted she and her team had never looked at. Perhaps the OBWC member didn't find the hand-written invoices because they were in boxes that Crowe didn't discover.

In any case, it appears that, especially early in the operation of CCF I, information that validated inventory transfers could have been available and transactions that were valid were therefore categorized as fake. Wilkinson made this clear in cross-examination:

> Q- "So, that means because you and your team at Crowe Chizek didn't find the records you were looking for, you don't really know what happened in relation to those transactions?
>
> A- "That's correct."[158]

Overall, while there is convincing evidence that Crowe's $12 million figure could have been inaccurate, there isn't reason to believe that there were no unsupported inventory purchases or that these inaccurately documented transactions changes the order of magnitude so that it was far off the $12 million given. Many of the examples – especially those from later on when the records were better — are convincing. Also, as we'll see shortly, Tim LaPointe testified directly to the fact that he and Noe used fake coin transactions to funnel money from the coin funds to VCC. These transfers were intended as advances or loans but LaPointe admitted that he and Noe failed to create appropriate documentation for that. And Noe himself admits this with respect to at least the final year or so.

While Ms. Neuman-Javornik and Crowe were effectively challenged on some aspects of their approach to documenting unsupported inventory purchases, the firm obliquely and continuously defended the overall integrity of their finding for recovery by arguing that VCC had the responsibility to keep accurate records and that any errors Crowe made were irrelevant because of VCC and Noe's failure to follow the law.

In summary, although the audit was shown to be shaky in some of its details, the fact of unsupported inventory purchases was effectively sustained in Ms. Neuman-Javornik's testimony.

After the Crowe testimony, various coin dealers and collectors/ investors were called to prove that CCF inventory records were false – they didn't sell the coins described as being purchased. And, the prosecution relentlessly got them to state that, by contrast to VCC, they kept accurate records.

In return, the defense focused on the fact that VCC and/or the coin funds made profits on most transactions, that holding checks to cash them was common, and that the other dealers mostly worked with Tim LaPointe for records and details.

— Crowe-Chizek and Check Applicability- "Use of Cash"

Intermingled with the testimony on unsupported inventory transfers was Crowe's assertion that, as described earlier, when a transaction moving money from a coin fund to VCC was shown to be invalid, it would then be possible to look at the VCC check register to see what the fraudulently obtained money was used for.

This technique of attributing checks was used to devastating effect early in the testimony when the Crowe accountant alleged that, because Noe and VCC had negative balances in their check registers when the first CCF I funds were deposited, that would mean that checks written after that would be effectively spending OBWC money. Specifically, Crowe argued that Noe paid off a line of credit and paid a number of personal bills with state money. This assertion was repeated many times for different unsupported inventory purchases.

The defense savaged this line of argument. Wilkinson again pointed out a practice in the coin industry for checks to be held and got Ms. Neuman-Javornik to admit they hadn't looked at that.[159] Even more important, he got the witness to agree that Crowe had ignored deposits from other non-coin fund sources in calculating what was state money: if Noe began with a negative balance just before a coin fund deposit, a subsequent deposit from a VCC sale unrelated to the coin fund would be ignored. In other words, all checks written on the account would be described as using state funds even though funds from other sources were also available in the account.

Q- "And if I understand it, you're telling us that on 3.1.3.1.3 [exhibit] with respect to all those deposits from non-coin fund sources, you disregarded those and assumed that all the checks during that period of May 12 through at least May 30 were funded with the Coin Fund deposit on May 12th; is that right?"

A- "Yes."

Wilkinson illustrated his point by using a set of four plastic buckets. Three were for deposits: the coin fund, VCC, and non-coin funds. The last was for payees. Moving checks from the various buckets to the payee bucket, he emphasized that it was impossible to look at the payee bucket and know which bucket the check came from. Ms. Neuman-Javornik agreed that it wasn't possible to follow "the exact dollar."

Later on, Prosecutor Weglian adroitly offset Wilkinson's point by going through checks in buckets to show that, in the early months –March to April of 1998 – deposits from non-coin fund sources hadn't been enough to keep the VCC account in the black. The last bucket was empty without CCF I funds.[160]

Using the limited tools available in cross-examination, Wilkinson responded by getting the witness to agree that the coin funds had grown in value to a level that exceeded the amount invested by the OBWC:

Q- "Are you aware of the fact that there were about three times that many transfers into the coin funds from non-coin fund sources during the period that Mr. Noe or Vintage managed the Coin fund?

A- "No sir."

Q- "About $44M worth, you didn't know that?

A- "We didn't total those, no."

Q- "So that if we looked at all the money that went into Vintage to fund these checks to the payees, you weren't aware of the fact that three-fourths of the money, approximately, came from sources other than the Coin Fund?"

A- "I wasn't aware of that."[161]

Weglian objected to this line of questioning. Judge Osowik, agreeing, sustained the objection and prevented Wilkinson from continuing.

MR. WILKINSON: I'm not sure I understand the basis of the – [not] allowing me to talk about that. Several witnesses have already talked about the recoveries. Mr. Tripp talked about recoveries, and with the witness yesterday. We've had at least two or three.

THE COURT: What relevancy is this?

MR. WILKINSON: He just tried to convince the jury that the Coin

Fund ended up broke.

THE COURT: No. No.

MR. WILKINSON: He left the bucket empty.

THE COURT: No, it's not. Just because he empties a plastic bucket, you're implying that's what he said?

MR. WILKINSON: Okay. I'll do it another way.[162]

This exchange was telling, since Weglian definitely *did* try to create that impression.

But Wilkinson failed to make clear to the jury that there was no requirement that the coin funds be balanced on a daily or even a monthly basis. The right period for this analysis of fund balances wouldn't have been two months, but at the time that annual reports were prepared. One could even argue that the contract only considered full accounting of profit and loss for the entire life of the coin funds, which extended from March 31, 1998 to May 27, 2005. Also, to be accurate, any annual or ending analysis wouldn't have been limited to coins but would have included other investments, such as stock holdings, loans, and joint ventures.

Another technical flaw in the Crowe method was that it used only VCC's internal check register and not VCC's bank account. Wilkinson pointed out that, for a variety of reasons, the bank account was almost always significantly higher than the business' internal QuickBooks register. Early on, the difference was $1.4 million.[163] Ms. Neuman-Javornik didn't have a coherent explanation for why her firm used the smaller number.

 — Crowe-Chizek and Allowability of Collectibles

Crowe asserted, both in the audit and in testimony elicited by the prosecution, that Noe did not have the right to purchase collectibles.

Q. And in your work, you also concluded that it was not permissible for the Coin Fund manager to invest in non-numismatic items; right?

A. Correct.

Q. And you also made finding of recovery about that subject?

A. Yes, sir.[164]

Although the defense later clearly established in other testimony that collectibles were allowed and were listed in the official inventory provided to the OBWC, the defense failed to highlight for the jury the fact that the audit was wrong and that the Crowe accountant had testified incorrectly.

— Crowe-Chizek and Allowability of Loans and Advances

In almost identical fashion to the issue of collectibles, Crowe asserted, both in the audit and in testimony elicited by the prosecution, that Noe did not have the right to take loans (and advances, which were usually lumped in with loans in testimony).[165] The defense quickly demolished this on cross-examination and the Crowe accountant admitted that she had been wrong, attempting to defend herself with the rather weak statement that she had only been referring to "undocumented" loans.[166] She emphasized many times, however, that the contract called for full and accurate records – something that would apply to loans – and that she and her team had found no evidence of "documented" loans.

But the Crowe testimony wasn't all that was important on the issue of loans. Anticipating that the defense would make the argument that Noe was using his contractual right to take loans (while for the most part also denying that he had the right to do this), the prosecution focused on documentation as being intrinsic to a legal loan. The VCC employees who took the stand early on said that they were unaware of any loan documents. The same was true of the witness from VCC's outside auditing firm.

After the accounting testimony was concluded, the prosecution called the much-referenced Keith Elliott of the OBWC, evidently with the goal of having him say that loans, to be valid, would have to be documented. He did say that, but on cross examination ran into something of a buzz saw from the defense.

Since Elliott's concerns, both earlier and in testimony for the prosecution, expressed doubt not just about coin fund operations but also the contract itself, in cross-examination, defense counsel John Mitchell was able to take Elliott all the way through the contract (AKA the "operating agreement." A key section concerned control:

Q. Okay. But you would agree with me that the authority vested by the operating agreement gave them all decision-making authority in the enterprise; do you agree with that statement, sir?

A. They would have the authority for any investments that the entity chose to invest in. Other operating decisions, things of that nature, yes.

Q. So the answer is yes; right?

A. Things of that nature, yes.

Q. I mean, anything — all the investment, all the decision making authority in the enterprise would be the Capital Coin Fund; right?

A. Subject to the operating agreement and the various other divisions that were included, yes.[167]

And a bit later, Mitchell asked if Noe had the right to make alternative investments to coins:

> A. Yes, that he had the ability to invest in other investments deemed in the best interest of the partnership.[168]

The discussion went beyond the issue of control by the managers to cover division of profits, self-dealing, closure of the funds, everything of importance. Elliott agreed that the contract favored the managers in all these things.

Mitchell then drove the nail in by taking Elliott through the internal discussion on his various concerns. It turned out that Elliott had been advised by his boss to talk to an OBWC attorney about the contract provisions. When he did, she took him to school, explaining LLCs and other legal vehicles to him. Contrary to Elliott's prior understanding, he learned that LLCs can determine their own characteristics.

The conclusion of these internal discussions included, in part, a letter (8/24/2000) from the head of investments Robert Cowman to John Annarino, the Bureau's chief legal officer stating "… the agreement gives the general partner the flexibility to invest in other vehicles."[169] Cowman also described the contract as being like one for a Venture Capital Partnership, where managers rather than partners hold assets and have control.[170]

Mitchell also took Elliott through a discussion of the section that allows two-year repayment if a distribution or profit distribution is made in violation of the agreement.[171] More on this later.

Finally, Mitchell pointed out that, although the OBWC did make some operational changes[172]*m* to its contract with Noe, it was subsequent to Elliott's review that the Bureau went ahead and made another deal with Noe (CCF II) in 2001 and was considering a third investment in 2005.

Mr. Buchman, who led the questioning of Keith Elliot for the prosecution, didn't have much to fire back with in his re-cross examination, but again got Elliott to say that there was no "explicit" ability to take loans in the contract and, that when Elliott had done his review (1999-2000), there was no evidence of loans and advances to Noe or VCC.

Importantly, although Buchman made no reference to the "in violation of" clause, he did draw attention to the fact that provisions of the contract were subject to the limitations imposed by the "Ohio Act,"[173]*m* arguing that, under Ohio law, the state, although not listed as an owner, nevertheless retained an "interest" in the property and could not therefore give its consent for a manager to do the things the contract allowed Noe to do. More on this in the appeals section (below).

Before leaving this section, it's important to return to the nature of the Crowe audit and why their report and their representative had to sustain such powerful attacks from the defense. Crowe, now Crowe Horwath, is currently the nation's eighth largest accounting firm and appears to be very well-regarded across the board. It's not reasonable to expect that it was their decision to provide a truncated and unbalanced report. On the contrary, it seems logical to assume that they were constrained to provide the kind of audit that their client wanted.

LaPointe Testimony

Tim LaPointe's testimony was much anticipated, not least because the defense, with the obvious intention of establishing that he was a key actor — and possibly the actual bad guy instead of Noe — had consistently brought him up in questioning. Typically, they would ask witnesses such as coin dealers and accountants whether they had dealt with Noe or LaPointe and the answer was usually the latter. This wasn't very effective, however, because on re-cross-examination, the prosecutors would establish that the witness considered Noe to be LaPointe's boss.

In fact, though, LaPointe's testimony wasn't very exciting. He quickly stated two things: 1) he and Noe had in fact made unsupported inventory purchases that had the effect of moving money from the coin funds to VCC without actually transferring anything of value in return; and 2) he and Noe both thought of these transactions as loans that would be repaid.

Although the jurors would surely have known at this point in the trial (day 14) that Noe and LaPointe had taken cash out of the coin funds and falsely described these transfers as purchases of coins from VCC, LaPointe's testimony wasn't anti-climactic: he described in convincing detail how the process occurred and in particular how he and Noe borrowed coins from other dealers to give the impression to auditors and later to the OBWC that the coins were actually in the coin funds' inventories.

Q. All right. When was the first year that you altered the inventory?

A. I'm not exactly sure the year was, but it was right after they decided on agreed upon procedures and we hired Plante Moran [the auditing firm hired by the OBWC] to come in and do the inventory.

Q. All right. And it would have been the Plante Moran inventory?

A. Yes.

Q. All right. And after these documents had been made, invoices, purchase orders, and after they'd been checked, what did you do with that documentation?

A. I put it with the coins in the safe, and when Plante Moran came in, we'd show them the coins and the inventories.

Q. All right. What if coins were missing or weren't there, what did you do?

A. If there were coins that — if we didn't get enough inventory in [by borrowing from other dealers], we would create sales invoices or approval invoices where sales were sent out for grading.

Q. When you're talking about sales invoices, what do you mean?

A. We'd make up an invoice that we sold coins to somebody, we were waiting for the money to come in, or we'd sent them out to on approval.

Q. When we talk about on approval, what are you talking about?

A. On approval is when you send a customer a coin that they haven't paid for yet, you let them look at them and see if they want to buy it. If they want to buy it, then you let — then they pay you.[174]

Jeff Lingo did a very good job for the prosecution with LaPointe, but there was one very awkward moment for his side:

Q. All right. After the coins are returned in 2004, how is business again at Vintage?

A. Business is up and down. Probably more down than it was up.

Q. When you say --

A. For Vintage itself. I mean, the Fund [sic] were doing fine. Vintage was having a rough time.

Q. By a rough time, what do you mean?

A. Well, we had to keep taking more money from the Fund to keep money in Vintage Coins.[175]

Lingo got the answer he wanted here – Noe and LaPointe were taking more money out of the coin funds and putting it into VCC during that time. But, since the prosecution's consistent implication was that the coin funds had been fatally damaged by Noe, he also got information he didn't want – the coin funds were "doing fine." Lingo rushed on, anxious to show the jury more trees so they would forget there was a forest. And Mitchell, who cross-examined, never brought the issue up.

It's not clear Judge Osowik would have allowed follow-up in this area since he could have considered testimony about the overall health of the funds as information on the overall valuation. But it would have been interesting to know what reason he would have given for disallowing questions on a statement given by a prosecution witness.

Much of the testimony and cross-examination focused on LaPointe's credibility in light of the state's formal support for leniency with respect to the charges against him if he testified fully and accurately. It's unlikely that the many defense challenges on this point had much impact on the jury. However, the defense also failed to register with the jury that LaPointe had already been given substantial benefits by the prosecution, even before he testified. For example, LaPointe testified that he had not reported for tax purposes substantial bonus income – but he was never charged with tax evasion. LaPointe was also never arrested.

Summary on Theft

The principal focus of the prosecution was on the "unsupported inventory transfers" and these must have seemed like theft to the jury. The defense's argument that they were loans was poorly laid out, primarily because the limitations of cross examination didn't give them much scope to express alternative ways of thinking. Also, the prosecution was skillful in employing the "use of cash" analysis as a vehicle that allowed them to bring to court people who had received supposedly tainted checks from Noe. The tedious and repetitive nature of testimony from swimming pool vendors and landscapers might seem silly in the abstract, but in fact it helped the prosecution focus on Noe's allegedly "extravagant" lifestyle.

Forgery, Money Laundering

To a person not familiar with the law, the money laundering charges seem more than odd. Money laundering, as used in this case at least, occurred whenever Noe spent money from his business or personal bank account that, according to Crowe's "use of cash" analysis, belonged to the OBWC.

Ignoring the bizarre nature of the "use of cash" analysis, to the layperson the money laundering charge seems like a kind of double jeopardy – being charged twice for the same crime. In other words, you are charged with theft for taking an amount of money, then again with money laundering for spending any part of that. Shouldn't the theft charge be enough?

Ohio law defines "money laundering" as to:

> ...conduct or attempt to conduct a transaction knowing that the property involved in the transaction was the proceeds of some form of unlawful activity with the purpose of committing or furthering the commission of corrupt activity, and/or conduct or attempt to conduct a transaction with the purpose to promote, manage, establish, carry on, or facilitate the promotion, management, establishment, or carrying on of corrupt activity.[176]

The prosecution spent almost no time explaining the money laundering per se. Rather, the fact of the money laundering charge allowed them to bring in for testimony people to whom Noe had written checks. They would then be asked to describe expensive purchases he had made and as a result the jurors had another window into Noe's "lavish lifestyle" – a favorite *Blade* term.

The forgery charges are similarly odd.

What happened here was that the investigators and auditors discovered that Noe had written a number of checks on the VCC account to a variety of other people and that he had described ("coded") the checks as payment for inventory purchases – in other words, VCC was shown as selling coins to these people. But there were no inventory transactions because the people didn't in fact buy anything, nor did they receive the checks. Instead, Noe signed the purported buyers' names to the checks and deposited them in his personal account. Effectively, he was moving funds from VCC to his own account for personal use. Neither the coin funds nor the persons whose names were on the checks were involved in any way.

As described in endless, boring testimony, the people named in these transactions as recipients of checks never knew that the checks were issued and weren't harmed financially or otherwise.

The prosecution tacitly admitted the lack of harm, and couldn't really connect most of the transactions to the coin funds – even with the dubious "use of cash" methodology. Instead, they asserted that Noe secured an illegal tax advantage from the forged checks and brought in the Noe family CPA, the person who prepared their tax returns, to describe the impact of under-reporting on state and federal income taxes.

The testimony of the CPA was brief but interesting. Despite adroit questioning by Wilkinson, the man was unshakeable that there would have to be some illegal tax advantage from the way the money was moved: Noe either under-reported distributed income or failed to report interest from a loan (likely a much smaller benefit). However, the defense attorney did get the man to agree that any tax advantage from the process wasn't the result of how the checks were signed, but in how they were coded – as inventory purchases rather than distributions.

> Q. Isn't it true that the improper tax benefit that you've described flows from the 500 coin inventory purchase entry in the accounting system as opposed to whatever name might appear on the back of this check?
>
> A. Yes.[177]

In other words, the defense substantially undermined the forgery charge but essentially admitted some level of tax evasion. Ironically, Noe remained in jeopardy from the former and was never charged with the latter.

Valuation

The prosecution filed a motion opposing the defense's desire to present evidence about the overall value of the coin funds and the related issue of profit on October 16, and the defense replied on October 27.

The Prosecution's motion (motion in limine)[178] was filed in response to the defense's plan to call an expert on valuation, David L. Ganz. According to the prosecution, a 70-page document prepared by Ganz (not available in the trial materials) argues that the coin funds lost value after the state-assigned liquidator, DSI, took over, and that this loss is more important than Noe's actions. The prosecution stated that evidence of this kind is "not relevant" to the charges against Noe, especially including theft:

> For example, if A gives $50 to B to invest for A and B immediately pockets $10 of that money for himself, whatever happens to the remaining $40 invested with B (whether there was a profit or loss) is irrelevant to the theft charge regarding the $10 taken beyond the scope of A's consent by B. In the same manner, the actions taken by DSI in managing the coin funds or the actions taken by the OBWC in divesting itself from the coin funds' assets (even if those actions adversely affected the value of the coin funds' assets), are not relevant to the theft offenses that occurred long before the day Noe was removed as manager of the coin funds. The State has not brought theft charges against Noe because he was a poor businessman or ineffective manager of the coin funds but because he knowingly took the OBWC's investment money (with the purpose to keep it for his own use) beyond the scope of the OBWC's consent (there will be testimony that the OBWC did not consent to Noe using its investment money for his own use).[179] [180]*m*

The defense brief in response[181] described the funds taken by Noe as "permissible advances" that "…were secured by adequate value so as to ensure repayment."[182] The defense went on to argue that "…the State has already placed Mr. Noe's decisions as the coin funds' Manager directly at issue in this case, citing as examples testimony about valuation by OBWC investigator Tom Wersell and by Sotheby's expert David Tripp.[183] Also, the defense argued, the state had placed Noe's expenditures such as investments in mortgages, non-coin collectibles, loans and other transactions at issue. As a result, "Mr. Noe is entitled to show that these investments made money for the Coin Funds, and were sound investments."[184]

The defense also challenged as misleading the state's reference to "post-Noe" coin fund assets, pointing out that no assets were purchased after Noe's resignation as manager, with the result that the value of all assets is attributable to Noe.

Judge Osowik ruled on the prosecution's motion on October 31 and, as expected, he supported the prosecution. The text of his order was extremely brief, with the following as the key point:

> The Court finds that testimony regarding the Coin Fund's [sic] valuation subsequent to the defendant's management and possession could not make any fact of consequence more or less probable. See Oakwood v. Makar, 11 Ohio App. 3d 46, 463 N.E. 2d 61 (1983).[185]

The prosecution successfully threaded a needle on valuation. They wanted a representative of Sotheby's, David Tripp, to testify, but styled him as a "fact" rather than an "expert" witness so that he couldn't be forced to testify on the larger issue of his firm's value estimates. The defense challenged this strategy at the time (and in appeals), but failed. And Tripp himself was not to be trapped:

> Q. Are you aware of the fact that the Florida coins sold for three times the amount of Sotheby's appraisal?
>
> A. I don't know what the amount was. I do not know any specifics as to what was what and when it was sold.[186]

The defense's argument here is strong with respect to the fact that Noe was contractually able to take loans (and advances), but weak on the "post-Noe" part. In fact, it can't be disputed that the value of the assets could have gone up or down after he lost control. What was important, and what the defense didn't emphasize, was that there was already good evidence as to the value of the funds prior to their closure: the numbers were estimates based on purchase prices and stated in ranges, but they were important evidence nonetheless. For example, as noted earlier, Sotheby's estimated the coins and collectibles alone as worth $21 to $27 million. In a later filing (Court of Appeals), the state effectively admitted that valuation was possible while Noe was still in charge: "The state can prove the value of stolen property in a theft prosecution by showing the purchase price of the property, especially where the property in question consisted of rare and otherwise valuable coins that tend to fluctuate in value."[187] Failing to energetically challenge the prosecution's characterization of the valuation issue as entirely "post-Noe" was a major flaw in the defense's strategy.

Judge Osowik's ruling is weak as well. Since the prosecution's motion relied extensively on evidence yet to be presented at trial on the key point of whether Noe was entitled to take loans and advances and on his ability to pay for losses in one part of the fund with assets from another, the judge effectively preempted the jury and made a decision on that issue on his own. However, by allowing valuation to be framed entirely as "post-Noe" management, the defense certainly opened itself up to this manipulation.

CLOSING ARGUMENTS

The Prosecution- Weglian

Prosecutor Weglian's closing remarks were superbly constructed. He offered the strong logical flow that had been obscured by the trial's jumble of witnesses and the enormously boring detail. In addition, his examples were clear and the style and language very accessible – Weglian's comments on reasonable doubt, though probably not original, were very well done. And, he effectively avoided tough issues such as the contract language that described taking money even if there was a violation. Finally, freed from having to deal with the question of profit on the non-coin side of the business, Weglian again managed to leave the impression that the coin funds as a whole had lost money.

The Defense- Mitchell

John Mitchell led off for the Defense, and was very solid on reasonable doubt: "If there's no intent to deprive in the theft, you don't have a theft. If there's no enterprise in the pattern of corrupt activity, you don't have a pattern of corrupt activity."[188] He reinforced the question of active consideration by quoting Ted Kennedy that, "too often we allow ourselves the comfort of opinion without the discomfort of thought..."[189]

Building on this point, Mitchell went on to point out that Noe had been judged guilty by politicians and the media long before the evidence was presented. "We don't try our cases in the press. We don't let politics dictate whether people are guilty or innocent. And in this case, more than any that's ever existed in this State, that's what happened."[190] Despite the heavy political overtones, there was, he said, no evidence at all of political involvement in Noe's contract with the OBWC. There were many implications of this, he said, but no evidence – jurors have to use the discomfort of thought to evaluate something like this where the suggestions are strong but the evidence isn't there.

Moving from overarching issues to specifics, the defense attorney emphasized that the initial prospectus for the funds made clear not only the overall risk but also that Noe and Greenberg had no experience as managers of this kind of undertaking. The OBWC knew what it was doing, and went ahead because it, quite reasonably, wanted diversification.

Mitchell emphasized that neither the state's Inspector General, Tom Charles, nor the lead investigator for the OBWC, Tom Wersell, knew anything about the business or had read the files when they started their investigations – they were just marching to the beat of the *Blade*'s drum.

There was much internal debate within the OBWC about the CCF I after the Keith Elliott review, but they still went ahead and gave Noe permission to continue, and then again chose to make another investment. Clearly, that's consent.

The only number among the vast sea presented to the jury that isn't contested is that Noe did give the state $8 million in profit.

Moving to attack the Crowe audit – and noting in passing that the Auditor of State paid them about $500,000 – Mitchell listed some 10 boxes that contained purchase orders and invoices that Crowe didn't look at. They never looked at these key boxes, he said.[191]

The attack on LaPointe was much stronger than in the cross examination. LaPointe, Mitchell said, is a tax cheat who was not prosecuted for that. By contrast to Noe, he was never investigated: no one searched his house or checked his assets. Also important, LaPointe constantly said "I don't remember." He didn't offer clear and assured testimony. The fact was, Noe was an absentee manager who left LaPointe in charge.

The Defense- Wilkinson

Picking up the baton from his colleague, Wilkinson began by saying that it was always clear that money was going to flow from the coin funds to VCC; this was in the contract and certainly not a crime.

Moving to his key theme of consent, he said:

> You haven't heard anyone testify in this case that's been put on by the State, you didn't hear anyone testify that loans, advances, advance purchase transactions, advance profit distributions were not permitted by the contract.[192]*m*

Back to another key theme, he observed that "If there's been a proof of some bad act by Mr. Noe in this case, it's bad bookkeeping."[193] This means, he said, that the issue is one for a civil court, not a criminal one.

Wilkinson took the jury through all the charges in order: theft; money laundering, forgery, pattern of corrupt activity (tampering with records, he said, had already been dealt with).

Wilkinson, after describing how theft and money laundering are essentially the same thing, went on to challenge the theft charges, again focusing on the OBWC's consent, as illustrated by the high degree of control and flexibility given to the managers in the contract.

Finally, the defense also put some focus on the "distribution in violation" clause, which Wilkinson cited as:

> A member who knowingly receives a distribution which is in violation of the agreement or the Ohio Act is liable to the company for a return of such distributions for a period of two years after it's made.

That clause might seem strange, he again said, but the contract was discussed at length internally in 1999-2000 and the language wasn't changed.[194m] And it was still there when the next contract was signed in 2001. In other words, Wilkinson stressed, the OBWC's consent was challenged, then affirmed, then renewed.

Attempting to get to the larger value of the fund, at least indirectly, Wilkinson told the jurors that the state had worked to give the impression that a "little red box" that the Sotheby's expert, David Tripp, had found when he entered VCC's premises in 2005 was all of the coin assets. But, Wilkinson asserted, that's not at all true. In addition to the $8 million in profit returned,

> "There were millions and millions of dollars of assets that came in from Broomall, Pennsylvania, from Wilmington, Delaware, the Delaware Valley location and the RCA location in Florida, from NPL out in Denver, and Mr. Roberts came in and testified about the, you know, the good profit that also came in from the Spectrum Fund transaction."[195]

In addition, there were mortgages, loans, and partnership interests. And also stock in NGC (a coin grading company) that had been moved to Noe's name for technical reasons, but for which a loan document was included in the papers.

Wilkinson concluded the consent theme by pointing out that the legal "owner" of coin fund assets wasn't the OBWC but the coin funds. And he dealt with money laundering in a few words: "The Judge is going to tell you that with respect to money laundering is to conduct a transaction knowing that the property involved in the transactions was proceeds of some form of illegal activity."[196] In other words, if you find consent [instead of theft], there's no money laundering.

Wilkinson emphasized that Noe was taking loans, just as LaPointe had said. Noe was wealthy, with a net worth of $8 million, and could repay. He had no intention "to take this money and run and never come back."[197]

The defense lawyer's remarks on the VCC staff member's ATM comment were confusing, but he offset that by emphasizing that all of Noe's staff people as well as the others he worked with had said that Noe never asked them to do anything illegal. This point obviously had to exclude LaPointe.

Like Mitchell, Wilkinson aimed heavy fire at the Crowe report. He started by trying to take the "full and accurate records" issue off the table: "We're not defending this case on the basis that contract requirements on record keeping were met. There's — that's conceded."[198]

From there, however, there were a lot of serious criticisms. Wilkinson mocked the "use of cash" methodology by saying that you (the jury) wouldn't rely on this.

> You have to ask yourself is that the kind of information that you would rely on in the most important of your own personal financial affairs if it was your money at stake with that kind of analysis?[199]

He again noted that Crowe had failed to check the overall balances, but simply accepted the QuickBooks [internal register] from VCC, which wasn't valid in part because of the coin industry practice of people holding checks.

Perhaps Wilkinson's strongest arguments went to the Crowe "use of cash" practice of ignoring deposits. The judge didn't allow him to present a document that summarized the bank statements (because it was new), so he had to read through an enormous array of numbers. But the conclusion was powerful:

> ...and if you want to add all those things up, you're going to find that there's about $60 million in total deposits that are shown right on that exhibit. $60 million went into that Vintage account. And Emy [the Crowe auditor — Emily Neuman-Javornik] disregarded every one of those dollars that didn't come from the Coin Fund to do her analysis when she said I can trace the money through that account to these people.[200]

Before leaving the Crowe audit, Wilkinson mocked the auditors for using an "adding machine supplement" to their documents, and went on to read from their own report the language that said it wasn't a real audit.

Unfortunately, the defense never asked if the state had provided instructions to Crowe on how — beyond the formal letter of charge — to circumscribe their analysis from the initial broad charge to one that just focused on Noe. Wilkinson could have said, but didn't, that something like this must have been done, either in writing or perhaps more likely orally, since the final Crowe report used in the indictment and in court was not consistent with the Auditor of State's charge to complete an identification and accounting of all coin fund assets.

On forgery, Wilkinson said little that he hadn't mentioned in testimony. He agreed, effectively, that the actual signing of the checks involved forging someone else's signature. But, he again emphasized that just doing that wasn't defrauding anyone. As for the possible tax benefit, he made a little fun of the CPA, Mr. Decker, "who said remarkably, I love tax."[201] But the issue wasn't in the forgery, Wilkinson said again. Rather, the charge, if any, should be false inventory coding – and there was no evidence Noe was the one who did that. He also observed that, despite the allegations, Noe was in fact not charged with tax fraud.

Wilkinson closed by addressing the RICO charge, "the count we didn't hear anything about in the trial."

"There has to be – you have to find that Mr. Noe somehow became affiliated with this mysterious enterprise that we haven't heard anything about during the case, as the evidence was presented, and that through the enterprise he engaged in a pattern of corrupt activity, meaning multiple incidents of various crimes under the law."[202]

In his concluding minutes, Wilkinson noted that someone from the prosecution will now get up and speak and he [Wilkinson] wouldn't have a chance to respond. As a result, members of the jury should ask themselves "...I wonder what Bill would have said, what the rest of the story is in response to the remarks you're now going to hear from the prosecutor."[203]

The defense's lawyer's final words were awkward and perhaps damaging. The jury, he said should "send him [Noe] off to Columbus to face the State's lawyers in the civil case...I'm going to ask you to find that the evidence that's presented, even if it suggests to you Mr. Noe probably did some things wrong, he's probably done something that he ought to have to pay for it, that's not the question for you."[204]

THE PROSECUTION'S REBUTTAL- KIROFF

Assistant Prosecutor Larry Kiroff employed the same factual approach as Weglian, though in an even more conversational approach. He started by going through numerous examples of things Noe did that weren't allowed in the contract and asked, if these are loans or advances, why are they "covert?"

Kiroff dismissed the "knowingly in violation" clause as only applying to profits and not loans or advances, and stated that OBWC was in fact the owner under Ohio law and did not consent.

In a surprise move that the defense protested and Judge Osowik allowed, Kiroff read from Noe's deposition on his political involvement (the document used by the defense to support the motion to disqualify local judges), and then asked whether someone this involved in major activities like politics is someone who doesn't know what's going on in his own business? It was therefore obvious, the jury was supposed to conclude, that LaPointe acted entirely under Noe's direction.

As for the ability to repay, the Assistant Prosecutor said someone can't rob a bank and then come back later and say I'm going to give you your money back with interest. He dismissed the check coding issue by saying that the circumstantial evidence all pointed to Noe as being the one who made the entries.

To once more hit on Noe's allegedly "lavish lifestyle," Kiroff again played a contractor's video of Noe showing of his luxury house as a way of showing that Noe had a motive.

Finally, Kiroff challenged Wilkinson's description of $60 million in deposits to VCC, by saying it didn't include expenses which, he implied, meant it wouldn't cover the $12 million stolen.

SUMMARY COMMENTS ON THE CLOSING ARGUMENTS

As noted, Weglian was exceptionally clear and with outstanding logical flow. The final points on reasonable doubt were also good.

The defense was sort of a mixed bag. Mitchell was eloquent in challenging the jury to think, though that may have gone over the head of this group. He also did a good job of illustrating how political and media motives drove the investigation and the trial. And, the shots at LaPointe's testimony were much more powerful than anything prior: Mitchell showed that LaPointe had a much stronger incentive than the state had mentioned to say what the prosecution wanted. And, again, there was much LaPointe couldn't remember.

Wilkinson was effective in restating the consent issue but, while he made some good points, wasn't able to deliver a clear framework on the overall funds that would provide essential context for Noe's falsely documented borrowing.

The validity of the Crowe audit was again destroyed, but Wilkinson didn't ask whether the report was off-balance because the state had told Crowe to make it that way.

Wilkinson made the point that Noe intended to pay off the loans and had the ability to repay, but the defense lawyer failed to describe the inventoried coins as being effectively the same as IOUs. Also, while the illustration of how much money was in the overall VCC account (the $60 million in deposits) could have helped to give the jury perspective, it wasn't delivered crisply or clearly enough to be effective.

The attack on the RICO charge likely gave the jury pause, but any qualms they developed would have been offset later by the judge's instructions: what Wilkinson presented as beyond the law was in fact well within it.

Finally, as noted, the awkward closing statement to the effect that Noe was guilty but not of criminal conduct could have left a sour taste with some jurors.

Kiroff's rebuttal was smooth and well-stated, but logically flawed – notably including an absolutely ridiculous explanation of Crowe's "use of cash."[205] Kiroff repeated Weglian's exercise showing there wasn't enough money in CCF I to cover Noe's initial checks, but used the same short early time period, a comparison that was calculated to mislead the jurors on the overall activities of the funds.

The attack on the "knowingly in violation" clause as only applying to profits was technically accurate – the statement is in the "Distribution of Profits" section of the contract. However, it's likely that, if the defense lawyers had had the opportunity to respond, they would have been able to point out that profits don't have to be distributed after the fact, they can also be taken in advance (not least because the contract specifically allowed that). And, given other language on loans elsewhere in the contract, a loan against a profit is also feasible. Finally, they would have said, "there's that 'knowingly in violation' wording that essentially trumps any restriction." Wilkinson might well have turned to the prosecution and said, "What part of 'knowingly in violation' don't you understand?"

Despite some important logical flaws, as with Weglian's presentation, Kiroff did a better job of connecting to the emotions of the jury.

THE JUDGE'S INSTRUCTIONS TO THE JURY

Judge Osowik's instructions to the jury comprised plain vanilla reading of legal definitions of the alleged crimes together with references to the specific acts: e.g., defining money laundering and referring to a specific transaction or transactions.

The defense asked Osowik to include definitions drawn from the state's commercial code, notably definitions of ownership and consent, but the judge refused.

THE VERDICT

The jury delivered its verdict on November 13, issuing guilty verdicts for 29 counts, including all of the important ones relating to theft and RICO. It found Noe not guilty of 11 counts, principally relating to money laundering and tampering with records. The logic behind the not guilty decisions is unclear. It might seem at first glance that the jury found the money laundering charges a little too much, but they did convict on four of those counts. Later commentary from the jury foreman (see below) suggests that the not guilty decisions were the result of compromises in a conflicted group, with at least some favoring not guilty verdicts on the more important counts. This issue of jury decision-making is also discussed in the section on the appeals.

Courts conduct hearings to allow the prosecution and defense, as well as various interested parties, to offer opinions on the nature of the sentence that should be imposed once guilt is determined. Judge Osowik held the sentencing hearing on November 20.

Tom Wersell of the OBWC read a statement which can be summarized as saying the Bureau was doing great before the Coingate crisis started but was now doing badly — "the pride was gone."[206]

> The department also suffered a 37 percent reduction in our return on investment, a measure that we were proud of when the department hit an all-time high in fiscal year 2005 when we reported a $12 return on investment. During the year of Tom Noe, we saw that drop to $7. The department also saw a reduction in our prosecutions. During fiscal year 2005, we obtained 143 convictions. During the year of Tom Noe, our convictions dropped to 90, a 37 percent reduction.[207]

It's exceedingly difficult to see how Noe could have been responsible for any of these problems experienced by the OBWC. Fortunately for Wersell, there was no cross examination.

The prosecution, in its brief to the judge on sentencing, offered a comparison with the case of a lawyer in Columbus who had just been sentenced to eighteen years for theft, including RICO. This case is discussed in some detail in the section on the Ohio Court of Appeals (for the moment, note that the comparison was disingenuous to the point of dishonesty).

By contrast, Wilkinson was eloquent in his appeal for the minimum sentence, which would be ten years:

> I think it's important to consider, Judge, that in terms of recidivism factors, that of this ten years, Mr. Noe's going to have to do every single day. There's no parole. There's no judicial release eligibility for him under that sentence. If you give him the minimum sentence in this case, he will serve every day in the Ohio Penitentiary. I think it's also important when you consider the overriding purposes of sentencing, Judge, there is an idea that punishment is something you must consider.

> When we sat down at the beginning of the case, the trial team in this case looked throughout the United States and throughout the State of Ohio to cases that were similar to Mr. Noe's that had an aspect of the political involvement that had an aspect of theft or embezzlement, and the one that we discovered and came up with was a case involving a gentleman by the name of Frank Gruttadauria. Mr. Gruttadauria had both a state and a federal case, Judge. I believe he stole somewhere in the

neighborhood of $130 million, ten times what Mr. Noe was alleged to have stolen in this case. In that state sentence, he was sentenced to a term of 54 months of incarceration in the state penal institution. Not even five years. And I believe he served seven years — and I don't think our sentencing brief is clear on this, Judge, and I want to bring it to your attention, but he received a sentence of seven years in the federal penitentiary for stealing ten times what Mr. Noe did. And I think it's important to consider, Judge, that when Frank Gruttadauria performed the acts that he did, he cleaned out the life savings of numerous people. He had millions of dollars entrusted to him and literally the next day this was gone. This was in contrast to what happened in the Coin Funds. We know from DSI, the witnesses we were to put on in this case, and we know from the recent articles in the paper the Coins Funds are going to return a profit and they expect to receive $55 or $56 million from the liquidation of those assets.

Now, if you add $7.9 that Mr. Noe has already paid back to the BWC over his management of the Coin Fund, that means on an initial investment of $50 million, regardless of what Mr. Noe did or didn't take, the Bureau of Worker's Compensation is still going to receive $63 million over the life of that investment. Which means, Judge — and we've heard no evidence that any injured worker ever didn't receive their just due or that their medical coverage wasn't there because of Mr. Noe's actions.[208]

Wilkinson went on to offer some personal perspectives and also to comment on Prosecutor Bates' statement to the *Blade* that Noe should get a longer sentence than offered in the plea deal because he chose to go to trial.[209]*m*

I understand that you have to punish him, Judge, and I'm going to ask you to consider the Gruttadauria sentence, which means 7 years for $130 million and you add 27 months for his federal case on top of that, that would still be less than the ten years Mr. Noe has to serve on his state case. I think that looking at other proportional sentences in this state leads to the belief the ten years that has to be imposed in this sentence should be served concurrently with his federal offense. That's not in no way, shape, or form minimizing any of Mr. Noe's conduct.

Judge, personal affect [sic] on Mr. Noe. I mean, his family's here. You've seen them come to the Court to support him. He's got five children. He's going to miss four weddings, three college graduations, and one high school graduation, and the birth of his grandchildren. I only bring this to your attention to let you know that this is a personal affect that that's going to have on him.

And I think the overall idea behind this, Judge, is that I read in the paper today for the first time that the plea negotiations involving Mr. Noe were made public, and it appears that — I don't know why that this would be leaked the day before his sentencing, but it appears that the prosecutor's asking you to put some sort of trial tax on Mr. Noe, that by executing his constitutional right to a trial he should be punished more than he could have plead [sic]) to at an earlier time.[210]

Immediately after the testimony concluded, Judge Osowik sentenced Noe to eighteen years in prison, served after the federal sentence was complete and with no real possibility of early release.[211]*m*

THE BLADE'S COVERAGE OF THE TRIAL

The *Blade*'s pattern of one-sided coverage continued throughout the trial.

For the opening statements, the article fully covered the prosecution's key themes, but gave much less attention to the defense. In particular, Wilkinson's theme that the OBWC gave Noe "consent" was mentioned only indirectly.

The first day testimony of the lead investigators, Tom Charles of the OIG and Tom Wersell was reported with no indication that there was defense cross examination at all — for example, no reference to the ambiguous testimony offered on why the investigation began or especially of the confusion on both sides at the time of the search warrant. Thus, readers would have falsely concluded that the investigators at that time were organized and purposeful while Noe and his lawyers were obstructive.

In this first article, the *Blade*, as always, put in praise for itself as the source of the investigation.

Coverage of the testimony of Noe's staff, including that of Sue Metzger, who said that Noe used the coin funds as an ATM, was generally fair –the *Blade* didn't have access to the defense's criticism of her very concerning inconsistency or evidence of the prosecution's failure to provide the defense in advance of her testimony about the newest – and potentially most damaging comments.

The *Blade* was also remarkably fair with the testimony of the Crowe accountant, Emily Neuman-Javornik, pointing out Wilkinson's devastation of the firm's "use of cash" methodology.

The *Blade* used a great deal of space to describe the appearances of people involved in the various transactions that Ms. Neuman-Javornik described as unsupported inventory purchases or when checks were written to personal vendors but coded as coin purchases in VCC's accounting. This was reasonable given that this testimony consumed a lot of trial time.

Coverage of Tim LaPointe's time on the witness stand was for the most part very straightforward and fair. Notably, however, the paper didn't mention

LaPointe's comment that the coin funds were "doing fine" at a key point in 2004. This is consistent with the *Blade*'s aversion to any mention of the overall success of the funds, but it's likely also related to the fact that the defense didn't bring it up in cross-examination.

Coverage of the Keith Elliott testimony began in a balanced way. The *Blade* made clear that Elliott had said the contract was very favorable to Noe, even mentioning that there was a provision that allowed Noe "to take money from the funds as long as he intended to pay it back within two years."[212]

However, the article then quickly entered into a discussion of how it was that Noe got such a favorable contract, and quoted various sources about Noe's GOP connections, including ties to the man, Paul Mifsud, who was chief of staff to Governor Voinovich when the first fund was approved in 1998. This departure from the main line of the trial into broader thinking about the workings of Coingate illustrates the fact that the *Blade* didn't feel locked down to the grind of testimony. On the other hand, the only occasions when the paper showed an ability to stand back and think analytically were ones that were negative to Noe.

Unsurprisingly, the *Blade*'s reporters seemed not to understand the state's purpose with the forgery charges. They mentioned that the prosecution said the reason could be tax evasion. Otherwise the coverage was largely favorable to Noe, pointing out that the people called to testify were mostly very friendly to Noe and that the prosecution failed to challenge Wilkinson's point that no one was harmed by the forgeries.

We've seen that the *Blade* was hostile to the idea of anyone knowing the full value of the coin funds. Its coverage of the press conference Noe and his lawyers had in December of 2005 focused on negative comments from various state or state-related actors to the near exclusion of Noe's perspective. The *Blade* published no investigative stories on this issue and simply reported Judge Osowik's ruling with no substantive comment.

The *Blade* jumbled the two closing argument presentations rather than taking them sequentially. It was a reasonable approach, but one that didn't give either side its full due. Taking into account its already entrenched biases, the *Blade*'s article on this part of the trial didn't add any new tilt.

It's hard not to describe the *Blade*'s coverage of the trial as anything other than strongly biased. Some of that was manifest, as noted above, in coverage of day to day testimony – usually as a result of omitting important defense points. But the key omission was the failure to consider the case openly and analytically.

The *Blade* by no means felt constrained to limit itself to the case's legalities. The editors felt it was important for their readers to know about wine and cigars in Colorado and about the history and current lifestyle of a former Noe partner in California. And it diverged –appropriately so --from mundane testimony to speculate about how Noe was able to secure such a favorable contract from the OBWC. Indeed, the *Blade*'s consistent probing into political connections wasn't just reasonable, it was courageous.

But, when speculation might have opened up another way of thinking about Noe's responsibility, the *Blade* suddenly became very shy. The newspaper that aggressively pursued the OBWC's inventory records all the way to the Ohio Supreme Court became very passive when it came to determining the value of the coin funds at the point when the state took control from Noe. Although the existence of the relevant documents was well known, the *Blade* appears never to have asked for the full Sotheby's appraisal. Nor did it ask why the Crowe audit never completed the Auditor of State's request to analyze all of the assets of the coin funds – including stocks, accounts receivable, etc. Somewhere between the Auditor of State's letter of charge and the indictment there was a major change of prosecution focus – but the *Blade* wasn't interested.

The most visible evidence of *Blade* bias, and what could be interpreted to be an attempt to influence the outcome, came in the paper's endorsement of judges just before election day, November 1 of 2006. Judge Osowik was running for a promotion – to Appeals Court judge – and the *Blade* strongly endorsed him. But it wasn't just an ordinary endorsement. Whereas, according to local observers on both sides of the aisle, judges were usually endorsed by the *Blade* as a group and on an inside page, the editors in this case chose to endorse Osowik by himself on the front page.[213] If "appearance of impropriety" is commonly described as a point that shouldn't be passed in ethics, the *Blade* exceeded it in a giant leap with this action, which immediately followed Osowik's critically important decision on valuation.

PERFORMANCE OF THE KEY PLAYERS

Both sides were effective in the actual trial. However, the prosecution had an advantage because the original framing of the charges, together with the judge's apparent bias, meant that it had been able to significantly outmaneuver the defense in the pre-trial.

Performance of the Prosecution

The prosecution's initial decision to include the RICO charge and oppose any reference to the value of the funds as a whole gave it a strong advantage, and was followed by a strong performance in the trial itself. Prosecutors sometimes showed a sly habit of leading witnesses into inappropriate territory – for example Weglian tried to get the Inspector General, Tom Charles, to talk about the federal case and the Noe-related ethics problems in Columbus.

The prosecutors were consistently skillful in keeping the testimony focused on their narrow niche – just the coins and just in Maumee. One example of this, one that was at a minimum devious, was to insist that the Sotheby's appraiser, Tripp, was to testify as a fact witness rather than as an expert. In doing this, prosecutors prevented the defense from bringing up his overall analysis. As will be seen later, a federal judge derided this strategy.

Perhaps most important, the prosecution was better at attending to the jury's emotions, largely with an excellent job of drawing attention to Noe's lifestyle. Prosecutors were also skillful in distracting attention from potential problems with the substance and logic of their charges by employing mind numbing practices such as having witnesses open envelopes to verify checks.

Performance of Noe's Counsel- Pre-Trial

The most important action of the defense, of course, was Wilkinson's "shortfall" statement. It wasn't brought up at trial, but it set a frame for the whole process that was enormously damaging to Noe. As well see in Part VI which describes the impact of media on jurors, it's virtually impossible that jurors didn't know of Wilkinson's comments.

Otherwise, the defense presented a thoughtful and energetic set of pre-trial motions including recusal of judges, change of venue, and (to a lesser extent) a challenge to the RICO charge. That they lost on all these points has more to do with the fact that the Lucas County deck was stacked against them than with the quality of their work.

Performance of Noe's Counsel- Trial

Both Wilkinson and Mitchell appear to have presented a positive face to the jury, and both were very effective in questioning the prosecution's witnesses. As noted above, they scored quite a few key points. However, they were less effective than the prosecution in part because their points were, by comparison, more logical than emotional. More important, they had a very limited scope of action once Judge Osowik took the issue of valuation of the coin funds as a whole off the table.

No witnesses for the defense – a valid strategy?

To a considerable extent, the defense's decision not to put on a case of its own could be attributed to the judge's refusal to let them discuss the overall value of the coin funds. As noted, this left them with a very narrow playing field. They were unable, for example, to demonstrate that Noe had the money in other areas of coin fund investments to cover shortfalls in coins.

The next most problematic failure of the defense was not to acknowledge the false record keeping. It must have been obvious to the jury early in the trial that Noe was taking loans (and/or advances) and not documenting them. If anyone had failed to connect on this point early on, they certainly would have been convinced after LaPointe's mostly unchallenged testimony. The prosecution's case was heavily focused on a line that went like this- "this guy's going to say he was taking loans but in fact he didn't have the right to do that and even if he did it was done fraudulently." The defense's response was to ignore whether Noe actually took the money while arguing that he did have the right to do it. This approach surely introduced a credibility problem with the jury – if he's denying the obvious, then maybe nothing he says is true?

The attack on LaPointe, as mentioned, is from the standard legal playbook: you can't prove that the other guy *didn't* do it. But simple logic – LaPointe obviously acted on Noe's orders – likely rendered this line ineffective. And, as with the denying that Noe took money out, it was most likely counterproductive with the jury.

Still, there were important opportunities left on the table. The defense did a great job of attacking Crowe's bizarre "use of cash" analysis and could have reinforced this by pointing out that the prosecution's rebuttal covered only a very narrow time period – the only logical way to analyze which monies funded what would have been to look at the entire time period. In the same vein, the defense could have driven home the point that the Crowe analysis treated the funds as if they had to be balanced on a minute by minute transactional basis –as a normal checking account — whereas the contract mentioned only annual reports and therefore implied only annual reconciliation.

The defense's dismissive statements in the closing arguments left far too much hanging. The most damning piece of testimony at the trial, that Noe paid off personal debts immediately after the state monies entered his checkbook, could have been countered in a defense case by Noe's explanation that he had been buying collectibles in advance of the deal so that he could be ready to make money. He had used personal funds, notably his line of credit, to do this and thus had to reimburse himself. Noe's personal and business accounts were so intertwined that it would have been hard to counter this. Even if the prosecutors had attacked fiercely, they wouldn't have had a clear line of fire and doubt would have been raised on a critical issue.

The defense also failed to mention that Noe, by providing an itemized and detailed inventory of coins that were supposed to be owned by the coin funds, was effectively leaving IOUs in the accounting system – very much by contrast to Weglian's consistent comments to the effect that Noe left no IOU in return for taking the State's money.

Performance of Judge Osowik

Judge Osowik doubtless sincerely believed he was unbiased, and nothing he did was overtly unfair. Generally, he was reasonable on technical issues, often ruling for the defense. Still he came to the trial with some obvious preconceptions and was also most certainly vulnerable to unconscious bias.

Osowik's overly narrow views about jury bias have been noted earlier; in Osowik's world all you need is to find a dozen people who are willing to say they can be fair.

Most important in the actual trial phase was the judge's decision about valuation – not to allow the defense to argue that the coin funds had made an overall profit. This ruling directly aligned the court with the carefully contrived and exceedingly narrow view of Noe's actions advanced by the state. As we'll see, the fact that it was sustained in the appeals process means almost nothing – on issues like this, appeals courts defer to the discretion of trial judges.

Osowik's decision to maximize the sentence – he gave Noe ten more years than necessary[214]*m* – is puzzling in the extreme. His boiler plate explanation –"you were a person of trust" – doesn't begin to address the enormous disparity between Noe's sentence and what others had been shown to receive for similar crimes. It's hard to escape the conclusion that Osowik wasn't thinking about justice in the abstract but was instead caught up in the media and political hurricane that had swept Lucas County.

As will be discussed later, Osowik was and is a well-respected judge and there's no indication and no reason to believe that he deliberately ruled against Noe on the basis of political or personal bias. But bias isn't always conscious. Some biases are natural human responses that allow us to filter information that doesn't conform to our beliefs from the environment. It's possible that the prospect of supporting the defense's position on valuation produced enough "dissonance" in the judge's mind that he couldn't allow the logic in. The timing of the trial shortly before the election surely influenced Judge Osowik in some way. And, he would certainly have known that a different ruling would have drawn the ire of the *Blade*, which preferred the view of the state as coin collector. And the *Blade*'s endorsement in the imminent contest for a judgeship on the Appeals Court was, like it or not, extremely important. The point here isn't that Osowik is more vulnerable than another person to bias, it's that people shouldn't be placed or allow themselves to be placed in a situation where unconscious bias can affect decisions. More on this in Part VI.

The Jury

Reading the voir dire, discussed in more detail later in Part VI, doesn't inspire one to be confident about the abilities of those in the overall jury pool.

The actual jurors may have been much more capable than their peers in the pool, but their foreman, James Petiniot, characterizes their performance in a very negative way. Petiniot, writing some years later, says in part:

> I presided over a group of people who tried their best to decide the case, but were completely overwhelmed with the mountain of material they had been provided. We received over 20 banker's boxes of this material,[215]*m* and we didn't have any auditors, accountants, or lawyers as jurors. In reviewing the evidence, we had to sift through financial spreadsheets, and PowerPoint presentations, contract provisions, bank records, inventory records, tax records, receipts, adding machine tape, and other items. We didn't have to just look at these items, but had to interpret provisions and (especially with the contracts) decide what they meant. Unfortunately, it was a task that we had little or no prior experience doing. I did not understand much of this material, and I know that my fellow jurors did not either.
>
> In short, we didn't decide the case on the evidence. We felt that if we didn't return a verdict soon, the general public would think that we were stupid. After all, according to the media and the politicians, everybody in Ohio knew Mr. Noe was guilty. What would take the jury so long to convict him? Under that pressure, we had numerous, heated arguments in deciding the case. After spending a couple of days trying to get through the evidence, we gave up and convicted Mr. Noe of crimes he did not commit. I am sure you know Mr. Noe received a sentence of 18 years.
>
> I never felt that the State of Ohio had presented evidence beyond a reasonable doubt regarding the RICO count. Still, I signed the verdict oath form even though I didn't believe Mr. Noe was guilty of that offense. I violated my juror oath, and I signed a verdict form I didn't believe in. I was not alone; other jurors voiced the opinion they just wanted to get the case over, even if it meant convicting Mr. Noe of offenses he didn't commit.
>
> My failure as a juror has haunted me since I learned much more about the "Coin Gate" scandal after the case was concluded. First, I learned that coin funds had actually made money for the State. During the case, the prosecution focused on how Mr. Noe had supposedly looted the coin funds. The jurors were led to believe that the investment was a disaster. I learned the truth was vastly different.[216]

Needless to say, there are a number of very good reasons why the legal system doesn't allow the post-trial perspective of jurors to drive any kind of decision. Still, from the point of view of fairness, this is powerful commentary.

NOE'S PERSPECTIVE

When the *Blade* did the original article on me and the Coin Fund in April of 2005, I knew that this was just the beginning of a long road. Little did I know at the time how long that road would be; full of speed bumps and craters. The quick follow-up articles gave me a taste of what was to come. I attempted to correct the record on a couple of the articles but hit a brick wall so I finally gave up trying. As soon as a number of political and personal "friends" started turning on me and running I knew there was little I could do to stop the bus from running over me. I knew our records for the Coin Fund were a mess but figured I'd have plenty of time to review them and correct the many issues. I couldn't have been more mistaken. I had numerous calls from clients and friends offering millions of dollars of financial assistance and other help but I knew by early May that this whole situation was as much to do with politics than just the coin fund, especially since people were saying they knew nothing about the coin fund until the *Blade* articles when, in fact, the awarding of both coin funds were done at more than one public meeting of the Ohio Bureau of Worker's Compensation Board and I had conversations with many of them about the coin funds.

I remember my first meeting with Thompson Hine, my new attorneys, the third week of May trying to explain the coin business and how the coin funds worked. One of the many issues we discussed was what would happen if the state held a fire sale on the coin funds' assets. I estimated that there could be a 10-15 million dollar valuation shortfall and told them that we had to do whatever was necessary to make sure that didn't happen. My lead attorney, Bill Wilkinson, went to meeting the next day with the state and federal investigators and prosecutors and two days later I'm served with a search warrant based on Bill's supposed statement at that meeting that there was $13 million dollars missing from the coin funds. At the time, a lot of people asked me why I didn't hire local counsel for the state trial. The answer was simple, Rick Kerger, Reg Jackson, and most other Toledo attorneys were conflicted out because they represented various defendants in my Federal Campaign Finance case. Once the conflicts were gone after a few years, and Thompson Hine and I agreed to part ways, Rick Kerger agreed to take over my appeals and did a phenomenal job, even though we weren't ultimately successful. The deck seemed to be always stacked against us but I've always wondered if I would have had the same outcome with Rick there from day one.

The day after the search warrant was served, Bernadette and I watched on live TV, from my sister and brother-in-law's house, as the state

backed a semi-truck to the front door of my office and loaded
everything on the premises, including some of the furniture, into the
truck. It was as close as I got to a breakdown over the course of the
next 12 years. Luckily, Bernadette and some close family and friends
helped me get through the ordeal. My doctor prescribed some effective
medications to regulate my mood swings. The bad side effect was that I
gained weight and my mind and memory weren't as sharp as I would
have liked. I was also carrying around the guilt of some loyal employees
losing their jobs. We were a close knit group and they were like family
to me.

Bernadette and I decided that the best thing for us to do was to move
to the house in Florida to get away from the media circus that ensued.
Bernadette had previously passed the Florida Bar Exam and was able to
put food on our table while the lawyers tried to sort everything out. I
have a somewhat fuzzy memory of the next 17 months but soon after
we moved to Florida, there was a picture on the front page of the Blade
of Bernadette and me in our van coming out of a car wash in Key
Largo. The headline said something like "Noe's spotted in Key Largo".
Not sure where they thought we would be because we did live there
now!! I tried my best to find some humor wherever I could.

My biggest concern was more for the kids and our families. We had to
uproot our youngest two kids and John had to find a different college.
A larger issue was the fact that the two oldest girls, my mom, my sister,
and Bernadette's family still lived in the Toledo area and had to endure
the constant barrage of negative articles. I'll always be haunted by what
I put everyone through. They always say that what doesn't kill you
makes you stronger. I'm not sure I believed that at the time but 12
years later I know that we have the strongest and best family and real
friends that anyone could ever hope for.

Once we got settled the biggest unknown was the "where and when" of
what I would be charged with and when they would do it. The first
indictment was the Federal campaign finance charges in the fall of
2005. Those alone would have been easy to handle without the
knowledge that a bigger shoe would drop in regards to the state issues.
On top of all the stress of the unknown, three hurricanes, Rita, Katrina
(yes, that same one), and Wilma, hit South Florida and Keys in the fall
of 2005. Rita was the worst and caused the most damage for us but
none of them were "fun". Bernadette was on call for the Department
of Children and Families for the upper Keys. I took the Red Cross
emergency and evacuation training in Marathon to be on call to help

with any rescue situations. It made the time go by but added more stress to an already difficult period. I do remember my sister, Beth, and her husband, Ron, visiting us when Hurricane Wilma hit us. We all survived and I'm sure Beth still has her "I survived Hurricane Wilma" t-shirt somewhere!

One of my most vivid memories soon after the hurricane season was the press conference that we held in Thompson Hine's Columbus office. The object was to make a case that all the money was there and that there was actually a profit if DSI didn't screw up the sale of all the assets. I didn't have much confidence in DSI, based on the observation of their first sale in Columbus. Beth Deisher, the editor of Coin World at the time, wrote an editorial about how DSI was liquidating these coins. The Blade actually printed it as a guest editorial. That was the biggest surprise! When we finished the press conference I got the distinct impression that my attorney, Bill Wilkinson, didn't believe me that all the money was there. It added to my weariness about the whole situation. It was always like pulling teeth to get them to respond to the negative press, mostly in the Blade, even if it was blatantly false or misleading. The false, bordering on slanderous Cayman Islands story that insinuated that I had money in an offshore account, was a typical example of what we were fighting against. The Blade bought their ink by the barrel and we bought ours by the ink pen full! TH saw no reason to respond to the article or try to set the record straight. I'll never understand TH's aversion to responding to the press. Once Rick Kerger took over my case at the appeals level with the Ohio Supreme Court, he would respond to any and all inquiries from the media. I, at least, felt like a had a chance.

Reality really set in when the state indicted me on over 50 counts in February of 2006. I was already very fragile emotionally but this took it to a new level. Bernadette was trying to work while all this was happening and it took a terrible toll on her, too. When the lawyers wanted a lien on the Florida house to guarantee their fees moving forward, it put a terrible strain on our marriage and caused even further stress. Looking back, I'm not sure Bernadette made the right decision (for her) by allowing the lien, but she put my best interests ahead of hers and acquiesced for a third mortgage, at $1.8 million. Almost 10 years later she had to file suit against Thompson Hine, and ultimately settle with them, to sell the Tavernier house. Maybe this lien issue in early 2006 should have been a sign of things to come in regards to TH... we will never know.

When it came time for my trial in October 2006 I didn't have the confidence in our defense that I would have liked. It seemed like every motion we filed was denied and every one that the prosecution filed was granted. I joked at the time that when I walked into the courtroom the first day the "Visitor's light" on the scoreboard lit up! It always felt like we were swimming uphill.

Even when I felt like our team made good points it seemed like the jury didn't get it. I knew that this was a very complex case, with a ridiculous amount of daily negative, almost slanderous, publicity in the local newspaper. When I would look at the jury during the testimony they seemed lost. While I felt like we scored some good points, I never felt confident that it was enough. After the prosecution rested, we met for a few hours and Bill and John convinced me that we shouldn't call any witnesses, especially me. I truly wanted to testify but they felt it was too dangerous. Given the outcome I'm not sure I could have made it much worse. Their reasoning was that the prosecution hadn't proven their case and that there was nothing to gain and everything to lose if we called anyone else. Would it have made a difference? We'll never know but given the jury foreman's letter to the Governor and subsequent affidavit that they never understood the issues and if they had known that the state made a profit on the funds (yes, the state knew before my trial that they would make a profit) they would have never convicted me. In his opinion, they convicted an innocent man on the RICO charge which carried the 10 year mandatory minimum sentence. Over 10 years later I still have nightmares over the decision to not put on a defense, including me taking the stand. Part of me will always wonder if Thompson Hine didn't want to spend the money on the witnesses. Money always seemed to be a battle with them.

When I was found guilty on the most serious charge along with many others I was definitely in shock. I was taken right away to Lucas County jail to await sentencing a week later. That was a really tough time for me and my family. Thank goodness I have a very strong relationship with God or I wouldn't have survived, not to mention the support of the greatest and strongest family and true friends in the world. As my late mom always told me, "Let go and let God". That became our family mantra for the next 10+ years.

BLADE REACTION TO THE SENTENCE

The *Blade's* reaction to the conviction and prison term can be summed up in one statement from its article on November 20: "The reaction across Ohio was nearly unanimous: A long prison term was well deserved for a man who deceived so many."[217]

This was a news story, not an editorial.

There certainly wasn't time for a poll to validate the "nearly unanimous" reaction in the state. Did the *Blade's* staff decide that the sentiment in their management offices was sufficient evidence?

PETRO RESURFACES

Attorney General Petro, who had been pumping out campaign-fueled press releases on Noe's "theft" up until about the time of the indictment in February of 2006, grew completely silent as the trial approached. The principal reason for this was that the civil case was suspended in order not to influence its criminal peer.

But another explanation for the Attorney General's silence could be that he didn't want to influence the jury pool with positive information – relevant in this case because Petro, as overseer of the civil case, had access to all of the information about the funds that had been recovered — and were expected to be recovered — from Noe and the coin funds. However, the conviction caused him to break silence and return to the PR trail.

In a November 21 announcement (the criminal trial ended November 13) Petro stated that the civil case against Noe would restart. He added that the state had so far recovered $40.8 million. That amount didn't include the $7.9 million in profits paid earlier, so the total recovered at that point was really $48.7 million. And the liquidators identified to a *Coin World* reporter at least another $4.5-$5.5 million likely to be gained from known assets.[218] In other words, at the time of the trial and likely well before, the state knew that it would recover more than its $50 million investment, even as it was arguing that Noe "stole" $12-13 million.

The *Blade* missed it, but the timing of Petro's announcement was not lost in the world of coin investing: *Coin World* led its December 11, 2006 article on the Attorney General's announcement about the value of the funds as "The best-kept secret about the state of Ohio's recovery of its coin investment is out."[219]

TRIAL SUMMARY AND FAIRNESS SCORECARD

The state managed throughout the trial to keep a distinction between a micro and a macro view of the coin funds, with the former getting intense focus and the latter being relentlessly hidden.

Thus, if a phony inventory transfer occurred in proximity to a personal expenditure by Noe, such as a home purchase or a landscaping bill, it was argued that public funds were being used to pay these personal expenses. The defense responded in vain that you can't do accounting that way. For example, Noe might have anticipated income from another source (e.g., a major coin sale by VCC) that would make up the difference later in the month. The prosecution's support for the auditor's "use of cash" analysis seems to have been intended to mislead the jury – indeed it's probable that this methodology originated with the prosecution (or the State Task Force) rather than from the auditor.

Moreover, although Noe was supposed to submit accounting information monthly, it's not clear that he was responsible for maintaining a positive balance during that interval. An assessment of profit and loss for distribution to the partners was made only annually – and even then, the managers could choose not to distribute.

In addition, Noe's contract did clearly allow him to take advances and loans from the funds, with a term of two years to repay the latter – even if taken "in violation" of the contract's terms. Thus, Noe was allowed to transfer money from the funds to himself and to Vintage. He certainly didn't properly document all of those –perhaps any of those. And the misleading nature of what he did in some cases could reasonably merit a charge of tampering with records or similar. But, in light of the contract, nothing the state presented supported a charge of theft.

The state's response to this was to argue that Noe could not in fact take loans and advances because his contract was improper – the state (in the form of OBWC and its legal department) should never have agreed to these things. What this means for Noe is that, many years after acting according to the rules of a contract that had been reviewed and approved by numerous state lawyers, he was now to find that the state had changed its mind — and done so retroactively.

Under no condition is this a fair action on the part of the state. And, as noted, it's not a precedent Ohio will want to make visible as it engages with its many thousands of vendors and contractors. Who will want to work with an entity that, after the fact, chooses to renege on clearly agreed contractual terms?

With its arguments in the Noe case, the state is acting like a bank that grants a mortgage under clear terms then, after you paint the house a certain color and remodel the kitchen, tells you that, because it has decided it retained "an interest" in the house, it can punish you for acting without its permission.

Finally, the greatest victory of micro over macro came in the nature of accounting for the OBWC's overall investment. The state contracted with an external accountant and also used many of its own analysts to examine all of

Noe's transactions. This process took ten months and should reasonably have led to an accurate balance for the total of all financial interactions between Noe, VCC, and the coin funds and their partners. In addition, the state contracted for an appraisal of all coins and collectibles held by the funds. Taken together, the accounting and the appraisals allowed an overall estimate, within a range, of the coin funds' assets. But the state kept that secret.

This approach of focusing on the micro and ignoring the macro is inconsistent with the one used for other managers of other OBWC investments, whose performance was assessed on *overall* profit and loss. It is also inconsistent with the concepts of fairness and justice.

Nothing offers better evidence of the political frenzy surrounding Noe than the fact that the *Blade* and many politicians called for Noe getting the "maximum allowable punishment" or words to that effect. Did they know that that meant 18 years with no reasonable expectation of early release?

Was There Theft?

At this point in the book there's enough evidence to evaluate the core question: did Tom Noe steal money from the OBWC?

The answer is clearly not.

As we've seen, Prosecutor Weglian said Noe couldn't say he'd taken loans or advances because he hadn't left an IOU. But Weglian then went on to describe the detailed invoice information Noe left – a very specific record of each coin and its value. Those were the same as IOUs.

"But," the critic will say, "these coins didn't exist! Noe took money and provided nothing in return!"

That sounds damning, but it isn't true. Consider this sequence of facts:

1) Noe *was* authorized to take loans and advances. The contract was clear on this in a number of places and a reasonable court would never have concluded that these provisions could simply be retroactively negated.
2) He was required to keep accurate records, but not required to designate loans or advances in any special way – a loan by any other name is still a debt. This may seem a technicality, but it's still relevant because...
3) Noe did document each advance/loan and did so in a way that made clear the amount taken and in addition specified in an unambiguous manner his responsibility to pay it back.

With reference to this last point, consider what happened with Noe's unsupported inventory transfers – he took money and in return gave the OBWC not a real coin but a note – a record in the accounting system — stating that it owned that coin. In other words, a form of promissory note.

There is no question that Noe was legally and visibly obligated to replace the promissory note with either the coin or the cash at some point in the future; he did nothing whatever to avoid or disguise that obligation.

Noe was the custodian of the funds, serving as manager of both the inventory and the books for investment vehicles that weren't intended to continue forever. When a fund expired or was closed, Noe was solely responsible for providing all of the coins and cash or other assets that the fund was shown to own. Only if he couldn't do that could he be charged with anything – civil or criminal.

"Well," our critic will say, "the funds were closed and Noe didn't have the cash –doesn't that answer the question? No, it doesn't. First, he wasn't in fact given the opportunity to repay. And second, the closure violated the contract and failed to give him time to put everything together in a reasonable manner – in this case to efficiently retrieve funds to repay the loans/advances. A hedge fund or a venture capital fund could be caught short if forced to suddenly close down in the middle of a long-term strategy. That's why such funds all have provisions preventing sudden, unplanned closure. Investors have to sign numerous documents agreeing that they can't take their funds out before a specified point. OBWC did that for each of the coin funds, with clear knowledge of what it meant.

Another interesting question, one alluded to in the earlier "Non-Political Noe " section, is whether Noe should have been allowed to cover the debt he'd taken on in coins with profits he'd made in other areas like investments and collectibles. The prosecution's view was that he definitely could not do that --recall Assistant Prosecutor Kiroff's statement that you can't rob a bank and then offer to pay it back. A more rational argument, one that would have been used in front of a judge rather than a jury, would have followed the line "yes, we made a profit, but we could have made a bigger one if the funds hadn't been diverted."

The "we could have made more" point is a reasonable one, but doesn't seem to be an approach that was applied consistently –or at all. As noted above, the OBWC seems to have paid no attention to what kind of investments its contractor, Allegiant, made before it was closed down. What if another bank fund's managers had taken money out of one area of investment for personal or corporate use, for example from bonds, and covered it with profits from another area, for example from stocks? In such a case it appears OBWC wouldn't have been the wiser because it wasn't its practice to look. And, based on its reporting on the Allegiant case, it seems clear the *Blade* wouldn't have asked any questions either.

It's also significant that the prosecution didn't like its "we could have made more" argument enough to present it to the jury.

But let's say the first of Noe's coin funds came to its agreed-upon ending point and the issue of diverted money did go to civil court. And let's also assume that OBWC eventually prevailed (these things take time and a lot of legal fees).

What would have happened to Non-Political Noe ? Well, he might have had to pay OBWC a lot of money. Or maybe only a little. There was more than $10 million of cash in the bank and accounts and notes receivable when the state took control, and the defense could have argued that these funds came, in whole or in part, from the "unsupported inventory purchases" thereby making them legitimate. The state would have responded with evidence of funds being moved to personal use, the defense would have responded that this was permitted and temporary. Etc. "What if" kinds of questions with an array of factors at play rarely result in big payments.

In any case, Noe would have certainly been allowed to repay from other personal sources. The whole "you can't rob a bank and pay it back" argument wouldn't have been even remotely relevant. And if Noe didn't have the money? Well, he would have had a debt to pay. Would he have gone to jail? No way. The *New York Times* recently told the story of a businessman who used money from investors in a newly formed public company to pay off a number of personal obligations, thereby shifting his debt to the investors. The amount transferred was huge – some $300 million. Although investors claimed he didn't have the right to do it and sued in civil court, the businessman, whose name is Donald Trump, faced no criminal charges for his actions.[220]

Although a rational analysis of Tom Noe's case suggests it should have followed the path of the Non-Political Noe one presented here, in the real world it didn't. That's because, in cases like this, where the verdict is crafted from a chain of prosecutorial and judicial discretion, the appeals system is set up more to sustain error than to reverse it.

Part IV- Appeals

Noe's first appeal was filed on July 15, 2009 and decided on December 31, 2009.[221] This was two and a half years after his conviction – an unusually long time in these matters. In fact, Noe's attorneys filed a notice of appeal immediately after the trial, and the delay was occasioned by the inability of the court reporter to get time to complete the transcript (something that occasioned an angry *Blade* editorial – in support of Noe).[222] Eventually, the Appeals Court ordered the lower court to give her the time and this final piece of documentation was completed.

THE OHIO APPEALS COURTS

Ohio's appeals courts are organized in districts. Lucas County is in the Sixth District, an eight county grouping in which Lucas is dominant as measured by population – and which very much falls in the ambit of the *Blade*. This district court had five judges including four Democrats, one of whom at the time of appeal was Judge Osowik, who had been elected originally during Noe's trial to a partial term and then again to a regular term. Another judge, a Republican, recused himself, leaving only Democrats to hear the appeal.

In Ohio, Court of Appeals judges are elected in even-numbered years to six-year terms on a nonpartisan ballot – though most will have been previously elected to a lower court in a partisan election. Cases are heard by a panel of three judges.

Appeals courts are limited in what they can do. Here's commentary from the Ohio State Bar Association on the role of the district appeals courts:

> These courts generally do not hold trials or hear evidence. They decide matters of law based on the record of the trial court, the written arguments called briefs (which are prepared by the attorneys), and the oral arguments before the court. After hearing arguments about the trial court's decision, the appeals court may either affirm or reverse the trial court, or remand the case to the trial court for further proceedings. Appeals courts issue formal decisions called opinions, which are based upon whether or not prejudicial errors were made at the trial court level.[223] *m*

In practice, appeals courts give considerable deference to the trial judge in issues where rulings are based on the judge's interpretation of the evidence rather than on his or her interpretation of the law. So, in Noe's case, the starting principle of a court of appeals would be to give deference on an issue like change of venue, because Osowik didn't determine which law to apply but how to apply it in this circumstance. The same would be true of the valuation issue where Osowik was determining relevance, not an issue of law.

The appeals process reverses roles: the defense becomes the Appellant, the person bringing the action, while the prosecution is the Appellee, the person (entity) defending the original decision.

Prosecutors also have the right to appeal if decisions go against them:

> Where more than one level of appellate review exists, whenever an intermediate court has held in favor of a defendant-appellant, the prosecution should be permitted to seek further review in the highest court.[224]

One important difference in the appeals courts is that the defense has an advantage in the number of briefs. Thus, the defense's brief comes first, the prosecution then replies, and the defense then has the opportunity to submit a "Reply Brief." Unless the court asks for verbal presentations, this is the final filing prior to deliberations by the three judge panel. This is the opposite of the process for closing arguments in the trial court, where the prosecution goes first, then the defense, then the prosecution gets a final shot.

Noe was still represented by William Wilkinson and John Mitchell of Thompson Hine in this appeal.

Introduction to the Issues

Overall, this section of *Coingate* uses four documents: 1) the Appellant Brief from Noe's lawyers at Thompson Hine; 2) the Appellee brief filed by Lucas County Prosecutors; 3) the Reply Brief from the Defense; and 4) the actual ruling issued by the Appeals Court's three judge panel.

The Appellant Brief (defense) creates the structure of the process by providing a list of what are known as "assignments of error." These are the particular issues from the trial court that the defense seeks to have remedied. For example, Osowik's ruling on change of venue is one assignment of error.

The defense offered a total of seven assignments of error, some of which have major subsections. However, as with the trial testimony, the official structure isn't the best way for the reader to understand the issues. Thus, the assignments will be considered in five groups: 1) Theft, RICO, Forgery, Money Laundering; 2) Jury Instructions; 3) Change of Venue and Disqualification of Judges; 4) Valuation and Expert Testimony; and 5) Sentencing and Restitution.

As an overall comment it should be noted that the appeals documents are generally clearer, with arguments that are easier to follow, than the transcripts or even the closing arguments. This is true despite the presence of numerous citations of case law. Of particular interest is the language used in the prosecution's brief: it's folksy, almost breezy. The prosecutors seemed very confident they would prevail in this friendly venue.

Theft, RICO, Forgery, Money Laundering

It's logical to begin with the key issue of theft, and linking it to the Assignment of Error on money laundering.

> Assignment of Error No. 1: The state failed to present any evidence on at least one element of each offense charged in the indictment in violation of Mr. Noe's rights under the Fifth, Sixth, Eighth and Fourteenth Amendments to the United States Constitution and Article I, Sections 9, 10, and 16 of the Ohio Constitution.

> Assignment of Error No. 6: Mr. Noe's convictions for theft and money laundering were allied offenses of similar import, and sentences for both offenses violated Mr. Noe's rights against double jeopardy guaranteed by the Fifth and Fourteenth Amendments of the United States Constitution and Article I, Sections 10 and 16 of the Ohio Constitution.

The defense began by taking on the theft charge with a familiar argument — there was no theft because the monies claimed to have been stolen were not taken "beyond the consent of the owner," and the owner was in every case a Coin Fund and in no case the OBWC (aka the State of Ohio):

> The Indictment charged theft offenses under R.C. § 2913.02(A)(2), which provides: (A) No person . . . shall . . . exert control over . . . property . . . in any of the following ways: *** (2) Beyond the scope of the express or implied consent of the owner . . .

> Who, then, was the owner of the money Tom Noe is alleged to have stolen by using it beyond the scope of that owner's consent? In drafting these charges against Mr. Noe, the State failed to recognize that the Coin Funds were legal entities separate and distinct from the OBWC. The State presented evidence that the Coin Funds were the owners of the money allegedly stolen by Mr. Noe, but offered no evidence that the Coin Funds did not consent to the transfers of their money to Vintage, relying instead on immaterial evidence that the OBWC did not consent to those transfers. Without evidence that the Coin Funds did not consent to the transfers to Vintage, the State's proof on the theft counts is fatally defective P. 8...But the State offered no evidence at all of the owner's non-consent, only evidence of the OBWC's non-consent.[225]

The prosecution replied that an owner is "any person, other than the actor, who is the owner of, who has possession or control of, or who has any license or interest in the property or services."[226] As a result, OBWC by virtue of its 80% of the profits has an "interest" and therefore is an owner. The prosecution went on to note that the Ohio Supreme Court, in its opinion on giving the *Blade* access to the OBWC records, described the OBWC as an "owner."[227]

The prosecution also attacked the issue of consent:

> If there had been such consent, Noe would not have created a set of books for CCF with which to deceive OBWC into believing it owned coins purchased from VCC and another set to show his VCC accountant for tax purposes. If he had been honest, he would have listed the transfers of money from the Coin Funds to VCC as unsecured, undocumented loans and then informed OBWC of exactly what he had done.[228]

The prosecution again noted overarching contract language that put everything within the "limitations imposed by the Ohio Act and this Agreement..." and also required the managers to act in the interest of the business.[229] The prosecution's idea in emphasizing these points was clearly to negate the sections of the contract that allow loans without limit and that give the option to repay if managers take profits in a manner that violates other provisions of the contract.

The defense's Reply Brief described the cases cited by the prosecution as irrelevant, and noted that the internal OBWC review, as well as their auditor Keith Elliott's testimony, made clear that Noe had the right to do the things the prosecution considers as theft.[230]

The defense also attacked the record-keeping issue more directly and effectively than in the past:

> Mr. Noe's alleged transgressions of keeping false records and misleading the OBWC may warrant a civil action for breach of contract or his removal as Manager, but there can be no theft when there is no evidence of non-consent by the owner.[231]

With respect to RICO, the defense repeated its theme that there was no "enterprise" within the meaning of the law, and as a result the RICO statute did not apply.

The prosecution's brief simply cited the law, noting that "The term 'enterprise' is broadly defined under § 2923.31(C) and incudes one or more individuals or other entities that operate, in some fashion, as a group,"[232] and goes on to say that a pattern "is present when the defendant commits a second act of corrupt activity within six years of the first corrupt act."[233]. Noe didn't act alone, the prosecution said, observing that "It would have been extremely unlikely that Noe, as an individual, would have gained access to any portion of the OBWC's portfolio, much less been able to have looted millions from it."[234] The prosecution goes on, in more florid language than usual, to describe VCC as a criminal "front" used by Noe to steal from the OBWC.

It seems significant that the defense's Reply Brief did not mention RICO.

On forgery, the appeal gave the defense an opportunity to expand on the arguments it made at trial that: 1) there was no intent to defraud; and 2) if there was anything wrong, it wasn't in the signatures of others that Noe placed on the checks, but rather in the coding that suggested they were for coin purchases. While the state had connected Noe to the signatures, it had presented no evidence, the defense argued, that it was Noe who entered the code on the check.

> However, no tax underpayments by Mr. Noe resulted from the allegedly unauthorized signing of payees' names on the back of the subject checks. The checks were written from a pad of business checks that had two parts, the check and the stub. The State alleged that Mr. Noe received tax benefit from the handwriting on the check stub that recorded the checks as coin purchases (account code 500), rather than as distributions of income to Mr. Noe. However, the State presented no expert or other testimony as to the identity of the maker of the "500" notations. Further, the alleged improper tax benefit would have been exactly the same for each of the checks if they had been made payable to Tom Noe and indorsed [sic] by Tom Noe in his own name-- because it is the "500" coding that confers the alleged tax benefit, not the name of the payee. That was the concluding testimony of the State's tax expert (Mr. Decker) on cross- examination.[235]

The defense argument here is interesting, but the prosecutors' succinct and direct response was very strong. First, the prosecution brief emphasizes that Noe did receive a tax advantage as a result of the forgery. Next, it derided the defense's use of the state's Uniform Commercial Code as a legal foundation by calling it "his arcane argument, silly as it is…"[236.]

The defense Reply Brief showed the relevance of the cases cited by the prosecution to be thin, and noted that the state hadn't effectively responded to the fact that there was no proof Noe was the one who had entered the "500" codes.[237]

The defense challenged the money laundering charges in two places. First, with respect to theft, with the idea being that if there's no theft there's no money laundering.

The second argument was made in Assignment of Error #6, where the Thompson Hine lawyers asserted that theft and money laundering "were allied offenses of similar import, and sentences for both offenses violated Mr. Noe's rights against double jeopardy…"

The prosecution first replied that the theft was in fact proven and therefore the money laundering was relevant. As for the concern about theft and money laundering being allied offenses of similar import, the prosecution cited case law to the effect that while theft requires the intent to permanently deprive the owner of property, money laundering "requires no such intent. Instead, money laundering requires either an intent to conceal the nature, location, source, or ownership of the proceeds of some unlawful activity or a purpose to promote, manage, establish, or carry on corrupt activity."[238]m

The defense's Reply Brief did not address this point.

The defense tried in the appeal to make essentially all of the arguments on theft, etc. presented at the end of the trial in its motion to dismiss. It got nowhere with Judge Osowik and, while the points were on the whole made much more effectively in the appeal brief, the results were the same.

The Appeals Court, citing Ohio case law referring to vehicle theft, agreed that the OBWC did have an ownership interest in the funds and also accepted that the overarching language in the contract that cited Noe's responsibility not to use "the funds or assets of the Company in any manner except for the benefit of the Company in furtherance of its business purposes…" effectively trumped other language in the contract allowing him to take loans and to repay profits if taken "in violation." The Appeals Court also cited the omnipotent "Ohio Act" as preventing the contract language cited by the defense.

On money laundering, the Appeals Court agreed that their decision to sustain the theft charges validated the money laundering conviction and also described the case law that supported the difference between the two charges stating that, the way the law is written, use of the two together doesn't amount to double jeopardy.[239]m

The decision on RICO was similar. The Appeals Court cited case law that allows the interpretation of RICO used by the prosecution. It should be noted, though, that clarity on Ohio's RICO law isn't easy to come by. Someone in the legislature was channeling Marcel Proust when the statute was drafted: it's a single 307 word sentence that cites some 20 other criminal statutes. The Ohio Supreme Court nearly threw it out on the grounds of incomprehensibility.[240]

The forgery charges merited a more complex response from the Appeals Court, but the judges believed that ultimately the law was clear cut, "Thus the question here is whether the state proved that appellant uttered [sic] the check in the names of acquaintances or clients and endorsed them with the knowledge and intent to defraud anyone, if so, then the forgery convictions were supported by sufficient evidence."[241] "Anyone' in this context referred to the tax authorities.

Jury Instructions

The Assignment on jury instructions should be grouped with that on theft, *et al.*, because it relates to the definition of theft.

> Assignment of Error No 5: The trial court abused its discretion in refusing to instruct the jury on essential components of Mr. Noe's defense, denying Mr. Noe a fair trial as guaranteed by the Sixth and Fourteenth Amendments to the United States Constitution and Article I, Sections 10 and 16 of the Ohio Constitution.

The defense asserted that Judge Osowik's narrow instructions to the jury deprived Noe of a fair trial:

> Mr. Noe's defense was prejudiced by the trial court's failure to instruct on the [sic] even the most basic requirements of Ohio's corporation law. For example, the trial court refused to instruct the jury as to the meaning of the words "owner" and "consent." As such, Mr. Noe could not establish critical portions of his defense: (1) that CCF I and II, as LLCs, were the owners of the funds allegedly taken by Mr. Noe, not the OBWC; and (2) that an owner can consent contractually. Without the instructions proposed by Mr. Noe, the jury could not possibly understand how ownership interest in an [sic] limited liability is limited to units or the basics of a contract. Thus, Mr. Noe could not present fatal flaws in the State's case – the absence of any evidence of the lack of consent by the coin funds. There is no question that Mr. Noe's proposed jury instructions were legally correct, pertinent to Mr. Noe's defense and timely presented. Therefore, the trial court abused its discretion and denied Mr. Noe a fair trial.[242]

In response, the prosecution argued that the trial court had the discretion on how to instruct the jury and the Appeals Court should not reverse that. It also argued that the defense's proposed instructions pertained more to civil than to criminal law, and that the key issues were in fact presented to the jury.

In the Reply Brief, the defense pointed out that "Mr. Noe's case was an extraordinary criminal prosecution and it would have been appropriate for the trial court to supplement the rote instructions given in other cases."[243]

The Appeals Court essentially ignored the defense's case by asserting that instructing the jury on consent would have been irrelevant because "there was no evidence to suggest that the operating agreements [contracts] or any other agreement between the parties permitted personal use of the funds by the appellant."[244]

Change of Venue and Disqualification of Judges

> Assignment of Error No. 2: The trial court violated Mr. Noe's right to a fair trial as guaranteed by the Sixth Amendment to the United States Constitution and Article I, Section 10 of the Ohio Constitution by holding this trial in Lucas County, Ohio, an area overwhelmingly saturated with negative publicity about Mr. Noe and his alleged guilt.

> Assignment of Error No. 3: The denial of Mr. Noe's affidavit of disqualification violated Mr. Noe's right to a fair trial as guaranteed by the Sixth and Fourteenth Amendments of the United States Constitution and Article I, Sections 10 and 16 of the Ohio Constitution.

The defense's arguments on the issue of change of venue were inspired, altogether much stronger than those presented in the earlier motion to Judge Osowik.

The defense began by returning to the example of the Sheppard murder trial and again cited the many categorically negative comments made about Noe by senior politicians from both sides of the aisle. If both Democrats and Republicans were against him, the public would have to think he must be bad.

The defense continued by pointing out that "The negative publicity directed toward Mr. Noe continued after his trial began."[245] In addition to newspaper articles, the brief points to the many political commercials which featured attacks on Noe. This point is significant because the jury wasn't sequestered.

Closing the initial brief, the defense made a telling point: "If the unceasingly negative publicity directed towards Mr. Noe before and during his trial were insufficient to require a change of venue or jury sequestration, one must wonder what circumstances would.[246]

The defense was succinct on the disqualification of judges, noting simply that "The denial of the affidavit [for disqualification] ensured that a jurist against whom Mr. Noe conducted and directed active political campaigns for judicial office presided over his case."[247]

On the venue issue, the prosecution's words were familiar, again citing the trial judge's obligation to attempt to seat an unbiased jury and, if successful, to proceed to trial. Oddly, the prosecution noted an important weakness in the process, "Even if a potential juror had expressed an opinion as to the defendant's guilt, the juror could still have been seated if the juror was able to set aside that opinion and render a verdict based solely on the evidence presented at trial."[248] This apparent problem was OK, the prosecution argued, "Because all of the jurors selected for jury service stated that they could be fair, impartial, and render a verdict based solely on the evidence presented, the trial court properly seated a jury in this case and correctly overruled Noe's motion to change venue."[249] As we'll see in Part VI, the research in psychology shows this assessment to be incorrect.

Finally, the prosecution stated the fact that the jury showed that it was paying attention and entirely fair because it found Noe not guilty of some counts, and because it deliberated for "approximately twenty hours."

This point, though made in passing, deserves some attention.

In fact, when the then deliberating jury asked questions on November 9, the judge said that "it's obvious the jurors are reading everything rather meticulously because they're noting dates, exhibits being identified [sic]."[250]

That sounds reasonable on the surface, and taken together with the fact that the jury took several days and found Noe not guilty of a number of counts provides the substance of the argument that the jury was discerning (in the words of the *Blade*).

On closer examination, though, the argument withers.

The first problem with this "sophisticated jury" defense is that it's confusing a physical progression through the counts with an actual analytical process. In fact, if the jury did nothing more than exercise its most minimal responsibilities, it would have taken several days to move through the counts and give each no more than a perfunctory examination. If a discerning jury is one that does more than just shuffle papers, that's not a high bar at all.

The real question is analysis. Did the jury reach different verdicts based on a careful interpretation of the evidence? Or, put another way, is there any reason to believe that the information that led to not guilty verdicts was qualitatively different from that which led to guilty verdicts?

A good place to start with this is money laundering counts 3 and 5 (not guilty) and 7 (guilty). These counts concern checks Noe wrote in the days after receiving the first deposit of coin fund money, a transaction that, because it was based on an "unsupported inventory purchase," would make subsequent expenditures from the same account qualify as money laundering.

Now, one could think that the jury found Noe not guilty on counts 3 and 5 because it agreed with the defense's devastating attack on Crowe Chizek's "use of cash" analysis. If so, that would certainly show a jury that was not merely meticulous but also insightful and independent.

Unfortunately, the argument doesn't hold up: the count for which the jury did find Noe guilty was in the same time period and would have fallen without question under the same "use of cash" theory.

The only difference between the guilty and not guilty verdicts appears to be that the jury didn't think checks to individual people in payment of debts constituted money laundering while paying off a debt to a bank did. This distinction exists nowhere in the statute, in the prosecution's and defense's arguments, or in the judge's instructions. Instead, the distinction between not guilty counts 3 and 5 on the one hand and guilty count 7 is something the jury pulled out of thin air. It appears to indicate nothing more than a sop offered to those who were reluctant to convict.

A similar analysis of the tampering counts shows the same lack of logical consistency.

In sum, the most likely explanation for the not guilty verdicts can be found neither in meticulousness or discernment but in the strong internal disagreements that jury foreman Petiniot described in his deposition — the hurried majority trading off some not guilty verdicts in order to keep the dissidents on board with what the public expected them to do. The fact that compromise would also get them out of the jury room sooner was doubtless important as well.

Moving on, the prosecution minced no words on the disqualification of judges: "This argument fails on every level imaginable."[251] The prosecutors did repeat the well-worn argument that there "was no evidence" of Osowik's bias, but relied on the more relevant point that the decision to reject Noe's effort to disqualify Osowik had been made by the state's Supreme Court and that an appeals court had no jurisdiction to overturn that.

The defense's Reply Brief is where its arguments really shined, beginning with the previously un-emphasized point that in law there are circumstances where prejudice must be "presumed." One such case is where pretrial publicity is sufficiently prejudicial and inflammatory and…saturated the community where the trials were held."[252]

The prosecution's idea that the voir dire showed a lack of bias was attacked mercilessly. The defense pointed out that half of the first 12 jurors were excused because the publicity had led them to pre-judge Noe as guilty.[253] Overall, 45 jurors were excused for this reason. This led the court to call another 75 jurors because the original group of 100 was insufficient. "Mr. Noe had more jurors excused for cause because of their pre-trial opinion of his guilt, 45, than jurors that survived the venire procedure."[254]

In conclusion, the Reply Brief quoted the United States Supreme Court as saying that the reasoning behind the doctrine of "presumed prejudice" is important because "our system of law has always endeavored to prevent even the probability of unfairness."[255]

In its decision on venue, the Appeals Court went through the various prior cases and concluded, as expected, that a change of venue was allowable only in cases where a community was so saturated with negative publicity that an impartial jury could not be empaneled. In addition, the Appeals Court judges went on to praise the voir dire conducted by their colleague, Judge Osowik: "During the course of voir dire, multiple persons were completely unaware of the case while several indicated that they were suspicious of the veracity and evenhandedness of the reporting of the story, particularly through the print media. After reading carefully through the entire voir dire proceedings, we can find no evidence of any pervasive prejudice or bias from those called for jury service."[256]

The Court of Appeals concluded its section on change of venue with the dry observation that, "Upon review of the proceedings herein and the relevant case law, and after reviewing the volumes of articles, editorials, and cartoons, it may be argued that the news media was not entirely unbiased with regard to the prosecution of appellant."[257]

But that was just an observation in passing, because the appeals court went on to say, "However, we cannot conclude that the pretrial publicity was sufficient to create a presumption of prejudice. Accordingly, we cannot say that the trial court abused its discretion when it denied appellant's motion for a change of venue. Appellant's second assignment of error is not well-taken."[258]

On the issue of disqualification of judges, the Court of Appeals simply agreed with the prosecution that it lacked jurisdiction.

Valuation and Expert Testimony

The issue of valuation was argued in two places in Assignment of Error #4. In the main one, the defense addressed the judge's ruling directly, while in the second the role of valuation was again challenged, but in this case on the decision to allow the Sotheby's expert, David Tripp to testify as a fact witness rather than as an expert – and subsequent to that to allow the OBWC investigator Tom Wersell to testify as to what Tripp told him.

> Assignment of Error No. 4: The trial court abused its discretion with regard to various evidentiary decisions that denied Mr. Noe a fair trial as guaranteed by the Sixth and Fourteenth Amendments to the United States Constitution and Article I, Sections 10 and 16 of the Ohio Constitution.

In the trial court stage, the prosecution had filed a motion to pre-empt the defense from discussing the overall value of the Coin Funds. A particular thrust of the prosecution's effort was that Noe could not claim credit for the value after he was no longer manager (after late May of 2005).

The first part of the defense appeal focused on Osowik's decision to allow Tripp and Wersell to testify on value. The defense began by pointing out that the prosecution "sandbagged" them on Tripp by originally describing him as a fact witness, which meant that he couldn't be compelled to meet with the defense before his testimony (in fact, he was asked to meet, but refused). Then, only at the last minute and during a sidebar, did the prosecution mention that Tripp would offer some testimony about the value of coins, not simply their presence. This left the defense unprepared.

More important, though, was Wersell's testimony since he spoke to the value of the coins found at all the locations, not just at Noe's Maumee store. The defense pointed out that this allowed the prosecution to have it both ways – they could use Wersell to present evidence about the overall value of the coins found in May of 2005 – which they needed to do in order to specify the amount alleged to be stolen. On the other hand, this maneuver prevented the defense from providing its own evidence of valuation – which would have included more than coins.

The defense also pointed out that Wersell's testimony was hearsay from Tripp, since Wersell himself had no knowledge of the coins' values.

The prosecution, taking advantage of the fact that the defense's initial brief wasn't clear on the "post-Noe" issue, focused on that aspect, hammering away at the irrelevance of Noe's role in creating value after he was no longer in charge:

> Noe has mischaracterized the States' motion *in limine*. The State did not seek exclusion of, and the trial court did not bar, Noe's proffered evidence as to the value of the Coin Funds at any time under his management. Rather, the State's motion asked the trial court to exclude only that evidence regarding the value of the assets of the Coin Funds that he managed – CCF, CCF II, and RCE –after he was removed as the Coin Funds' manager on May 24, 2005, and after Development Specialists Inc., (DSI) took over management of the Coin Funds.[259]

The prosecution's response on Tripp and Wersell relied on two points: 1) the value that Tripp testified to was only the purchase price and therefore not expert testimony; and 2) Noe should have requested a continuance of the trial to prepare for Tripp once they reached the view that his testimony had gone beyond fact.

The defense's Reply Brief demolished the obvious falsehood of the first of these arguments, noting that Tripp did testify on his opinion as to value (Weglian— "I'm going to ask… [about the number provided in the inventory] and ask him whether or not that's somewhere in the ballpark"). On the second issue, the defense drew attention to the obvious: it would not have been possible for them to get a continuance to secure expert testimony at that point in the trial.

Overall, the defense started well on the larger issue of allowing valuation testimony in the appeal — "One must wonder, if the value of the items recovered by the state was not relevant, why the state chose to introduce a portion of this information."[260] And it also offered this damning thought in the Reply Brief:

> The State was offering the value of some Coin Fund assets to demonstrate the Coin Fund losses because of Mr. Noe's actions, but the trial court persistently refused to allow Mr. Noe to present evidence of the value of all the Coin Fund assets to show that nothing was missing. If the State was permitted to present this information, fundamental fairness would dictate that Mr. Noe should be allowed to use similar value information to dispute the State's theft figures. Allowing the jury to hear only half of the story regarding Coin Funds' assets' value was a decision that was arbitrary and unreasonable, and, as such, was an abuse of discretion.[261]

Despite these strengths, the defense continued to be remarkably vague about the "Noe in charge" vs. "post-Noe" issue. The language of the appeals brief does appear to refer to value while Noe was still in charge, but isn't explicit about that. Instead, the focus is on Noe's ability to repay.

The Appeals Court's decision began ominously: "We first note that a trial court's ruling to admit or exclude evidence will not be reversed on appeal absent an abuse of discretion."[262] An abuse of discretion, the court notes, "connotes more than an error of law or judgment, it implies that the court's attitude is unreasonable, arbitrary, or unconscionable."[263] This is an amazingly low standard for evaluating a judge's performance, and effectively telegraphs the conclusion of not just of this but of several Court of Appeals rulings.

On the question of Tripp and Wersell's testimony, the appeals court ignored the defense's sophisticated arguments about the manner in which the state was trying to have things both ways on valuation and described the decision to allow them to testify as fact witnesses rather than as experts as "harmless."

Taking advantage of the defense's vagueness about the "post-Noe" issue, the Court of Appeals moved quickly to put the valuation appeal in hostile territory: "In particular, Appellant wished to demonstrate that the Coin Funds actually returned a $10 to $13 million-dollar profit. The State counters that appellant was permitted to present evidence of the value of the fund during the period in which he was a manager; their motion only excluded the period after May 24, 2005, when appellant was removed as a manger."[264]

The Court of Appeal's categorization of the valuation issue wasn't a fair one, and this approach allowed it to rule that the information wasn't relevant, again based on the argument that the information was "post-Noe."

Sentencing

Assignment of Error No. 7: The trial court's cumulative trial and sentencing errors violated Mr. Noe's rights under the Fifth, Sixth, Eighth and Fourteenth Amendments to the United States Constitution, Article I, Sections 9, 10 and 16 of the Ohio Constitution and Ohio sentencing framework.

The defense argued two technical points in the sentence: first, that Judge Osowik failed to follow proper procedures in determining the sentence; and second, that the judge didn't follow the law in specifying Noe's "post-release obligations."

On the first issue, the defense argued that the law required the judge to give Noe the minimum sentence in addition to the ten-year minimum for RICO (the range was from a minimum of three to a maximum of ten additional years). On the second, the defense pointed out that Osowik failed to follow the rules on describing post-release requirements; a very technical issue.

Although the length of sentence was obviously important, the basis on which it was argued and decided was primarily technical – e.g., did Osowik have the right to do what he did.

Nevertheless, the defense did characterize the sentence as "harsh" and the prosecution chose to respond, drawing attention to the Sentencing Memorandum it had given Judge Osowik prior to his determination of the sentence back in 2006. In that document, the prosecution argued that Noe should get at least eight years in addition to the RICO ten. The reason given was comparison to a Franklin County case, State v. Silverman, in which the defendant was convicted of RICO and other crimes and given an 18-year sentence.

The State submits that this case [Noe's] is similar enough to the Silverman case to be of assistance in the Court's sentencing decision. Silverman occupied a position of trust as an attorney and used that position to steal from his clients. Noe also occupied a position of trust as a manager of the coin funds in that he managed assets provided by the Ohio Bureau of Workers' Compensation (BWC) on behalf of injured workers throughout Ohio. Noe used that position to steal, at a minimum, an amount of money of $100,000 or more and, like Silverman, then engaged in a pattern of corrupt activity that facilitated his crimes and prevented the State or the OBWC, for a time, from discovering his criminal activity.[265]

The comparison between Noe and Silverman is disingenuous in the extreme.

One important difference is that Silverman's case wasn't about accounting and loss in the abstract: he actually stole the money.[266] Also, there were actual victims whose lives were affected by financial loss. Most of the people from whom Silverman stole had been in automobile accidents and had suffered injuries that made it impossible or difficult for them to work. Not receiving their settlements had a significant negative impact on their lives, for example by losing a house.

And, as it happened, Silverman had served only about four years when then Governor Strickland first granted clemency:

> Strickland also revisited a case he decided a year ago when he granted conditional clemency to attorney Perry R. Silverman of Columbus.
>
> At the time, Silverman was ordered to repay clients $1 million and pay $155,000 in fines. In 2005, he was sentenced to 18 years in prison for multiple counts of theft, forgery, falsification, tampering with evidence and engaging in corrupt activity, all related to defrauding clients, including some disabled adults.
>
> In his new decision, Strickland gives Silverman the chance to get out of prison so he can earn or borrow money to repay the clients and fines. The Ohio Parole Board will keep "an accurate determination of the status of restitution ordered by the courts and the restitution paid to victims regarding Mr. Silverman's crimes.
>
> Silverman can be rearrested and thrown into prison if he fails to make the required payments.[267]

In its Reply Brief, the defense extended its efforts to show the extreme disparities. These examples will be discussed in Part IX, which addresses the larger issue of contrasting sentences.

The appeals court fully agreed with the prosecution on the main issue of length of sentence, supporting the defense on only one aspect of "post release control obligations" —a minor issue having to do with how a convict is overseen after leaving prison.

ANALYSIS OF THE COURT OF APPEALS DECISIONS

The "assignments of error" can be divided into three categories according to how the Court of Appeals dealt with them: 1) denied on the basis of clear-cut law; 2) denied on the basis of vague law; and 3) denied on the basis of obvious error by the Court.

The "vague law" reference requires some explanation.

Most people think of the law as being fairly precise, with judges relying first on the language of the law and then on previous decisions – "case law." In fact, as was definitely the situation here, the legal language required interpretation and the case law left open a lot of options that lacked an obvious conclusion. Put another way, it seems clear that a number of the Sixth District Court of Appeals decisions on Coingate could have been decided differently by a different court. It's this author's opinion that they *would* have been decided differently by a court not influenced by the political and media environment of Toledo. One would normally think that such errors would be reversed on appeal. The fact that this didn't happen can be ascribed to a "chain of discretion," in which the upper courts offer near absolute deference to the discretion of lower courts.

Denied on Clear-Cut Law- RICO, Sentencing, Money, Laundering, Forgery

The average person, certainly even a well-informed one, would agree with the defense's arguments that this was not a RICO case. Nevertheless, the law clearly and unambiguously gave the prosecutor the right to use this statute.

The defense put together a nice argument on sentencing, much better than that of the prosecution. Notably, in defending the comparability of sentences, the prosecution, to quote its own brief, offers an argument that "fails on every level imaginable." Still, the prosecution had the technicalities of the law on its side and this was an easy technical, if not moral, win.

The verdict on money laundering is the same as for RICO. To a thoughtful citizen, the money laundering charges sound like double jeopardy. But the law allows it.

Some might see forgery in the "vague law" category, but it seems clear cut on close examination. It's true that Noe didn't harm anyone, and it's true that it was the coding of the checks rather than the actual forged signature that made the difference. Still, it's evident that the process was designed to deceive and could have had a benefit to Noe of avoiding tax, and that seems enough to fit the statute. The prosecution treated the defense dishonestly with the CPA's evidence, but honest behavior wouldn't have changed the outcome.

Denied on the basis of Vague Law- Jury Instructions, Theft

This is the only area in the appeal where a legal background would seem to be useful. To a non-lawyer, there doesn't seem to be any reason why Osowik couldn't have instructed the jury on corporation law – which isn't to say that he would have said exactly what the defense wanted him to. And, therefore, it seems that by ignoring the topic, Osowik strongly tilted the case to the prosecution's side. Still, greater knowledge of legal precedent might lead to a different conclusion.

Theft is a tough one, but here's a summary.

The state argued that the language of the contracts allowing Noe to take money "in violation" and have two years to pay it back was irrelevant for four reasons: 1) there was no language in the contract allowing Noe to take money for personal use, 2) it contravened the larger purpose of the business as stated elsewhere in the contract; 3) the OBWC really was an "owner;" and 4) Ohio law as a whole doesn't permit a contract that allows the kind of language employed in the "in violation" clause or, more generally, for a state entity to give up an ownership interest in its funds.

In response, the defense essentially said that, while you might not like the contract, it said what it said. The idea that an investor isn't an owner is inherent in all kinds of contracts, from mutual funds to venture funds and was something that the OBWC had specifically accepted. And, while the permissive language might be odd, the first contract passed numerous legal reviews and the second one contained the same language. Given all that, Noe had reason to believe he could use it.

The appeals court's decision, including the case law it cited, would seem to invalidate structures like mutual and hedge funds where investors sign a contract that explicitly precludes any ownership or management rights.

The decision by the Court of Appeals against Noe here seems highly discretionary rather than based on any obvious, unambiguous interpretation of the law. To illustrate what this means, consider a hypothetical situation in which the appeals court ruled the opposite way and dismissed the theft charges against Noe (taking most of the other charges, including RICO, down as well). And to continue the hypothesis, assume the prosecution could have appealed the decision to the state's Supreme Court. Would the prosecution have been able to secure a reversal? It seems very unlikely. It's most probable that the Supreme Court wouldn't have found any problem with the legal analysis and would therefore have simply deferred to the judgment of the appeals judges: same facts, same law, different judges, different rulings.

Denied on the basis of Obvious Error by the Court of Appeals- Change of Venue, Disqualification of Judges, and Valuation

Taking change of venue and disqualification together, the argument against the appeals court is simple: the law provides for the disqualification of judges and for changes of venue. The purpose is to avoid bias so strong that a reasonable person would conclude that it could affect the outcome of the trial. If Noe's case doesn't meet the standard of avoiding excessive bias, then nothing will. The Court of Appeals decision either: 1) effectively makes these two provisions of Ohio law irrelevant or, 2) shows that the justice system in Lucas County and Northwest Ohio was in fact biased.

As for valuation, there seems nothing in the law that would have prevented Osowik from considering the larger enterprise and its earnings while under Noe's control as relevant to the charges.

Again, the state is trying to have it both ways. When it comes to the RICO charge, it finds an enterprise. But when it comes to theft, the enterprise as a whole is ignored and deemed irrelevant; instead, it's OK to look at just one aspect of the business – coins – and to look in only one physical location – Noe's store in Ohio (a clear contradiction to the argument made in the search warrant hearing). The overall number of people in the enterprise helps define the criminal charge, but the overall amount of money in the enterprise has to be kept secret from the jurors.

The issue of "post-Noe" vs. pre-Noe appears to loom large here, but it seems doubtful that Judge Osowik would have allowed the latter to be presented because he effectively precluded discussion of "valuation with Noe in control" in his ruling. The Court of Appeals decision to uphold Osowik's characterization of valuation evidence as entirely "post-Noe" represents simple acquiescence to a clever rationalization.

As with the other issues in this section, this appears to be strictly the judges' call rather than a question of law. If Judge Osowik had allowed valuation testimony, no court would have overruled him.

Summary- the Ohio Sixth District Court of Appeals

On RICO, the defense had common sense but the prosecution had the law. The same was true for money laundering and forgery. But in the case of the other issues – disqualification of judges, change of venue, theft, valuation, sentencing – the Appeals Court affirmed decisions that were discretionary on the part of the trial judge and that ought reasonably to have gone the other way. It's difficult not to forget that the judges of the Sixth District Court of Appeals were all elected in the *Blade's* circulation area and that all were vulnerable to the paper's decision whether to endorse them rather than an opponent. If change of venue and disqualification of judges were valid issues for the original trial, they were valid here as well.

THE OHIO SUPREME COURT

The Ohio Supreme Court, like the US equivalent, doesn't automatically hear appeals. Instead, the judges vote on whether to consider cases presented to them.

When Noe's case arrived in 2009, the Ohio court, whose seven members are elected on a statewide ballot, had long been politicized, especially on the hot button issue of "tort reform," which pitted Republicans vs. Democrats on the issue of business liability.[268]

The Court had been involved in the case of Noe and the OBWC's coin funds twice before, once when the Chief Justice ruled against Noe's motion to disqualify Toledo judges, including Osowik. The other time was in a case filed by the *Blade* and other newspapers seeking access to OBWC records about the coin funds. In the latter case, five of seven judges had recused themselves because they had received contributions from Noe or because they were connected to him politically.

Two of the seven recused themselves for the state appeal, which included most of the same arguments presented to the district court. The Ohio court doesn't provide detailed reasons when it decides not to hear a case, so this report from the *Columbus Dispatch* is as definitive as it gets:

> There were 11 propositions of law in Noe's appeal, and the court ruled 5-0 to reject nine of them. [Justice] O'Donnell said he would have heard the appeal on the question of pretrial publicity, while [Justice] Brown would have taken the appeal on the issue of whether the lower court exceeded the maximum sentence for Noe.[269][270]*m*

There will be more on the Supreme Court in Part X.

THE FEDERAL APPEAL

Appeals obviously get more challenging as one works up the ladder, and the jump to the federal level is especially difficult. Federal courts hear appeals from state courts in *habeas corpus* proceedings and consider cases only according to whether the state decisions were so egregious as to violate the US Constitution.

The federal court actually employs a two-tier system. In the first level, a decision is made by a "magistrate judge," someone who has the credentials of a judge and who is employed by the court, but who isn't a full-fledged judge and only has jurisdiction to decide matters referred to him or her by the Court.

In Noe's case, the magistrate initially ruled against allowing him to introduce new evidence in 2012[271] and then not to hear his case in 2013.[272] The federal appeals were handled by Toledo attorney, Rick Kerger.

In October of 2014, the regular judge, John R. Adams, affirmed the magistrate's ruling.[273]

One can argue that Judge Adams' ruling was the first that wasn't biased by the Ohio political context, and as such it's worthy of some careful examination.

The various assignments of error involved in the state appeals were reduced to three for the federal court:

- Ground One: Improper denial of motion to change venue.
- Ground Two: Improper allowance of expert testimony on behalf of the State.
- Ground Three: Improper denial of Defendant's expert testimony.[274]

The first interesting points in Judge Adams' consideration of the case can be seen in the transcript[275] of a hearing he held on April 1, 2014 (the hearing was done by telephone due to bad weather).

Kerger[276]*m* made many cogent arguments on venue in just a few moments of oral presentation, observing sarcastically that the only public official not critical of Noe was the Pope.[277] Earlier, in his brief to the federal court, Kerger said:

> ...the *Blade* was well within its rights to report on him [Noe] in its news and write editorials about him. But what this unrelenting barrage of publicity did was create an aura around Tom Noe that even honorable persons trying to be honest in the jury selection process simply could not forget. How anyone in Northwest Ohio would have had a neutral image of Tom Noe at the time his trial started is beyond belief.[278]

Kerger continued with sharp points about the Sotheby's expert, David Tripp, pointing out that the prosecution had offered seven pages about his qualifications but then said he wasn't an expert, just someone who was present when coins were found in the Maumee location. And, Kerger noted, Mr. Weglian had actually described him in closing arguments as "a man who's an expert in coins."[279]

Building from there Kerger finally tied the role of Tripp to the larger issue of valuation: "Well, here the error in letting Tripp testify was magnified when the court then refused to allow counter-evidence saying that, 'Look, [the] state didn't lose any money on this coin thing, they made $13 million.'"[280]

Kerger agreed that the prosecution would have responded that the profits came after Noe was no longer manager, but emphasized that they [the defense] would then have been able to explain why they had reason to believe that the value would be higher.[281]

The lawyer representing the Attorney General's office responded on venue that to show "presumed prejudice, he [Noe] has to show that the conviction was obtained in a trial atmosphere utterly corrupted by press coverage, and as the Sixth Circuit has noted, it has to be kind of a carnival atmosphere and there's no evidence of that here."[282]

Judge Adams was more than a little skeptical of downplaying the bias:

Well, we have 1,500 pages of news coverage according to the briefing. I went back and looked at the record. The record is replete. This was a constant drumbeat of negative publicity against Mr. Noe. It started April of 2005, up to and including the trial, which sort of incidentally or coincidentally occurs right before the 2006 election cycle, which I don't know that I can take judicial notice of.[283]

Judge Adams pressed the Attorney General's lawyer on whether she thought Tripp was a fact or an expert witness, and when she said "absolutely" a fact witness, he asked, "Did you read the record in this case?"[284] and then went on to say, "A fair reading of the record is there's no dispute this person was called as an expert in my view."[285]

As to allowing evidence on valuation, the AG's lawyer stuck to the prosecution's line:

Mr. Noe — the motion in limine was only to the fact that he could not bring in anyone in to value the coin fund assets after May 24 of 2005. If he wanted to establish that the coins had a certain value before May 24 of 2005 or even on May 14 of 2005, he was permitted to do so under the order. What he wanted to establish was the liquidation process done by DSI and how the coin fund made money based on a liquidation process that no one knows the terms of that or what was liquidated. That would require an entirely different process to be brought into court and with what relevance?[286]

As with all of the judges in the appeals process, Judge Adams was limited in what he could do — deference to the trial judge still obtains at the federal level.

Judge Adams walked a fine line here. He criticized Noe's argument about jury bias: "In other words, Noe contends that the jurors' statements during voir dire that they were not swayed by media coverage should be given less weight because these jurors were in fact *subconsciously* prejudiced by the coverage."[287]

On the other hand, Adams affirms that, had he presided over the trial, he "would have granted Noe's change of venue request."[288] However, he did not propose to reverse the decision because his belief that prejudice should be presumed sits on a permissible spectrum and does not "render the decision of the trial judge unreasonable."[289]

Although Adams certainly believed that Tripp was an expert witness, "he has fallen well short of demonstrating that it was so prejudicial that it deprived him of due process and a fair trial."[290] Adams went on to state that Noe "admitted that the valuation evidence was tangential at best to the charges

191

against [sic]."[291] In fact, Noe hadn't admitted that. Rather, during and prior to the trial, the prosecution had so effectively removed from consideration any discussion of the overall value of the coin funds that Noe's defense was only able to allude to it in the appeals.

NEWSPAPER COVERAGE OF THE APPEALS

The *Blade* paid little attention to the Appeals Court ruling, which appeared on New Year's Eve,[292] but used almost every stage after that to solicit chest-thumping quotes from the prosecution:

After the Federal Magistrate's Ruling:

> Kevin Pituch, an assistant Lucas County prosecutor, was thrilled to hear the magistrate had denied Noe's petition for a new trial, though he said it did not surprise him.
>
> I was expecting this," he said. "Twelve jurors heard this case and found that there was overwhelming evidence of guilt that Tom Noe was not only a thief, but a swindler.[293]

After Judge Adams' Ruling:

> I'm pleased and satisfied that the trial judge here saw what every other judge that took a look at this case has seen — that Tom Noe got a fair trial and he was fairly convicted of stealing $13.7 million from the Ohio Bureau of Workers' Compensation," said Kevin Pituch, an assistant Lucas County prosecutor who tried the case.[294]

The *Blade* article did admit that Judge Adams would have granted a change of venue if he had been the trial judge.

The Blade Compared to the Dispatch

Compare the *Blade*'s stories to this article published in the *Columbus Dispatch* after the Supreme Court's decision not to hear Noe's case. While the *Dispatch* did cite the prosecutors' criticisms of Noe, it also added this:

> But in a prison interview with The Dispatch in February, Noe insisted that his contract with the bureau entitled him to 20 percent of the profits and allowed him to take "advances" to make coin purchases or in anticipation of a profit.
>
> Noe said there always were enough coins, collectibles and other assets on hand to cover the advances, and if authorities thought he owed money, they should have sued him for breach of contract.
>
> The fact that the bureau recovered more than the original $50 million investment when the fund was liquidated proves that, Noe said. His lawyers wanted to discuss the value of the investment at trial, but prosecutors objected.

"Yeah, it was a sweet deal; it was a good deal for me," Noe said, noting that his lawyers wrote the contract. "What I'm saying is, is that not one dollar was taken that wasn't either going to be paid back or that I didn't think I took under the terms of the contract."

Noe admitted that he falsified the inventories of coins and other holdings that were submitted to the bureau each year, and he couldn't explain why his previous attorneys announced there was a "valuation shortfall" of up to $13 million when the coin fund was shut down in 2005.[295]

THE APPEALS AND THE FAIRNESS SCORECARD

Given the deference appeals courts give to a trial judge, they aren't the place to right the kinds of wrongs Noe faced, with the result that the fairness scorecard doesn't change. It's nevertheless disappointing that the prosecution chose not to reconsider its use of the Silverman case as a comparison; there is no honest equivalency.

Garrison Walters

Part V- Tom Noe in Prison

Visiting a prison, an early task in researching this book, is an unsettling experience for most people. The idea of being in a space where the normal rules of society don't apply puts the world out of focus. It's definitely an occasion for taking stock of one's life.

Ohio's Hocking Correctional Facility is a particularly mood-altering place. After driving through the beautiful green hills of Ohio's portion of Appalachia, a visitor passes through the charming, mostly restored town of Nelsonville. This first stage is pleasant, but a few blocks from the center one climbs past houses that were doubtless comfortable when built but have seen little maintenance in 90 or so years of unrelenting economic depression. The gloom of four generations of poverty hangs over the hillside like a morning fog.

Coping with the rules for entry is difficult, at least the first time. As at an airport, you have to take everything from your pockets before going through the scanner. But the difference is that your pockets stay empty. You are allowed to take with you only your driver's license and a card for the vending machines. No pencil or paper, no photos or mementos. And, of course, you can only visit when you have been approved and for a specific time.

The staff are not unfriendly. But these local people appear to view you as alien – someone not like them and not trustworthy until proven otherwise. Their near universal look – heavy frame, dark hair, brilliant blue eyes – must be worrisome to minority families.

The visiting room is small with numbered tables and a bank of vending machines along one wall. A guard sitting at the back gives you a seating assignment and, once you're seated, "your inmate," who has been strip searched earlier, is frisked and allowed to enter.

Tom Noe, now just over 60, is trim and moves with the agility and quickness of a much younger man. He has a ready smile and an engaging manner, sharing jokes with the guards and other inmates as he navigates the cluttered area of tables and chairs. It's obvious that people like him.

On my first visit, Noe and I did some reminiscing about my former workplace and the colleagues we had in common. But beyond this, personal conversation was limited since we hadn't been friends beyond work and had little knowledge of each other's family or hobbies and such.

The conversation quickly turned to life in prison. Noe was philosophical about this. It wasn't so bad, he said. He was able to exercise and the food wasn't terrible – though he later allowed that the very ordinary products disgorged by the vending machines were a huge treat for him.

Noe is by no means cut off from the outside world. Ohio prisoners have limited access to phones and a restricted, externally screened form of email. They are allowed to keep small devices that retain electronic documents, including photos. And there are visiting slots available most days. Noe has a lot of friends and he is kept busy with people from around the state and across the country.

The state of Ohio's approach to prisons seems remarkably enlightened, at least for those considered to be on their way to "reintegration." Noe later, when he had been moved to the reintegration camp at the prison in Marion, described the requirement to keep a log book of daily activities of substance – the state does not want inmates moving toward release to just sit around watching TV. Among other things, Tom teaches a course on personal finance and assists with church and with entertainment projects, particularly those connected to singing. Singing religious music is a part of his identity.

Noe skipped quickly through the hard part of life in prison. He said he felt safe, noting that the average age of prisoners here was over 50 and nearer 60. In passing, he mentioned that they don't have cells here, but that the bunks are very close together. If you reach out to either side you'll touch another person. Ear plugs are the biggest sellers in the commissary.

The lack of freedom wasn't a topic in our initial meeting or later. Other visitors have told me the same thing. Noe clearly doesn't want to burden friends with the emotional challenges of incarceration and indeed appears to be quite upbeat. But later conversations with his sister reveal that he has experienced serious down periods, especially around holidays. I don't know him well enough to gauge moods from a distance, but it's easy to appreciate that the more emotional times of year would stress anyone's reserves of mental energy – in fact, Noe was treated for depression beginning well before the trial.

Interestingly, Noe's comments about life don't dwell on what he'll do after he gets out. He talks about that, of course, but his emphasis is on the here and now and especially on helping other inmates. This is something he works hard at.

In later visits I learned that Noe's journey to Hocking was far from easy.

Immediately after being found guilty, Noe was handcuffed and taken to the Lucas County jail, then was transferred about a week later to Milan, Michigan where he entered the federal system. Milan was the first of many difficult experiences:

> Between the weight I had gained from inactivity and the medications the doctor had put me on, and the stress of the unknown (where I was going and what the real prisons would be like) I was as low as I had been since May of 2005. The first person I meet on the bus to Milan

from Toledo was a very large older man from Toledo by the name of Rodney King. I thought he had made that name up too but that was his real name. He had already served a 25 year sentence for robbery and was back in for a parole violation. He became my "guardian angel" at Milan for most of my 3+ month stay there. Because of the constant sensationalism of my case in the *Blade* everyone knew who I was.

Luckily for me, Rodney made sure that no one tried to bully me or take advantage of me. I'll always be grateful to him for his advice and friendship. The first altercation there was a fight over fried chicken. One of the cooks thought someone had stolen some of his "stash" and a fight pursued. One guy got hit and his momentum took him across the table I was seated at and all our trays flew everywhere. All the guards ordered us to our cells while 3 or 4 guys continued the fight over the chicken. As I tried to move away without getting in the middle of the fray, I felt a large body shielding me and moving me slowly towards my cell. When I looked up there was Rodney making sure I was OK before he went to his cell. That was the first of many altercations I witnessed over the years.

After about three months in Milan, Noe was put on a federal prison flight to Oklahoma City.

My first trip on "Conair" [nickname for the air service used to transport federal prisoners] was from Detroit to Oklahoma City with a stop in Chicago to pick up and drop off inmates. Once we landed in Oklahoma City we were told that the Federal holdover prison there was full so 30 of us were bussed (still handcuffed, belly chained and leg chained) to Grady County jail in Chickesha, Oklahoma. One of my bunkies over the next 6 weeks was a Cherokee Indian who was serving a 15 year sentence for the murder of another guy as a result of a fight outside a bar (yes, less than I received for my state case). I asked what he killed him with; a gun, knife or his fists, and he told me that he had killed him with a shovel!! He told me that his mother only got 5 years for holding the guy while he killed him. I decided not to ask him any more questions after that but we got along pretty well...

The worst place I have ever been was the Atlanta federal holdover. Anyone trying to get to the southeastern US ends up in Atlanta. We were locked down 23 hours a day and only came out for that hour a day to shower and make a phone call or two. They had rats the size of small kittens (ask anyone who has ever been there) and very large bugs. We would put a towel under our cell door at night to keep the rats and bugs out. When they were overcrowded, which was often, some guys had to sleep on mats on the floor. Remember that the toilets and sinks were in the cell too so it made for very close quarters. Luckily I only had to be there a couple weeks until I went to my parent [permanent assignment] institution, or so I thought…

Noe's initial assignment was to Edgefield, South Carolina.

When I arrived there [in Edgefield] I thought I had hit the jackpot. Nice, open, air-conditioned dorms, free movement and lots to do. But less than 24 hours after my arrival, I was called to the office and informed that the classification bureau had made a mistake and because I had a detainer [an additional sentence] back to Ohio after my Federal time that I should have been sent to a "low" security prison not a "minimum" camp. I was then handcuffed and taken to the "hole" (24/7 lockdown) until I could be re-classed to another institution. I spent 2 weeks there while the wheels turned slowly to transfer me.

Because Noe couldn't be in a minimum security facility and because the prison administration didn't yet have a place to send him, they put him in their maximum security area. He wasn't allowed to have any of his medications there, and as a result went through a medical and mental crisis. The combination of extreme isolation, and having no access to his asthma medication, and no antidepressants, brought Tom to what he describes as a 'near death experience.' He said only God could have saved him from his dark night of the soul.

When his wife, Bernadette, found out about the situation she appealed to everyone she could think of. And help came from a surprising source:

If it wasn't for Bernadette and the *Blade's* (yes, the *Blade!*) [296] constant inquiries and pressure on the Federal Bureau of Prisons I would still be in the hole at Edgefield.

Noe went from Edgefield to the Coleman prison in Florida. The Coleman camp had many activities, including an active Catholic ministry.

There were two full time chaplains and one was a wonderful Catholic priest, Fr. Bui, an immigrant from Vietnam. He was a political prisoner for years in Vietnam so he could relate to what we were all going through. In fact, his time in prison was much worse than we could all imagine. Being able to go to Sunday mass, weekly rosary with an outside deacon on Tuesday nights, and a fellowship night every Friday really lifted my spirits. Besides cantoring at mass, I sang in a 10 person band that did quarterly concerts out in the rec yard.

The time in the federal camp was also valuable in other ways. Tom lost nearly 30 pounds and restarted a reading habit. He estimates he's received, read, and, through the generosity of family and friends, donated around a thousand books since he's been in prison.

Noe was released from the federal system after two years and moved to the State of Ohio system.

> I was transferred to my parent institution at Hocking Correctional Facility (HCF) in Nelsonville, Ohio on December 9th, 2008. It was at HCF that my life was changed for the better. In October 2009 I was picked to make a Kairos weekend retreat. There were 24 inmates along with the 26 outside guys that taught us all what was important in our lives....God. While my spiritual life was always important to me, God had not been my major focus and highest priority. When I finished that weekend my life changed for the better in ways that are hard to describe. In my 10+ years in prison, I had lost my freedom, my material wealth, been through a divorce, my mother and father-in-law passed away along with many other family and friends, my daughter got married, two more grandkids were born and I lost numerous appeals and a filing for clemency. Most people would have given up but not me. I finally realized that I had to come to prison to find "true freedom"; The freedom that comes from putting my life in the hands of Jesus Christ and trusting Him that whatever I am faced with is His will. It's often said that people plan and God laughs. I became the poster child for God's laughter!!! I continued to ask God to show me His path. I began teaching classes, got very involved in the Kairos Prison Ministry with a praise band and the next almost 8 years flew by.

Noe was at Hocking from December of 2008 until the late summer of 2016 when he was transferred to a larger prison in Marion, in the middle of the state. This prison has a large high security area, but also one area that is much more hospitable.

> I was moving to the honors camp.....say what?? I didn't even know about the camp. But less than 24 hours later I was on my way to a separate building that housed Marion Reintegration Center (MRC). God hit these answers to my prayers out of the ballpark!! There are fewer than 400 guys housed in 2 dorms at the camp and we have our own rec yard, exercise area, dining hall, vending machines, laundry, library, chapel, etc. After almost 10 challenging years in prison I had finally been assigned to the lowest and best security level and housing available in Ohio. I now wear an all khaki uniform, instead of the standard blues, and the inmates and staff treat you with respect. I'm back to teaching a couple of classes and I continue to look for ways to reach out to the other guys here to try and make a difference in their lives to give them the tools to not reoffend once they are released.

Marion has a different feel from its sister prison down south. At least from the perspective of visitors, the guards here seem much less suspicious, more open and personable – this is true despite the much more hardened overall inmate population.

The visiting room in Marion is perhaps twelve times bigger than the one in Hocking, and spending the better part of a day there is a fascinating experience (visits are normally around seven hours). There are many children and a special play area for them. The mood is usually festive, with lots of laughter. It's quite a contrast with the very somber little room at Hocking. Still, this is a different kind of world: Noe points out men who will likely never leave this place because they have a number of "bodies" on their resumes.

Noe knew about the idea of a book at our first meeting and seemed enthusiastic. But my closer read at the time was of a well-calibrated reserve. He'd had seven years of disappointments with the appeals, and just recently also the unsuccessful request for clemency. So his expectations were limited, but he was certainly willing to cooperate and curious about the approach I planned to use.

In fact, at the outset of the book project I was not at all certain of the facts of Noe's case and told him that. My initial premise – based on people who knew the law – was that the sentence was wildly disproportionate. But I had little knowledge of exactly what Noe did and didn't do, nor did I have direct personal knowledge that the sentence was wrong.

In those initial meetings, when I hadn't read much except for a few newspaper articles, I encouraged Noe to limit his comments to general terms, since I wanted to have a much better understanding of the background before getting into specifics.

Noe framed the situation at the outset by first volunteering that he'd done things that he shouldn't have done with the coin funds. Certainly, he accepted the charges of tampering with records. But he didn't think he was guilty of theft. The coin fund contracts, he said, gave him the right to take loans and advances and to trade with his own business. Also, since the OBWC did an extensive internal review and then agreed not only to the existing investment but to another fund as well, Noe had become confident that he had a great deal of flexibility to take loans and advances on profits.

I was puzzled by this description of the contract initially, thinking that his characterization couldn't be accurate. Later, of course, I discovered that these points are in fact crystal clear in the documents. Actually, I came to disagree with the idea that it was a "dumb" contract for the OBWC. Except, perhaps, for the "knowingly in violation" clause, the various provisions were consistent with the venture capital-like operations of businesses in this field.

Noe also emphasized at the outset that he had intended to cover all the advances and/or loans and that he would have been able to do that if allowed to close the fund himself. He spoke with certainty that the liquidation under state control was not well done and that it lost many millions for the state, probably more than ten (see the table at the end of Part VI for details).

In later interviews, when I had greater knowledge and was able to press on details, Noe was more specific. He accepts that he'd underestimated the cost of running both the coin funds and his own business at the same time, and that the idea of refusing to take any operating costs up front was a bad one. That was especially true once he realized that investing $25 million in a continuously productive way was going to be very hard, not least because the coin market was soft when the money was first made available in the Spring of 1998. He would have liked to hold money until things improved, but believed he really couldn't do that because then he'd be reporting very weak returns and feared the coin funds might be characterized as low performing and subsequently withdrawn.

This early situation explains, he says, several aspects that became controversial. For example, the real estate investment with John Ulmer (whose business seemed entirely legitimate to him at the time – see below in Part IX). Noe emphasizes that the OBWC knew all about this and that his contract with Ulmer fully protected the funds – and that the coin fund made a considerable profit.

Noe also says that the weakness in the coin market caused him to buy collectibles on his own account before the coin fund money arrived and that he took out a line of credit to do that. This, he says, explains why much of the initial transfer of money went to his personal or business' accounts – it was to pay for assets that would later become part of the coin fund.

But this point raises a more challenging one: why wasn't all this shown in the books?

Here Noe is candid, embarrassed and contrite. In running a comparatively small business he had never been focused on accounting and never been careful in separating business and personal funds on a regular, daily basis. Instead, he allowed things to pile up until a frantic end of the fiscal year struggle when numbers needed to be sorted out and put straight for the tax returns.

One of the worst aspects of this, Noe says, was that as a small businessman he'd come to rely on an excellent memory as a way to manage assets. So, instead of documenting everything in detail as it happened, he'd done things like keep assets for different accounts in different parts of his secure storage area. Based on past experience, he felt he could remember what was what. His memory was especially important for the collectibles, which his assistant, Tim LaPointe, didn't have much to do with.

The size of the investment Noe had undertaken magnified the problems of a very haphazard approach to accounting. And this already serious issue was exacerbated by Noe's accelerating involvement in politics, public affairs, and charity. By 2000 or so he was spending the majority of his time on these and paying far too little attention to the business. He was relying on LaPointe more and more and that was a problem because, although his senior assistant was skilled in the coin business, he had a very poor memory and was even less capable than Noe in the accounting area.

So, what about the false coin transactions? The "unsupported inventory transfers" that Crowe Chizek identified and that were the heart of the prosecution's case?

Noe admits that these occurred and agrees that the reason was to disguise his need to get operating cash. He also accepts that some of those funds did go, at least temporarily, to pay for personal expenses, though he's mystified at Crowe's decision to ignore his other, non-coin fund deposits in concluding that OBWC money went for personal things. Noe says that many of the transactions that Crowe cited as state money going to personal expenses in its "use of cash" analysis were ones which were quickly covered by non-OBWC deposits.

In any case, Noe doesn't think that the "unsupported inventory purchases" were at all the same as theft. He acknowledges that his personal spending was excessive at some points but he also believed, again based on past experience, that he could cover the loans that were allowed in the contract.

Whatever the explanations, however, he doesn't deny the basic fact that he shouldn't have used any coin fund money for personal expenses – even temporarily.

Theft, in Noe's mind, would have been attempting to cheat with the books in a way that would be designed to fool an auditor – to make it so he could permanently keep the money he'd borrowed and never have to pay it back. But, he says, that was obviously not the case here. Any complete audit would have quickly found exactly what he owed. The undocumented withdrawals were clearly listed in the set of books available to the state and so weren't really hidden at all. He'd have had to cover at the end of the contract as specified. But he hadn't worried about that in the near term because a complete audit wasn't scheduled until each of the funds was terminated and he would have had plenty of time to cover before then – indeed, he is confident that he could have even covered in 2005 if he had been given the chance.

So does Noe believe that what he did was OK? No.

He accepts responsibility for misleading the OBWC and the falsification of records that made that possible. And, although he does regularly cite the contract when discussing his actions, he acknowledges that he shouldn't have acted in the way he did and that some punishment for this would be reasonable. Of course, he also very much regrets allowing himself to drift into a situation in which falsification became an attractive option.

Again, though, Noe doesn't accept that what he did was theft or that in submitting falsified records he stole money from the state or harmed its injured workers. He carefully follows the news, especially those stories that cover comparable cases. When he sees that many of these are never given prison sentences, or very short sentences, it is hard for him to escape the conclusion that his harsh treatment was for political reasons.

Interestingly, I never heard Noe speak angrily or vilify any individual. Rather, he seems to feel it was timing – really just bad luck — that caused the system to react so harshly toward him.

As agreed, Noe didn't talk about these issues in depth until my research was drawing to a close because, as mentioned earlier, I wanted to be at least mostly finished with my research when I asked for his side. As it happens, his statements fully matched my own conclusions.

On the other hand, to hear the *Blade* tell it, Noe is sitting in prison defiantly refusing to admit any guilt at all. And, according to the editorial page, he spends his time in prison counting the money in his Cayman Islands bank accounts – though there has never been evidence of any kind that such exist.

Readers of independent news sources know this unbalanced characterization of Noe as rejecting any guilt isn't accurate. For example, in a 2010 prison interview with the *Columbus Dispatch,* Noe clearly accepted responsibility for a number of the state charges and this was strongly repeated in his clemency application.[297]

As we know, the *Blade* has spoken resolutely about the appropriateness of Noe's sentence and, during the appeals, stressed the need to keep him in prison. One editorial was actually titled, "Keep Noe in Prison."

The *Blade* also editorialized against his clemency petition and commented approvingly when it was denied. It's very clear: unless Noe accepts that he stole money, the paper's management will assertively oppose his release.[298]*m*

One has to wonder about the real purpose of this sustained and implacable journalistic anger – is the *Blade* seeking closure for the people of Ohio? Or vindication for itself?

Part VI- Rewind: A fair trial?

The previous sections of this book, Parts I to V, have offered an overview of Coingate, from the first *Blade* article to the end of the appeals. These sections allude to, but don't fully answer, key questions about whether the process – from the first decision on charges to the final sentence — was fair.

This section, by contrast, deals directly and in depth with the issue of fairness, doing so primarily by considering Noe's legal process in the light of psychological research on bias. Since most of that research has been done in the context of media influence and juries, that setting will be used to introduce the key psychological factors. However, because issues of bias apply in many situations and to all individuals, and because decisions of prosecutors and judges were as important or even more determining than that of the jury, we'll also discuss how the various dimensions of bias affect the entire legal structure and the people in it.

RECAP: ROLE OF THE *BLADE* AND OTHER MEDIA

The role of local media, notably the Toledo *Blade*, has been mentioned on numerous prior occasions, so this section is just a quick recap.

By any measure, the level of coverage was extraordinary – a total of some 750 articles and letters from the initial allegations in April of 2005 until the defense moved for a change of venue in mid- 2006. There were on the order of another 250 articles published before the trial finally began in the fall of 2006. The pervasive nature of radio coverage has already been mentioned.

Television coverage is much harder to count, but it's safe to say that there were at least short segments on each of the local stations on average about once a week during the almost year and a half before the trial. Television coverage was strong because, while the stations did do some interviews, they relied on the *Blade* for much of their information – in fact, one of the strongest local channels had a news pooling agreement with the *Blade*.[299]

The focus of the *Blade's* coverage is described in depth in earlier sections, and this author – as well as judges in the state and federal appeals courts -- believes that a reasonable person considering the coverage would find it consistently negative toward Noe.

To be fair, however, the nature of the *Blade's* coverage wasn't entirely dependent on the attitudes of its management. As discussed, within weeks of the initial stories, the political environment had shifted such that both political parties were strongly critical of Noe: leaders of both regularly described him as guilty. In simply reporting what these individuals said, as was certainly appropriate, the *Blade* was necessarily conveying strongly negative information.

There were no individuals or organizations of prominence speaking in favor of Noe, except for occasional comments from the defense team (which were regularly, and for the most part with reasonable fairness, covered by the *Blade*).

In addition to the direct coverage of Coingate, there was also extensive writing on Noe's federal trial and, since he pleaded guilty, these were inevitably negative (all Noe-related topics are included in the 750 count given above). And, of course, many articles connected Coingate and the federal crime.

Simply put, when Noe's trial began, the region from which the jury pool was drawn had been saturated for about a year and a half with an almost entirely negative coverage that characterized Noe as a high-level criminal.

PSYCHOLOGY AND DISCRETION: JURIES

Most of the psychological research on bias focuses on the role of the media, though other possible sources will be covered later.

Media bias is a concern because the research shows that a significant part of the population from which jurors are drawn is unable to distinguish biased from unbiased information.

Juries: Media Bias and Prejudgment

There has been substantial research on media bias and jurors, and a survey article published by two university researchers in psychology in 1997 is unequivocal about the effect of pre-trial media bias on juries:

> Prejudicial pretrial publicity has been found to influence evaluations of the defendant's likability, sympathy for the defendant, perceptions of the defendant as a typical criminal, pretrial judgments of the defendant's guilt, and final verdicts.[300]

The research cited by the two professors includes both field surveys of actual jurors and experimental work. In one field survey, researchers found that:

> The respondents in the venues where the cases were scheduled for trial were more likely to know details about the cases, including inadmissible information, and were more likely to believe defendants were guilty (with differences between the venue and alternative sites ranging from 16% to as high as 40%). These results clearly suggest that the possibility of juror bias is greater in venue counties than in other counties.[301]

Another field survey example reinforces these conclusions:

> In each of these cases, Costantini and King found a strong relationship between the amount of information a participant could supply about a

case and the measures of prejudice. Respondents were asked to indicate whether they had formed an opinion about the defendant's guilt in each of the cases. These responses were then correlated with several variables, including gender, educational level, general attitudes about crime, and knowledge about the specific case. Although the results suggested that each of these variables was a significant indicator of the respondents' tendencies to presume defendant guilt, by far the best predictor was knowledge about the case—most of which was presumably gained through newspaper and television pretrial publicity. Specifically, in the three different cases 30%, 2%, and 2% of "poorly informed" respondents thought the defendants were guilty versus 54%, 66%, and 61% of "well-informed" respondents. Indeed, the more media sources to which a respondent reported attending, the more he or she knew about the case. Consistent with the findings of Simon and Eimermann (1971), respondents with greater knowledge about a case were found to be more pro-prosecution. Costantini and King concluded from these results that pretrial knowledge was the best predictor of prejudgment.[302]

The research not only strongly connects an individual's prejudgment to media exposure, but also finds that those who have prejudged also have high confidence that they could be impartial:

> Unfortunately, however, participants' knowledge of the case was not inversely correlated with their self-reported ability to be impartial. Regardless of the amount of knowledge about the case, a significant proportion of individuals thought they could be fair and impartial. In fact, the group that most strongly endorsed the proposition that there was "a lot of evidence" against the defendant also had the highest proportion of respondents who thought they could be fair and could set aside the knowledge gleaned from the news.[303]

Experimental studies, ones in which researchers simulated trials so that they could get strong comparisons, also showed that exposure to added information such as that about other crimes by the accused had a strong biasing effect:

> More than 72% of jurors exposed to the stories containing inadmissible information voted to convict, whereas less than 44% of the jurors not exposed to this information voted to convict.[304]

> Overall, these studies reveal that evidence or information casting doubt on the character of the defendant, such as reports about prior convictions and confessions or reports implicating the defendant in other crimes, is one of the principal vehicles through which pretrial

publicity exerts its effects. Jurors who have heard about prior bad acts by a party or who have reason to question the character of a party are more likely to convict or find fault with that party.[305]

In considering the above point about bias coming from prior convictions, recall that Noe was sentenced in federal court just weeks before his state trial began.

The research opens up the question of how well courts protect against bias.

> As can be seen from the review of research above, field surveys and experimental studies both consistently reveal an effect of pretrial publicity on people's attitudes about a publicized case. One response to these results may be "So what? The courts are aware of the potentially biasing effects of pretrial publicity. That is precisely why they have implemented various safeguards designed to eliminate media influence on juror and jury decision making." Although the courts have implemented these safeguards to combat the possible influence of pretrial publicity at various stages of the trial process, most of them have been shown to be ineffective...[306]

Despite this research —which was available at the time --Judge Osowik was unshakeable on the power of voir dire, believing the process would find people who did not follow the news and were therefore not influenced by any media bias.

> This Court has found out from other cases people use a number of different variety of news sources to run their daily lives. They're very busy, whether they're going out to soccer games, picking up their children, many people work from 3 to 11, don't even watch television, some people don't read the newspaper until just the weekends. So, I think we have to at least try to at least get and impanel a jury and find out what the answers to the questions are.[307]

There are several flaws with this line of thinking. A very important one is the idea that people only get news from news sources. In fact, many people get information about current events from other people.[308]m In a situation like that which existed in Lucas County, with many hundreds of newspaper articles and an unknown but certainly vast number of television and radio mentions, it would be a very rare person who would not encounter and hear some comment from a person who *did* read or hear the news – family member, friend, co-worker. Given the volume of media attention, a person who had no such contacts over the year and half preceding the trial would have to have lived an almost hermit-like existence.

The source of these personal news contacts – other people rather than news sources – also means that many people exposed in this way would often not remember the contact. Thus, voir dire would almost certainly miss a substantial number of people who had been exposed not just to information but to opinion about Noe.

Further, available research does specifically conclude that voir dire is not an effective remedy for bias.

> Jurors who claimed that they could disregard the pretrial publicity simply did not—despite their apparent belief that they could.[309]

> …the effectiveness of voir dire as a remedy for pretrial publicity rests on at least two assumptions: first, that jurors have cognitive access to their source of bias—that is, that they can remember having seen or heard news accounts of the trial accurately—and second, that prospective jurors are willing to report on any bias that may have arisen from exposure to pretrial publicity. In light of the research findings, both these assumptions appear extremely tenuous ["extremely tenuous" is academic-speak for "false."][310]

In sum, it appears that the effects of pretrial publicity:

- can find their way to the courtroom,
- can survive the jury selection process,
- can survive the presentation of trial evidence,
- can endure the limiting effects of judicial instructions, and
- can not only persevere through deliberation, but may actually intensify.[311]

Although more research is needed for solid conclusions, researchers cite two reasons why people who have been exposed to biasing information can't overcome that experience and render a truly impartial decision.

One explanation is that "when people are initially exposed to pretrial publicity, there is usually no reason for them to tag the information as unreliable or inadmissible."[312] Information acquired in this unconscious way can be hard to erase because people don't know or believe that they've acquired it.

A second reason for inability to overcome bias is that "…people find it very difficult to actively suppress a thought upon instruction, particularly when that thought is vivid or emotionally arousing."[313] Psychologists use the example of telling someone not to think about a pink elephant, which immediately causes them to visualize that mythical creature. Suppressing "a thought on instruction" refers in this case to a judge's admonition to a jury not to consider evidence not presented in court. Such an instruction is likely to be counter-productive, especially if bias is actually present.

In summary, in the case of juries exposed to extensive media bias, the research offers a negative view of the ability of courts to ensure a fair trial.

> Courts are aware of the potential problems that pretrial publicity can create, especially in regard to defendants' Sixth Amendment right to a fair trial. However, courts' assessments of the likelihood that pretrial publicity has resulted in prejudice against a defendant and of jurors' ability to disregard any prejudice are often based only on judicial common sense. Unfortunately, judicial common sense often reflects a misappraisal or misunderstanding by the courts of the capabilities and weaknesses of human inference and decision making. The courts' assumptions and expectations about jurors' decision-making processes and ability to disregard pretrial publicity are not consistent with social science findings concerning these matters.[314]

Although the main research cited here dates from 1997 and earlier, a review of the literature since then suggests that the initial conclusions have been reinforced rather than contradicted by subsequent analysis and experiments.[315]

Juries: Unconscious Bias- Media and Other Sources

While media bias is important in causing prejudgment, it's also a fact that many people enter the jury process with preexisting biases that they are unaware of. Psychologists, eschewing their normally polysyllabic ways, refer to this as simply "unconscious bias." This term may include bias acquired from a variety of sources, including media.

Unconscious bias, also called "implicit bias," is most often associated in the legal context with racial bias and there is a strong consensus that unconscious racial bias exists – even the Supreme Court recognizes it.[316] But there is also ample research in psychology on the phenomenon of unconscious bias in general.

The acquisition of bias doesn't necessarily occur consciously:

> Social behavior is ordinarily treated as being under conscious (if not always thoughtful) control. However, considerable evidence now supports the view that social behavior often operates in an implicit or unconscious fashion. The identifying feature of implicit cognition is that past experience influences judgment in a fashion not introspectively known by the actor.[317]

Unconscious bias is often seen in the form of "stereotyping," in which people make judgments "outside of conscious cognition," that is to say, on association. Thus, in the case of Tom Noe, people might develop a negative attitude about someone who had different political views.[318]*m*

Additional introductory information on this important topic can be found in a recent book, *Blindspot: Hidden Biases of Good People,* by Mahzarin R. Banaji and Anthony G. Greenwald.[319]

In thinking about unconscious bias, consider two relevant points from the research described previously: 1) bias that is acquired unconsciously, and therefore not evaluated as an attempt to persuade, can be very difficult to eradicate; and 2) those most confident they were unbiased were most likely to be biased.

Juries: How Did the Actual Voir Dire Go?

In light of the above about both media and unconscious bias, it's reasonable to ask if the phenomena observed by the researchers in psychology affected jury selection in Noe's trial. That's a question that can be answered, since the voir dire for Noe's jury is included in the transcripts.[320]

For the most part, the voir dire is not an easy read. Much of the text consists of lawyers extracting not particularly interesting personal information from people very slowly, in a long skein of short and simple questions. It's also difficult to evaluate the process when, as was the case with this author, one doesn't have access to the jury questionnaires and therefore doesn't know much about the characteristics of the people who were dismissed on the basis of their answers (Prospective jurors were given a questionnaire that covered key topics such as: 1) availability to serve 2) conflicts with the parties (e.g., positive or negative contacts with Noe or his family); 3) sources of possible bias such as having read about the case in the newspaper or watched news stories on TV; and 4) ability to be impartial.).

Also, the documents from the defense and the prosecution specifying their reasons for objecting to particular jurors aren't available.

Within the context of the caveats mentioned above, here are some impressions from the voir dire:

— Many of the prospective jurors said they knew a lot about the case from the media and thought that what they had read or heard was strongly negative toward Noe. Four of the first five were dismissed because their exposure had led them to form firm opinions of Noe's guilt. It's not clear from the transcript, but it appears that many more were dismissed because they had expressed the same opinion in their questionnaires.

— Some prospective jurors claimed not to follow the news and to have no knowledge of the case – some of these came off as credible, some not.

– One particularly amazing statement came from a man whose family subscribed to The *Blade* and often read it but claimed never to have read anything there about Noe. This is reminiscent of the O.J. Simpson neighbor who came forward months after the murders to say he'd been walking his dog the fateful night and remembered seeing the Bronco parked askew, but hadn't come forward previously because he hadn't known anything about the events occurring a few blocks away from his house. As noted elsewhere, it's reasonable to wonder if someone who lacked even minimum curiosity about the world around them would be competent to deal with the complex evidence presented in a trial like this.

    – A more credible answer from a prospective juror was simply: "Because it's not on ESPN, I don't pay much attention to it."[321]

– The voir dire turned up sloppy questioning and a lot of bias:

    – Crucially, given what we know from the research, few were pressed on whether they had heard family, friends, or coworkers discuss the case.

    – Most prospective jurors did agree to having at least some exposure to news about Noe, and many mentioned the federal case, which had just been in the news a few weeks earlier when Noe was sentenced in federal court. This is relevant when considering change of venue: jurors in other parts of the state would probably not have known about Noe's federal case since it was not treated as major news outside the Toledo area.

    – There were quite a few negative comments about the media and some special cynicism about the *Blade*.[322] [323] The following exchange might have worried *Blade* reporters in the room:

Prosecutor: "…you say you're an avid reader of The *Blade*?"

Prospective Juror: "Yes."

Prosecutor:	"Do you believe everything you read in The *Blade?*"
Prospective Juror:	"Absolutely not."

In fact, though, this person's antagonism toward his local paper apparently stemmed only from the fact that it had "a lot of typos."[324]

The biggest concern, however, was with the substantial number of jurors who said that they had read or heard negative views about Noe, and who had formed some tentative conclusions, but who nevertheless said they could be impartial. For example:

- A woman said, "...when I first heard about him with all the news and the reading of newspapers and that, I'm like, oh, he's guilty, but now I just haven't kept up, so my mind's just back and forth."[325]

- And a man who said, "The *Blade* prints a really pretty picture of him being guilty of everything he's being accused of." [326]

- And a man, an accountant, said that in his opinion based on reading about the case, "most likely there's something here."[327]

- Another, a woman, said she'd heard people, including family, say Noe was guilty but no one say he wasn't.[328]

- Another reported her understanding that there was theft, but that it wasn't clear who had done it.[329]

- A man who was clearly biased against Republicans associated Noe with them.[330]

In fact, in most of the cases mentioned here, as well as in a number of other similar ones, the defense expressed concern. An example was the person who said she understood there had been theft – this was a big deal for the defense, which was arguing not directly for innocence but for the fact there had in fact been no theft.

A particularly interesting episode involved a man who said he knew all about the case –including the federal conviction — and was a "news junkie." In response to whether he had an opinion, he said that he thought that "where there's smoke there's fire" and stated his belief that the state had invested in the coin funds as a result of "influence peddling." Overall, he gave the strong impression that he thought Noe was guilty of some crime (in addition to influence peddling). But the prosecutors and judge kept pressing, and eventually the man agreed he could "suspend his opinion" and be fair. The defense objected, but Judge Osowik left him in the pool, observing that Noe wasn't charged with influence peddling.[331] [332]*m*

In fact, Judge Osowik left in the potential jury pool almost all individuals cited above who said they'd formed an opinion. His consistent reason for this was that all that mattered was if the person was willing to say that he or she could be fair and impartial. Anyone willing to agree to this statement was legitimate by definition.[333]*m* Osowik repeatedly cited precedent from the Ohio Supreme Court that, if people with initial biases were systematically excluded, it would not be possible to empanel juries as needed:

> ...the existence of preconceived notions of guilt or innocence of an accused without more is not sufficient to rebut the presumption of prospective jurors' impartiality. Otherwise, we'd be held to an impossible standard.[334]

Existing research in psychology, for example the studies cited above that show stronger media exposure means stronger bias, were never referenced.

It's worth noting at this point that keeping obviously biased individuals in the jury pool forced the defense to use up its challenges quickly, meaning that Noe's lawyers were eventually forced to accept jurors who did not appear to be impartial.

The Stealth Juror Problem

The legal profession acknowledges that there is a problem with what are known as "stealth jurors," i.e., jurors who lie about their connections and their interests and biases in order to get on a jury. By contrast to the previously discussed group, these are people with "conscious bias."

Many in the profession think that the problem is very small, but others disagree:

> Los Angeles based jury consultant Philip K. Anthony blames dated voir dire procedures for complicating this most serious of guessing games. Anthony says stealth jurors are a real problem, not just in high profile trials. He says his research indicates that between 15 percent and 18 percent of potential jurors who are summoned for service have a biased mindset and actively seek out jury service as a way to comment on or influence a trial.[335]

A better voir dire process, and specifically one that allows for more specific and/or private questioning of jurors, is seen as a way to avoid this problem. But psychologists are skeptical:

> Psychologists have long been interested in detecting lies (William Moulton Marston introduced his first polygraph in 1915), yet research continues to show that trained professionals in law enforcement are rarely better than novices at detecting deception.

Given trained detectives' difficulties in deception detection, attorneys would be hard pressed to discover juror dishonesty during voir dire.[336]

The issue of stealth jurors becomes especially important because the intense media coverage in Lucas County focused on two factors. First, Noe's supposed "lavish lifestyle at the expense of injured workers" was a key feature of the *Blade* coverage that was echoed by the electronic media. In an economically depressed area with a strong blue-collar component, this aspect could certainly have caused angry individuals to lie in order to get on the jury. Second, and overlapping with the first factor, the endless portrayal of Noe as a Republican kingpin would certainly have drawn the attention of partisan Democrats looking for revenge, especially for the perceived fraud in 2004.

Stealth jurors, again, are people with conscious bias. If you add this category to the undoubtedly important number of those affected by unconscious bias, the probability that Noe's jury was truly impartial diminishes greatly. It also demonstrates the absurdity of the statement by Assistant Prosecutor Kevin Pituch that, "The people who were truly prejudiced against Tom Noe were excluded, and there weren't that many."[337]

It's important to emphasize that, as with the other dimensions of bias, the stealth juror issue scales with local circumstances and especially with media intensity. In other words, with normal media coverage the potential effect would be so small that there would be no need to change a trial's venue.

Juries: The Role of Peer Pressure

Peer pressure is one other very important aspect of psychology to consider in the context of a jury that's convened in the presence of intense and strongly biased media coverage. It's an issue that wouldn't show up in voir dire but could strongly affect the verdict. Interestingly, it's a factor that's already been mentioned in this narrative by James Petiniot.

Recall that Petiniot, in a later deposition to a lawyer for Noe, said:

> In short, we didn't decide the case on the evidence. We felt that if we didn't return a verdict soon, the general public would think that we were stupid. After all, according to the media and the politicians, everybody in Ohio knew Mr. Noe was guilty. What would take the jury so long to convict him? Under that pressure, we had numerous, heated arguments in deciding the case. After spending a couple of days trying to get through the evidence, we gave up and convicted Mr. Noe of crimes he did not commit.[338]

Peer pressure is often thought of as an adolescent issue. But, as the brilliant author Tina Rosenberg points out in her book, *Join the Club*,[339] peer pressure and the role of peers in helping create values and opinions is a critically important factor in the psychology of groups; one quote says it all: "In the face of strong public pressure to conform, most people conform."[340]

The issue has resurfaced in discussions about a recent film on the O.J. Simpson trial. Petiniot's point that the jury worried about what outsiders were thinking of them is certainly illustrated by Simpson's "trial of the century." The decision of jurors in that case was subject not just to local ridicule but also to withering criticism from national commentators and even late-night comedians.

Of course, Noe's trial wasn't at all comparable to Simpson's in media attention nationally. However, the voir dire alone shows that in Lucas County and other parts of the Toledo media service area, knowledge of the case was extremely high and the idea that a juror might be subject to criticism from friends and neighbors wasn't at all far-fetched.

Some will say that taking media influence and the psychology of bias and peer pressure into account will make it too hard to seat a jury. The same sentiment would be conveyed in the sentence "it would be too hard to give him a fair trial." In fact, in most cases, and especially in that of Tom Noe, moving the investigation and trial to a place where these issues wouldn't have important impact wouldn't have been difficult or expensive. A great many of the witnesses, for example, were based in Columbus.

DISCRETION AND PSYCHOLOGY: PROSECUTORS AND JUDGES

Although the most important part of this section concerns research in psychology, the relevance of that knowledge is closely premised on the freedom that key individuals have to make decisions. Since most people know what scope of action juries have, but few appreciate the broad latitude given to prosecutors and judges, this section will begin with a focus on the discretion – and therefore the vulnerability to biased action — of individuals who hold those jobs.

Despite the public perception that people in the justice system "just follow the law," the fact is that there is an enormous amount of discretion applied at all levels, and where there is discretion, bias can play a major role. The justice system isn't a smoothly functioning computer; it's a very human process that is highly susceptible to human emotions.

Since Noe's saga started with prosecutors, we'll begin there as well, starting with a recap of some previous information.

The Prosecutors and the RICO Charge

Prosecution of crimes in the US involves a confusing series of overlapping entities – not surprising because that's the way the courts are organized. At the federal level, the Justice Department oversees (though somewhat loosely) the US Attorneys who are distributed around the country and who prosecute federal crimes. States have Attorneys General (or similar) who do the same for the state level. Localities have prosecutors (or district attorneys or similar) who deal with issues at either the county or the municipal level.

There are no records detailing how it was decided who should prosecute what in the various concerns about Tom Noe and the coin funds, but it's reasonably certain that decisions were made in the task force that oversaw the investigation. Members of the task force at the state level were the offices of the Attorney General, the Inspector General, the State Auditor, and the OBWC. The group's apparent decision was that civil issues would continue to be handled by the Attorney General, with criminal charges devolving to the local entity, which in this case was determined to be Lucas County. The FBI was involved, but no federal charges were filed; many have wondered about this, since other OBWC cases were dealt with in the federal system.

In the case of Lucas County, Ohio, prosecution is in the hands of a Prosecutor, who is elected every four years and who appoints a professional staff to assist her. The prosecutor at the time of Noe's indictment and trial was Julia R. Bates, who was first elected to the office in 1996, though she had been employed there since she graduated from law school in 1976. Mrs. Bates, who continues in office at this writing (2017) is a Democrat.

The public doesn't generally appreciate the discretionary power of prosecutors. Many crimes, especially violent ones, are investigated by law enforcement (police, sheriffs) who then present charges to prosecutors. But prosecutors can also initiate investigations and, as was the case with Coingate, manage them as well. Prosecutors don't have to file charges in cases presented by law enforcement and often decline to do so, usually if they decide there is insufficient evidence to succeed at trial. Prosecutors may consult with police when dropping charges but are not required to do that, nor are they required to keep records describing their decisions.

The question of exactly what charges to file is also at the discretion of prosecutors. They may take the recommendation of the police or they may not. No one has standing to challenge their decision on what to file.

In many cases and in many but not all places, prosecutors must take their case to a grand jury before filing charges. But, as noted in the famous phrase that "you could get a grand jury to indict a ham sandwich,"[341] grand juries rarely constitute a significant barrier if prosecutors are determined to pursue a certain type of charge – the main reason for this is that grand juries only hear one side of a case – that of the prosecutor.

Prosecutors are, of course, challenged by defense attorneys and can be checked by judges who may choose to throw out charges even before a case is heard, as well as during its course. And, ultimately, it's a jury or judge that decides guilt, innocence and (to some extent) the level of punishment.

But the role of judges and juries shouldn't be taken to mean that prosecutors don't have tremendous discretionary power. In particular, the level of charges they file shapes the process in important ways. For example, a strongly worded indictment alleging serious crime can have a powerful influence on public opinion – and this can be significantly reinforced by statements prosecutors make to the media. Also, the nature of the charges can impose serious economic harm on a defendant who has to deal with major, complex charges.

Nowhere is prosecutorial discretion greater – or more controversial – than in the class of crimes introduced in 1970 and usually categorized under the federal acronym: RICO, which stands for "Racketeer Influenced Corrupt Organization."

The original purpose of RICO, and the explanation for the word "racketeer," was to deal with organized crime figures who were winning acquittals in court because they weren't personally and directly involved in criminal activity. So, a Mafia boss might not be involved in loan sharking or extortion himself, but would cause others to carry out those acts. Absent specific orders telling someone to commit a crime, convictions were becoming increasingly hard to get. As a result, the federal statutes targeted people who led or had a key role in "organizations" that "engaged in a pattern of corrupt activity."

RICO had a very important role in taking down various Mafia structures, and has been widely celebrated as a result.

The general public is often surprised when RICO statutes are used against anything other than Mafia or similar criminal entities, but the law was always intended to be useful in a wider context, and was very flexibly written as a result. Wider use quickly became common at the federal level, notably when the law was used against financier Michael Milliken in 1989.

Success at the federal level caused states to follow suit by passing comparable laws on their own, and a majority, including Ohio, had done so by 1990.

As RICO and RICO-like laws became more widely available and more widely used, their inherent flexibility began to cause concern. A 1988 article in the *New York Times* observed that "The discretion available to prosecutors under RICO-type laws has generated considerable controversy."[342] Two years later, a law review article carried the title "The problem with RICO – Excessive Prosecutorial Discretion" and led with this quote: "The major problem with adopting RICO at the state level is that it provides the prosecutor with extensive but unchecked discretion to seek potentially severe penalties and to label someone as a racketeer in cases where the defendant is not part of any organized crime."[343] Indeed, a few years later an annoyed person actually sued a group of federal judges for being part of a "criminal enterprise."[344]

More serious challenges to the use or RICO and RICO-like statutes point out that both the terms "organization" and "pattern of corrupt activity" are subject to a great deal of interpretation, with the result that prosecutors, by means of designating an organization and a pattern, can use the law to attack fairly ordinary activity, sometimes perhaps not even criminal. This alone wouldn't necessarily be a major concern, except for the fact that RICO-type statutes usually carry severe penalties, often including mandatory minimum sentences. The very tough penalties were added quite deliberately because RICO laws were designed to target individuals who were directors and overseers of criminal organizations.

Ohio's RICO-like statute carries the more appropriate name of EPCA for "Engaging in a Pattern of Corrupt Activity," but this book will still use RICO because it's more commonly recognized. The RICO charge was Count 1 in the indictment handed down against Tom Noe on February 10 of 2006.

Count 1 specifies the "corrupt enterprise" as including Noe and his assistant Tim LaPointe, in concert with Noe's business (VCC- Vintage Coins and Collectibles) and the other businesses Noe had engaged in the coin funds. It also tosses in the two coin funds as part of the "organization" as well as, in lawyerly "throw in the kitchen-sink" fashion, "others known and/or as yet not identified." The alleged offenses in the "pattern" of crimes include theft, forgery, tampering with records, and money laundering. Interestingly, although the companies affiliated with Noe and the Coin Funds were a part of the "organization" defined to invoke RICO, none of the individuals involved in those businesses was charged with a crime. Indeed, prosecutors were eager to avoid mentioning any activities in the other businesses.

The exclusion of anyone other than Noe and LaPointe from the "organization" certainly makes the indictment problematic from the perspective of the intent of the law, not to mention fundamental fairness.

If you exclude the allied entities that were not charged with crimes and therefore obviously not proven guilty of them, all you have left is the charge that two men and a business knowingly committed crimes. Criminal operations of this scale and type were common before the RICO laws appeared, and were easily susceptible to charges and convictions at that time. RICO was designed to deal with something very different. An objective interpretation in this case, therefore, is that the only reason for using the RICO-type statute against Noe was to secure a heavier punishment.

In light of the enormous amount of discretion available to them, did the prosecutors charge Noe as they would have anyone else in a similar case? Would Non-Political Noe have faced a RICO charge? The answer, as stated previously, is obviously no.

A related question is whether it is reasonable to assume that this prosecutor and her team could reasonably act in an impartial manner?

There will be more on the role of prosecutors in the conclusion to this section.

Judges, Prosecutors and Impartiality

As noted earlier, in late February of 2006, Noe's attorneys filed a motion asking the Ohio Supreme Court to disqualify all ten judges on the Lucas County Court of Common Pleas. The motion targeted not just the judge who had been randomly assigned the case, Democrat Thomas Osowik, but also all of his Democratic and Republican colleagues (though the latter had already recused themselves). If approved, the request would have required the state to appoint a visiting judge for the trial (moving the trial to another location in the state, known as change of venue, was a separate issue that was dealt with later).

The affidavit for disqualification emphasized Noe's and his wife's activities on behalf of Republicans and, among others, mentioned actions directed specifically against Osowik.

The decision by the Supreme Court was handled by its Chief Justice, Thomas. J. Moyer. In a terse, 3-page document, Moyer relied on two points: 1) Judge Osowik says he isn't biased and there is nothing he's said or done "that might convey personal bias or prejudice against the defendant;" and 2) the law doesn't require that campaigning against a judge is grounds for disqualification: "We elect judges in Ohio and we must ordinarily assume that an attorney's or a party's vocal opposition to the election of a judge will not cause that judge to harbor bias when the attorney or the party later appears before the judge."[345]

Was Chief Justice Moyer correct in assuming that Judge Osowik could be impartial?

The research on bias cited above suggests that Moyer was wrong in this decision. The same research suggests that Judge Osowik should have made the decision to recuse on his own – certainly when he learned of Noe's role in filing an ethics charge against him.

Of course, it will never be possible to isolate prosecutors and judges from biased information, whether from the media or from that acquired by the hard wiring that all humans experience. But the research on jurors strongly suggests that it is desirable to limit to the extent possible the exposure of all people to bias – "all people" would include prosecutors and judges. In the case of Tom Noe, this would have taken the form of both the prosecutor and the judge recusing themselves from a situation in which, because of important personal factors, they were much more exposed to bias than normal.

This last point is strongly amplified by the fact that people are known to rationalize actions taken in their own self-interest.

Everyone rationalizes some things, and psychologists observe that we usually start the process by placing ourselves positively with reference to some important principle. Thus, when the principle is fairness, someone might start with saying, "Fairness is important," then proceed to "I'm a fair person" and then go from there to the rationalizing conclusion-- "and as a result I can ignore pressure of any kind." We hear this argument often when legislators and politicians argue that they are good and fair people and as a consequence can make impartial decisions about legislation while completely ignoring the fact that people and/or organizations with an interest in a particular outcome have given large sums of money to their campaigns.

A recent book, *The Rationalizing Voter*, by Milton Lodge and Charles S. Taber,[346] summarizes the research on rationalization and makes for very scary reading. A reviewer notes that the authors' model "suggests this process of automatic, hot cognition results in a cascade of biasing effects, whereby one's initial affective response to a political object or person will influence all subsequent thoughts related to the same object or person."[347]

Remember that the public, thanks in large part to the *Blade*, thought of Noe primarily as a political person.

The fact is that people often cannot ignore their self-interest, especially when they attend to it subconsciously. Thus, there's no reason to believe that Prosecutor Bates ever said to herself "I have to act in a certain way or my family and I will be punished by the *Blade*." Similarly, there's no basis to argue that Judge Osowik made a conscious decision to rule in a certain way because the *Blade* and *Blade*-fueled anti-Noe public opinion might punish him in the upcoming election for the Court of Appeals (even though the *Blade* itself did argue that it would).[348]

Prosecutors and judges are, of course, in a very different situation from jurors. People who serve in these official roles are highly aware of the presence of biasing information and are trained – sort of – to deal with it. But knowing about the possibility of unconscious bias and subsequent rationalization doesn't make implementing such recusals easy.

Rationalization brings up this example: In December of 2005, Prosecutor Bates strongly attacked Noe's attempt to describe his coin fund investments as profitable. He was, she said, "trying to put spin into the world" and through that hoping to influence the public, including future jurors.[349]

Bates' vigorous condemnation of Noe's press conference sets an extremely high bar for what is allowable as freedom of speech, especially when you consider that Noe had not yet been charged with any crime related to his business.

But this high bar was nowhere in sight just a month earlier when, lacking any good evidence, Bates enabled the *Blade's* story about Noe having an account in the Cayman Islands. If Noe's attempt to explain his business took some modest steps toward influencing potential jurors, the *Blade* story that Bates participated in was a giant engine of bias.

To be fair, one explanation is that for most of us, when we're pressed to provide an instant comment, the words don't always come out the way we intended. But it's also reasonable to think Bates didn't consciously decide to draw these lines. Rather, it's probable that she reacted in both cases to an unconscious belief that Noe wasn't to be trusted so she needed to counter him. And that's exactly why she and her office should have had no role in this case.

While it's true that people in law enforcement and in the judiciary start from a different point than jurors, it's also the case that, as humans, they are subject to the same pressures as everyone else.

But, did these individuals *unconsciously* rationalize the self-interest of some of their actions? There's no way to know the answer. However, again, given what's known about the propensity to rationalize, the best solution is to prevent people from being in these situations. And, again, these are not situations that will appear often; most likely only a handful of judges or prosecutors will ever face a similar situation in their entire careers.

FAIRNESS SCORECARD: JUDGE, JURY, AND PROSECUTOR BIAS MEANS THREE STRIKES AGAINST JUSTICE

Recent problems with local prosecutors' failure to indict police officers accused of brutality and even murder have caused some cities to suggest that specially appointed prosecutors should handle police misconduct cases. The logic is that the regular prosecutors, because of their close working relationship with police, aren't sufficiently neutral to file charges when needed.

Political affiliations can also matter in these situations, primarily because the police commissioner (or similar title) is normally appointed by an elected mayor and he or she may want to avoid scandal. Or, and this is more likely, the mayor may not give any kind of explicit order, but people in the chain of command may instead choose, perhaps unconsciously, to avoid taking actions that could create problems for the boss. When prosecutors are themselves elected, the problem is magnified. Michael J. Ellis, writing in *The Yale Law Journal*, observes in a history of elected prosecutors that "Not long after prosecutors became elected, however, prosecutors quickly became involved in and co-opted by partisan politics."[350]

An opposing view comes from a (then) student at Harvard Law, Colin Taylor Ross, who argues that an election "gives voters tremendous leverage over how prosecutors perform their duties."[351] The vast majority of Americans, who probably can't recall who their prosecutor is or whether they voted for him or her, will likely think this view is nonsense. Ross points to elections in which voters were "galvanized" and threw out local prosecutors in elections. Indeed. But these were egregious cases that generated a huge amount of publicity. What about the more ordinary cases where prosecutors take actions that, although very consequential for the people involved, generate little or no negative publicity?

Arguments over the relations of prosecutors and local police will continue, but one point stands out from a very lively and increasingly emotional debate: no one really disagrees that prosecutors can be biased, including by local politics.

The same issue of potential bias clearly applies to elected judges. Consider these facts: 1) Lucas County was the focus of unrelenting political strife that affected not just the area but also the state and the nation, with Noe and his trial judge on opposite sides: and 2) the trial judge was preparing to enter what would certainly be a bitter and (indirectly) partisan race for a Court of Appeals Court judgeship (against a candidate who had been actively and visibly supported by the Noes) and would benefit enormously from the support of the newspaper that was regularly proclaiming Noe's guilt. Research in human psychology tells us that relying entirely on Osowik's sincere statement that he could be fair is flat out wrong. The Ohio Supreme Court erred egregiously in supporting this line of thinking.

The argument for error in 2005 is strongly reinforced by a complete reversal of the Court's philosophy in 2017.

In 2005, the *Blade* was scathingly opposed to recusal of judges in a case like Noe's, and the Ohio Supreme Court was literally dismissive.

But that was then. We've seen that the *Blade* was OK with a visiting judge just a year later when the accused person wasn't Tom Noe. The Supreme Court took a little while longer to reconsider, but when it did the change was dramatic.

In a 2017 ruling, Ohio's Supreme Court considered a case in which a man who had been convicted of fraud argued that he didn't get a fair trial because the judge, named Crawford, knew someone who was once a political opponent of the accused, named Knaus. Judge Crawford had said that the friendship with the opponent was casual and not in any way political and, like Judge Osowik, Crawford averred that he could "impartially and fairly" preside over the case. Just saying so was enough for the 2005 Supreme Court, but not the 2017 version, when Chief Justice Maureen O'Connor wrote:

> Nevertheless, even in cases where no evidence of actual bias or prejudice is apparent, a judge's disqualification may be appropriate to avoid an appearance of impropriety or when the public's confidence in the integrity of the judicial system is at issue. [352]

And here's what the 2017 version of the *Blade* had to say in an editorial:

> Now suppose Judge Crawford honorably ruled against Kraus. Suppose that that's exactly what the evidence requires. Even if any judge looking at the same evidence would reach the same conclusion, and even if Judge Crawford is a man of perfect integrity, that ruling would be hard to distinguish from one affected by bias.
>
> These problems don't arise with a new judge who there's no reason to think has a conflict of interest.
>
> We should all hope that Judge Crawford, and all our judges, have the integrity to follow the evidence and the law even when it leads them to personally unpleasant conclusions. But a casual observer can't judge a person's integrity. It's much easier to see the integrity of a system when it avoids a situation that might, in the worst-case scenario, lead to a biased result. Chief Justice O'Connor made the right call.[353]

Moral principles aren't temporal. If the "appearance of impropriety," so much disparaged in the political and media firestorm of 2005, is not merely acknowledged but asserted in 2017, that ought to be a factor to consider in reviewing the case of someone who has served ten years in prison with eight more to go.

The evidence is also clear for juries. Given a certain level of publicity, bias will be there and voir dire will not be able to detect it. And the judge's instructions will not be enough to offset bias, especially if people don't know they have it. In fact, instructions to ignore bias could very well introduce it.

Taken together, a careful reading of the research, plus what is known of the political climate in Lucas County, demonstrates the high probability that a number of the jurors in Noe's trial were strongly biased against him before they were seated and didn't consider the evidence presented by the defense with an open mind.

Prosecutor: Okay. Let me ask you. Have you watched any media coverage in regard to Mr. Noe?

Prospective Juror: I think you'd probably have to live under a rock to say no to that. So I'm sure I've seen things, yes.[354]

It's obvious that routinely disqualifying prosecutors and judges, and regularly moving trials to a different venue, would be a huge burden on our system of justice. But it's equally obvious that the scale and intensity of bias will rarely be sufficient to require such deviations from the normal system. Prosecutors and judges don't often confront active political rivals. Nor do they often encounter a local media storm that coincides and overlaps with intense local political issues —on the order of 750 stories in the space of a year is orders of magnitude beyond extraordinary — and that's before taking into account the relentless wave of anti-Noe television commercials paid for by both political parties. When such extreme variances from the norm do appear, higher courts should disqualify the local players and move the trial to another community; in some cases, the move needs to occur in the investigatory stage, i.e., well before a prosecutor considers filing charges. It takes only a few simple steps to ensure that the kind of "legal perfect storm" that engulfed Tom Noe doesn't happen again.

Garrison Walters

Part VII- The State Processes and Valuation

As we've seen, "valuation," the overall value of Noe's Coin Fund assets was a key issue at trial. The judge refused to allow Noe's attorneys to present evidence that the coin funds held far more money than the state had invested. Judge Osowik's rejection of the valuation argument rested on two points: 1) the only focus of the trial was theft in the form of the "unsupported inventory purchases" and therefore anything related to valuation wasn't relevant to the charges; and 2) any information on valuation presented after Noe gave up management of the coin funds in May of 2005 would not be attributable to the work of Noe but to the efforts of the liquidator, DSI. Noe should not be allowed, the judge said, to take credit for someone else's work.

The appropriateness of using only the "unsupported inventory purchases" as the basis for theft charges has already been discussed. And, it's already been emphasized that, by seizing all his records, the state effectively prevented Noe from doing his own overall valuation of the funds when his management ended (though a generalized attempt was done with the aid of his attorneys and presented at a press conference in December of 2005). With respect to this last point, it's important to emphasize that the state, which had hired auditors and appraisers, itself had the ability to determine what the overall valuation had been when it took over. Indeed, it appears that doing so would have required a trivial amount of effort –nothing more than adding up numbers from a few different sources. But no such addition was done (or if so it was not released), and this appears to have been deliberate. Perhaps the most telling evidence of the state's strategy of hiding the value of the coin funds was the fact that it allowed DSI to release information that showed the funds would make a profit only on November 14, 2006: exactly one day after Noe's conviction.[355]

It's not possible at this point to determine with accounting-level precision the valuation number that the state could have and should have found and published, but it is possible to come close by characterizing the assets shown in the breakdown the Ohio Inspector General used in its report of April 24, 2014.

FINAL VALUATION REPORTED TO THE STATE

An annotated version of the original table presented by DSI and published in the Ohio Inspector General report of April 24, 2014 is shown below.

The table lists assets of $55.8 million, of which only coins and collectibles were truly variable. "Variable" in this case means things that might have changed in value from the seizure in May of 2005 until the liquidation was mostly complete in 2008. The other categories, such as accounts receivable at around $20 million, cash at $3 million, stock at around $8 million, and a few smaller categories aren't likely to have changed from 2005 to 2008.

Type of Asset/ Liability	Actual Sale by DSI In millions of $
Fixed- cash, accounts and notes receivable, stock	33,154
Variable (collectibles and coins)	22,720
Subtotal	55,874

The table next lists liabilities, of which just over $6 million was in "operating expenses," which appear to be primarily payments to DSI for its fees. When about $1.5 million in debts Noe owed is added, the liabilities come to $7.7 million. Then, adding back in the earlier profit distribution of just under $8 million yields a total return to the state of $56 million.

Type of Asset/ Liability	Actual Sale by DSI In millions of $*
Fixed- cash, accounts and notes receivable, stock	33,154
Variable (collectibles and coins)	22,720
Subtotal	55,874
Operating Expenses and debt	-7,758
Previous profit distribution	7,903
Total to OBWC	56,019
Amount above original $50 million	6,019

CAN WE CALCULATE THE VALUATION WHILE NOE WAS MANAGER?

DSI's original table states that it reflects values as of 2011, when the liquidation was formally completed. But, again, most of these numbers were fixed at the time of seizure in mid-2005 and shouldn't have changed: it's difficult to see how DSI's management ability could have enhanced the amount of cash received from VCC's bank accounts, or its accounts receivable, or the value of stock or other investments.

The only important variables here, therefore, are the operating costs and the values of the coins and collectibles. We'll consider these separately.

Were the Operating Costs Reasonable?

If Noe had been able to manage the sale and closure of the funds himself, would it have cost $6 million? That seems very unlikely.

The $6 million in post-Noe operating costs – estimated at $9.5 million at one point[356]*m* — is far too high even if we assume the state would have done some kind of special investigation as a result of its concerns. We could assume that, in response to concerns raised about Noe, the state might have spent perhaps $500,000 for accounting, appraisals, and those ever present legal costs.

The only other operating cost at this point would have been Noe's profits. This number is really not possible to reliably estimate based on available data – there are too many unknowns. Instead, previous profits can be a guide. Noe directed profits of $8 million to OBWC for CCF I. Since the OBWC's share was 80% of the total, his share would have been about $2 million. The profits for CCF II and continued access to CCF I would not have been greater than that.

Recalculating operating costs, then, gives Noe $2 million for profit plus $500,000 to OBWC for auditing and related costs and yields a total of $2.5 million. Subtracted from the $6.1 million figure given by DSI, that's $3.6 million less than what operations cost the way the state did it.

Was the Amount Recovered for Coins and Collectibles Reasonable?

DSI's actual return on coins and collectibles was well below Sotheby's high estimate in 2005. Would it be reasonable to expect that DSI could have done better?

The experts consulted by the author think DSI could have easily met and almost certainly exceeded the highest Sotheby's estimate.

The experts aren't able to provide precise figures for what might have been, but their conclusion is that the Sotheby's estimates were themselves low and that securing at least that much would have been easy for a company more experienced in the coin market than DSI (recall the defense pointing out that a batch of coins sold for three times the amount estimated by Sotheby's).

Several of the experts consulted are in fact former colleagues of Tom

Noe, so their observations could be discounted. But there is independent evidence to support skepticism about DSI's ability to maximize returned value from the coin funds: the hobbyist publication, *Coin World*, which covered the Coingate saga from its beginning until the final reports from the OIG.

For example, *Coin World*, as well as nearly all those experts it interviewed, were very critical of an auction DSI conducted in March of 2006. The criticism began when the Attorney General announced in February that the state had a "reserve bid" for a batch of coins and currency from a company called Spectrum. The bid, the AG said, would guarantee the OBWC a profit of $1 million although the state would still go ahead with an auction (remember the Attorney General was still running for the gubernatorial nomination at this point).[357]

Coin World and its constituency had a lot of concerns about the auction. Criticisms included: the fact that individual coins weren't available (the total was divided into lots, but there were multiple coins in each lot); that a $10,000 deposit was needed to view the coins and another 10% of the bid had to be forwarded with the bid; those paying to view had to do so in a high security facility operated by the Ohio Highway Patrol; there was no real catalog and the poor quality of the images on the website didn't make up for it. All this was in addition to the fact that the "reserve" bid allowed Ohio officials to decide to ignore the individual bids and sell the whole thing to Spectrum as previously agreed – and that's what they did.

Coin World editor Beth Deisher published an editorial on the affair, which said, in part:

> While the state of Ohio may require competitive bidding, the hired guns directing this show have come up with the most hostile and bidder unfriendly method yet devised.
>
> In all likelihood, the taxpayers of Ohio have been shortchanged again by bumbling bureaucrats and politicians diving for cover.
>
> The 3,400 items for sale deserve the dignity afforded in a grand format numismatic catalog, with proper descriptions. And each coin and paper note should be offered individually. How else can true market value be established?[358]

A DSI representative defended the terms of the sale by saying that it was necessary because of contract provisions between the coin funds and Spectrum, but provided no explanation of what those terms were.[359] However, in another interview, the CEO of DSI, William Brandt, said that the deal with Spectrum was as much a legal settlement as an auction – though again with no explanation.[360]

DSI is a business that specializes in liquidating assets, and has a long-term track record of success, though had no significant experience to that point in coins – or collectibles. One area where Noe feels the liquidation failed badly was in the collectibles. He says that the Sotheby's evaluator was not at all familiar with this area and that his estimation of $2.5 million was far below the $6-7 million actually paid for these items. Then, Noe says, DSI compounded the error by selling them for $2.5 million to a single purchaser – without any auction or similar comparative assessment.

CEO Brandt emphasized at the outset that it wouldn't make sense to sell the coins too fast, saying to *Coin World* in October of 2006: "There's no hurry to sell these (5-7 years, he said)." [361] However, despite Brandt's statement that they would take their time, it appears that almost all of the coins were sold by 2007, with most in 2005-2006. One point of contention was that DSI refused to use Heritage, the largest auction house in the world, because it had previously done business – all of it entirely legal --with Noe. This decision could have cost the coin funds a lot of money.[362]*m*

To be fair to DSI, the Ohio Supreme Court made things harder with a ruling requiring the release of all coin fund records, including the inventory and prices paid:

> They can count on losing at least another several million dollars of their holdings, he [Robert Higgins, a coin dealer] said." .. "If I buy a coin for $75,000, how can I sell it for $150,000 if people know what I paid for it?" ... If we revealed what we paid for every item, what do you think our success rate would be in selling it [for the amount we want]?[363]

DSI's contract, which appears not to have been publicly released and which is not available now, had some positives and some negatives. On the one hand, the company was given an incentive to maximize value by taking a share of profits [amount unspecified] over $50 million. On the other hand, a cynical observer would think this was negated by the fact that DSI got to operate like a law firm by charging $175 an hour, with the meter running as determined by the contractor.

Type of Asset/ Liability	Actual Sale by DSI	Actual Sale by DSI with Lower Operating Cost	Sotheby's High Estimate and Lower Operating Cost	Experts' Estimate at 15% over Sotheby's and Lower Operating Cost
Fixed costs and liabilities	33,154	33,154	33,154	33,154
Variable (collectibl es and coins)	22,720	22,720	27,000	31,000
Lower operating cost with Noe retained as manager		3,600 (benefit from Noe managing the sales directly	3,600 (benefit from Noe managing the sales directly	3,600 (benefit from Noe managing the sales directly
Total to OBWC	$55,874	$59,474	$63,754	$67,754
Amount above original $50 million	~$5.6 million	~$9.4 million	~$13.8 million	~$17.8 million

The bottom line here is that DSI thought it did a great job, while many experts in the industry thought they missed a lot of value in a strongly rising market – by selling too quickly and not using the most effective mechanisms. It's also worth noting that one of the estimates given here is very close and two are higher than the much derided figure of $61.8 million Noe's attorneys offered in their December, 2005 press conference.

SUMMARY

So let's reconsider the totals.

DSI says it recovered $56 million dollars from sales of assets, net of liabilities and operating costs but including previous profit distributions.

But, that number is almost certainly much lower than would have been the case if Noe had retained control. A rough estimate is that leaving Noe in charge, as would have been done in a negotiated settlement, would have saved some $3.6 million.

If we assume the lower operating costs, then first add in the returns at the high end of the Sotheby's estimates, the total returned is just shy of $64 million, or an estimated $7.9 million more from Noe than from DSI. And almost $14 million more than the $50 million the OBWC put in.

Further, if the experts are correct, as shown in the far right column of the table above, the total returned should have been around $18 million.

Would that return have made the coin funds a good investment? Again, there are too many variables to say for sure. If the funds had been wrapped up right away after June of 2005, as was done for the most part, then the answer would probably have been that the investment was just OK. But if the liquidation had proceeded according to a careful and strategic plan, with a good part of the coin and collectible sales extending past the start of the 2007-2008 financial crash, OBWC's choice of rare coins (and collectibles) would have been seen as an incredibly smart decision. In other words, the funds would have met the objective of hedging the stock market.

Part VIII- A Contrasting Case- Paul Mifsud

EARLY HISTORY

Paul Mifsud was an interesting character. Of Maltese origin, he was rumored to have been a clandestine agent for the CIA prior to working with George Voinovich when the latter was Mayor of Cleveland. Mifsud was subsequently Chief of Staff during much of Voinovich's 1991-1999 term as Governor of Ohio.

ALLEGATIONS DURING TERM AS CHIEF OF STAFF

Ohio's system of selecting architects was widely alleged to be infected with politics, which is to say that critics said that architects seeking state contracts were asked to donate to politicians and political parties. Allegations of this version of "pay to play" extend far back in Ohio history — long before Voinovich became Governor and include both Democratic and Republican administrations.

Fairly early in Voinovich's administration, Mifsud's name became associated with this alleged system of forced donations. The rumors grew into allegations and the Ohio Inspector General, David Sturtz, investigated. Some reporters thought he was close to bringing major charges against Mifsud. Then something happened:

> In 1995, Mr. Sturtz was investigating whether Mr. Mifsud had offered a contract to William Cargile, an African-American businessman suing the state over the administration's decision to include Asian Indians in a minority set-aside program.

> The governor refused to re-appoint Mr. Sturtz, who felt that the choice was made to squelch his ongoing inspection of Mr. Mifsud.

> "I have been personally told that [that the decision to not renew Sturtz' appointment was made to protect Mifsud] by numerous sources inside and outside of state government," Mr. Sturtz said at the time.[364]

Sturtz was bitter about Voinovich's decision:

> Mr. Sturtz told Mr. Voinovich in a letter: "You preached ethics, you promised more, but in the end you failed to deliver. For a politician, I cannot think of anything more damaging than not keeping your word to the people who entrusted you with their vote to make you the state's leader."[365]

Conviction

Sturtz's replacement as Inspector General did not file charges, but trouble eventually found Mifsud:

> MARYSVILLE, Ohio [September 4, 1997]- Gov. George Voinovich's former chief of staff, Paul Mifsud, pleaded guilty Wednesday to charges that he tried to cover up a $100,000 deal on home remodeling work performed by a state contractor.
>
> Two months after pleading not guilty to five felonies and three misdemeanors, Mr. Mifsud accepted a plea agreement that could land him in jail for three days. He also faces 100 hours of community service, $1,750 in fines and two years' probation.
>
> In return, Special Prosecutor Anthony Heald dropped the most serious charges, including tampering with evidence and forgery. Mr. Mifsud could have faced 11 years in prison if convicted.
>
> "I don't think anybody who looks at this kind of circumstance can conclude that . . . it appears like there wasn't something going on," Mr. Heald said.
>
> Mr. Mifsud, 50, will be sentenced Oct. 9 on two misdemeanors: obstructing official business and violating Ohio's ethics law. The plea agreement acknowledges that Mr. Mifsud obtained free home remodeling work from Columbus contractor Thomas G. Banks. As the work was being performed, companies controlled by Mr. Banks received $3.7 million in no-bid state contracts.
>
> Mr. Mifsud later removed and altered a building permit to lower the project's estimated cost from $210,000 to $110,000 - closer to what he and his wife have said they paid Mr. Banks.[366367]

Mifsud's case was considered sensitive enough that, unlike Noe, he got a special prosecutor and a visiting judge.

The most important difference, though, was in the plea bargain. Mifsud faced a charge of five felonies and three misdemeanors, totaling a possible eleven years in prison, but was able to get a bargain that reduced it to two misdemeanors. The reduced charges normally wouldn't have required any jail time. In fact, Mifsud got a six month sentence, but was mostly on home release and spent only a few days in jail.

Another important difference is the attitude of the *Blade's* co-publisher, John Robinson Block. The following is from a *Blade* article related to a new bridge in Toledo:

> "Mr. Mifsud's private sector career was sidetracked in 1997, when

he pleaded guilty to two misdemeanors for state ethics violations. He ended six months of a jail work-release program in April, 1998, just in time to advise Toledo officials about the Skyway. He died in 2000 from lung cancer.

The Paul Mifsud remembered by Mr. Block was ethical, a shrewd Renaissance man of state government. "He was so very effective and so capable that he was able to do multiple roles," Mr. Block said. "He could serve as the chief of staff. He could serve as the Karl Rove to Voinovich, his main political guy." ...

"Paul Mifsud made that happen," Mr. Block said. "He brought [it] in like a brilliant orchestra conductor, who points to the violins and they start to play. And he points to the brass section and they start to play."[368]

The praise continued in an article published by the *Pittsburgh Post-Gazette* (a Block Communications paper) on Mifsud's death in 2000:

Mr. Mifsud also was a friend of John Robinson Block, co-publisher and editor-in-chief of *The Blade* of Toledo, Ohio, and the Pittsburgh Post-Gazette. Block said Mr. Mifsud was the man "who began to understand the problems of the rest of Ohio beyond the three C's [Cleveland, Columbus, and Cincinnati]."

"He understood that this state was being held back by the parochial political bullying by the three C's. He's the guy who got it. I'm not sure that any other statewide official fully understood it. It's a great loss for us because if Paul had been around for some more years, many of the problems related to the inequities would have been solved."

Block described Mr. Mifsud as a "remarkable personality, a thoroughly enjoyable man, and a man I'm proud to have had as a friend."[369]

Part IX- Contrasting Sentences

The case of Paul Mifsud, discussed in the last section, raises the larger question of comparability: was Noe treated differently from others charged for similar activities?

To lead off with something close to home, Mifsud's situation offers a stark contrast. Being chief of staff to Ohio's Governor is also a "position of trust" – arguably a much higher level than managing an investment for the Bureau of Workers' Compensation. Mifsud and Noe's charges were similar in comprising multiple felonies (including forgery). But the plea bargain for Mifsud dropped all the felonies, while the equivalent for Noe reportedly retained enough felony counts to mandate a minimum of ten years in prison. Mifsud got six months but served three days, while Noe is still incarcerated.[370]

Perhaps the best explanation for the radical difference between the two politically-connected men is that Mifsud got an avalanche of letters requesting leniency in sentencing from leading people – including the Governor and the President of Ohio State.[371] Noe, on the other hand, got press releases from politicians calling for maximum punishment.

Similar situations + very different political circumstances + a vastly different media environment = different decisions.

This formula appears to represent an unbroken pattern. Assuming comparable criminal allegations, there are no sentences even roughly similar to Noe's. On the contrary, there is a huge archive of sentences that are radically different.

It's interesting that in calculating amounts lost for financial fraud charges, this author hasn't located a single case in which law enforcement followed Ohio's example and considered losses in one part of the business to be theft while ignoring profits in another. Instead, prosecutors and judges in other jurisdictions appear always to use the *net* losses to calculate the gravity of a crime. Chopping business activity into pieces in order to find something that looks criminal appears to be a strategy unique to Ohio and to Lucas County.

To save space in the printed version, the following list of comparable crimes and sentences contains just the basic information. Note that no one got anything like 18 years and the amounts lost were far greater. This list is just a precis of recent events; a comprehensive example would be much longer. To get more detail, please go to the website.

Name	$	Sentenced /Served in years	Notes
Andrew Casperson	$95 Million	4	Ponzi scheme; took $25M from a charity
Walter Forbes	$ Billions	12	His company lost ~$14 billion in value due to deliberate fraud
Steven Chen	$51M	No criminal charges	Defrauded many poor and older investors
James Fastow	$ Billions	10/6	Devised a fraudulent scheme that wiped out the retirement accounts of thousands of employees
John Ulmer	$15 Million	10/6	Many poor and elderly investors lost their savings
Delton de Armas	$2.9 Billion	5	Deliberate theft- i.e. no indication of intention to repay
Monroe Beachy	$17 Million	6 ½	Deliberate theft- i.e. no indication of intention to repay
Robert Sacco	$27 Million	6	Deliberate theft- i.e. no indication of intention to repay
Joanne Schneider	$60 Million	9	Deliberate theft- i.e. no indication of intention to repay
Phil Falcone	$18 Million	No criminal charges	Misappropriation of client assets/ theft
David Murdock	$148 Million	No criminal charges	Misappropriated funds for personal gain
Hannes Tulving	$15 Million	2 ½	~380 victims

Part X- Conclusions and Recommendations

WHAT SHOULD HAVE HAPPENED- DIFFERENT CHARGES

The theft charges against Tom Noe weren't valid in law; they were political constructs that will likely live in the legal curriculum as an example of what *not* to do.

To get to theft and the other allied charges including RICO, the State Task Force and the prosecution had to do three things : 1) effectively declare the signed contract in effect at the time as irrelevant; 2) parse the enterprise down into smaller and smaller pieces until it was able to find a segment where charges could be brought; and 3) stop the clock and seize control of the business assets from the defendant so that reimbursement was impossible.

Invalidating and/or ignoring the terms of the contract as was done for Noe and the coin funds isn't going to be any kind of legal precedent. As observed earlier, the State's interpretation asserts an ownership interest even when the contract explicitly precludes one, and in consequence would invalidate contracts for hedge and mutual funds. This interpretation even conflicts with the fundamental concept of a mortgage. Under the thinking imposed by the State Task Force and Lucas County, a bank holding a mortgage retains an ownership interest that extends to management of the property. The mortgage holder would therefore have the right to determine – or retroactively object to – anything it determines would harm its ownership interest. This could include improvements as well as your color choices for walls and carpets, etc.

The contract had explicit and careful provisions to prevent sudden liquidation and subsequent fire-sale-like losses. The state simply steamrollered these clauses out of existence, forcing a loss in valuation and preventing Noe from covering his debts. This was a purely political act and isn't going to be repeated in normal –i.e., politically untainted — prosecutions.

Similarly, don't expect prosecutors in other jurisdictions to model the legal gymnastics used by the State Task Force and Lucas County to segregate coins in Maumee from collectibles and investments at the same location — as well as from coins elsewhere. To get Noe, Mrs. Bates and her team employed the legal equivalent of gerrymandering: valid in law, but not fair and not going to win approval beyond this one-time use.

Finally, it's not reasonable to accept the argument that, even if Noe's real-world sentence was far too high, it was important in the context of corruption in state government to "set an example" that this kind of politically-related crime wouldn't be tolerated.

It's sometimes appropriate to use a case to set an example, but such an approach isn't at all valid in Noe's situation: he wasn't charged with political corruption with respect to the OBWC investment and no evidence was presented to support such an allegation.

The worst kind of public example to set is convicting someone and giving them a harsh sentence for a crime they weren't charged with and therefore couldn't defend.

In an environment lacking the political hysteria that obtained in Ohio at the time, Noe could legitimately have been charged with tampering with records and perhaps tax evasion. But that's it. Period.

WHAT SHOULD HAVE HAPPENED- CHANGED BEHAVIOR BY THE PLAYERS

If Coingate were made into a film, it would be the rare drama with no heroes.

Tom Noe

Noe's decision to take loans/advances from the coin funds was technically valid from the point of view of the contract. But, like the prosecution's use of extreme legal origami to get the theft/RICO charges in place, being technically legal doesn't make something right. Noe knew that the OBWC wouldn't have wanted him to take large amounts of money as profit advances, and this caused him to obscure his actions. As a result he did tamper with records and this act probably did have a role in allowing him a more comfortable lifestyle for a number of years. Some punishment for the tampering – likely civil but conceivably criminal at a very low level --would have been reasonable. And, coding checks as inventory purchases did lead to tax evasion (though he wasn't charged with that – probably because LaPointe wasn't). Finally, while Noe would probably have been able to cover the balances and show a profit if the funds had been wound up normally, he wouldn't have achieved that goal according to the spirit of the contract.

However, it's not certain that Noe would have been the loser in a civil suit over lost profits. In such a suit, Noe would have been able to show that his advances were in fact documented, even if they weren't called that. Indeed, because the advances were denominated in coins rather than cash, they would have come with a substantial interest rate. Put another way, with Noe's documented but misnamed advances, the OBWC was, in fact, successfully investing in coins.

The Prosecution

People the author spoke to almost unanimously describe Prosecutor Bates as honorable and competent, and a reasonable person would conclude that they are right.

Nevertheless, it's also true that:

1) Mrs. Bates was a Democrat who had to run for reelection on a partisan ballot that included Republicans strongly endorsed by Noe and his wife;

2) her husband was the supervising judge on the court that Noe would be scheduled to appear in and had himself been the target of very active opposition from the Noes (Noe helped file an ethics complaint against Judge Bates in 1994 and also was successful in convincing the *Blade* to endorse his opponent). And Mrs. Bates was well aware of these actions because they were listed in Noe's Affidavit of Disqualification.[372]

3) she and all politicians in Lucas County were vulnerable to losing their jobs if they were opposed by the *Blade*, which was outspoken in describing Noe as guilty; and

4) her stepdaughter and her husband worked for the *Blade*.

If you take these together, and if the phrase "appearance of impropriety" means anything, Mrs. Bates should have asked, long before Noe's indictment, that the case be sent to another county (the phrase "appearance of impropriety" is so ingrained in our culture it even has its own Wikipedia entry).[373] Of course, had she contemplated doing that, she would have had excellent reason to expect that the *Blade* would turn her into a villain and that her career and that of her husband and other family members would be in severe jeopardy. There's no reason to believe she made a conscious decision based on these facts, but she would be a very unusual person if she didn't spend some unconscious time in rationalizing.

Even though Mrs. Bates bears some responsibility for her failure to recuse herself, it was the Supreme Court that had the greatest responsibility here (see below).

The Judge

Judge Osowik was in an impossible ethical situation and his behavior showed it. He should have recused himself (as should all of the local judges).[374] Instead, he did not recuse himself and went on to ignore common sense by denying a change of venue. His ruling on valuation was based on acceptance of the prosecution's desire to keep the overall picture of the coin funds from the jury. And Osowik's sentence of ten years more than the minimum was difficult to justify morally given that judges certainly know what years in prison mean.

All of Osowik's rulings were legal, as demonstrated in the appeals. But, as described earlier, judges have a great deal of discretion, and Osowik could have taken the larger picture into account. Then, realizing the essentially political nature of what was happening, his rulings should have been very different. And, remembering the deference that appeals courts give to trial judges, he wouldn't have been successfully challenged if he'd issued different rulings.

That Judge Osowik acted as he did reflects the fact that he wasn't a truly independent actor. Like Prosecutor Bates, he would have faced the wrath of the *Blade* if he'd decided differently. There's no reason to believe he consciously considered the consequences of *Blade*-fueled public opinion (although, as previously mentioned, the *Blade* itself argued that he could be reasonably expected to do that). Again, though, the effects of unconscious actions are the same in the real world as conscious ones.

All things considered, however, the larger responsibility for Osowik's actions rests, as with the prosecution, not with him but with the Ohio Supreme Court. A discussion of that entity is next.

The Ohio Supreme Court

When things get out of control as they did for Noe in Lucas County, there has to be the legal equivalent of the adult in the room – in this case that should have been the Ohio Supreme Court. This court had two shots at Coingate. In the first, it should have approved Noe's request for disqualification of local judges and gone beyond that to order a change of venue. Chief Justice Moyer's "we elect judges in Ohio" is a rather pitiful way of avoiding the fact that the situation at hand was politically extraordinary. His decision, like those of many others in this case, was certainly political, even if unconsciously so.

In refusing to overturn Osowik's decision on venue in the second appeal, the full Supreme Court essentially invalidated the concept of change of venue. The court might as well have added an opinion saying something like, "a change of venue can be obtained in Ohio only in very small communities where everyone knows the defendant and each other."

Looking at the overall context, it's naïve to think that the Ohio Supreme Court wasn't affected by the politics of Noe's situation. As mentioned, judges of this court are elected on a statewide ballot, and the contests had become very bitter in the years before Coingate. The Republican members, who dominated the court, would have certainly known there would be political repercussions to any action they took with respect to Noe.

In theory that wouldn't be the case, because even if Republican justices favored Noe — early on with disqualification of local judges or later support for a change of venue — Republicans would still vote for Republicans and Democrats for Democrats. In reality, though, it would be different because turnout is the key issue for Democrats. Many don't vote except in presidential years and even then many don't vote for offices other than the highest ones.

If the Democratic party made a big issue of Republicans on the Supreme Court protecting their own, as they surely would have done, the controversy could easily have been big enough to drive turnout that would affect not just the court but all contests on the ballot. If Chief Justice Moyer didn't consciously think of this as a factor, it would be extraordinary if his unconscious mind didn't have it high on the agenda.

The Supreme Court sets an important part of the state's legal framework, and it should have foreseen the kind of exceptional situation that obtained with Noe and issued appropriate guidelines (see below). Although such changes won't necessarily isolate the justices from the situation they faced in Coingate, they should help mitigate the unfairness.

The Blade

Over the years, the *Blade* has done an admirable — perhaps an exceptional — job in investigative journalism. Both the co-publishers and the various people who have worked there have reason to be proud of their record. They also have reason to believe that their approach of bringing truth to power will be even more important in the future.

The *Blade*, which was a Pulitzer finalist for the Coingate story in 2006,[375] certainly started on a winning track. It was right to question possible political connections in Noe's OBWC deal, and its investigation of the coin aspect led investigators and journalists to uncover many other problems; those in turn resulted in a number of criminal convictions. And the *Blade* both investigated and created momentum that revealed numerous ethics violations and led to a number of positive changes in state government. A really amazing set of achievements in less than a year.

But the *Blade's* strong start was quickly marred by biased coverage that appears to have been based on personal animosity.

For example, the *Blade* pursued the possibility, weak though it was, that coin fund money might have been used for wine and cigars in Colorado. But it showed no interest in the far more important fact that the state had restructured its special audit away from the planned (and logical) overview of transactions and assets in order to instead focus almost exclusively on Noe. Even when the *Columbus Dispatch* attempted to get an explanation, the *Blade* was uninterested. The prosecution was determined to tell only part of the story about the OBWC's investment with Noe, and the *Blade* seemed wholly complicit.

Despite its past credentials in investigative journalism – and they are truly significant --the *Blade* is not exempt from the popular observation that with power comes responsibility. As essentially the only voice on local affairs in its large and populous region of Ohio, the *Blade* has a unique ability to shape popular opinion. And, if not done properly, this shaping can effectively close off balanced thinking. That's what happened in the case of Tom Noe and Coingate, and those in charge at the *Blade* should consider how best to achieve fairness in the future.

CONCLUSION: RECOMMENDATIONS

A year of work on Coingate necessarily leads the author to make some recommendations.

Clemency for Noe

In a fair judicial process, Tom Noe would likely not have served any jail time. The fact that he not only went to prison but is still there is the result of a purely political situation. Noe did mislead the state about his investments, but the state in turn actively misled the public and the jury in order to get a conviction and harsh sentence. Noe should be released as soon as possible. Also, a reasonable argument can be made that the State of Ohio did recover its costs[376]*m* — and probably much more.

Oversight of prosecutors

There's national evidence to suggest that prosecutors, especially those in state and local jurisdictions, require some form of structured oversight.

The case of the Duke lacrosse players provides one vivid and famous illustration.[377] A recent but less well-known case in Texas is even more horrific.[378]

Many more such cases could be described, but that isn't the point – what's relevant is that these cases suggest to any reasonable observer that there are many rogue prosecutors whose actions aren't reported.

It doesn't seem at all probable that a significant proportion of prosecutors regularly and consciously distort justice. But it does seem obvious that people with this extraordinarily broad discretionary power can be put in situations where they are pushed to act in a manner that might be improper. The best way to guard against these situations, whether they occur consciously or unconsciously, is for prosecutors to know that someone independent will review their behavior. Everyone needs some kind of external scrutiny, some process to ensure that they behave appropriately, and exempting prosecutors from this oversight is dangerous to a society that values fairness.

For all its flaws and challenges, our society allows its members an unprecedented amount of leisure, much of which has been channeled toward an infatuation with sports and through it an obsession with winning. Whether this is good or bad is a topic for another forum, but what's certain is that a single-minded drive to win isn't appropriate for all endeavors. Prominent among these exceptions should be the criminal justice system, and particularly the prosecutorial system. Prosecutors should want to win and should try hard to be successful. But winning should always be considered in the context of both law and fairness. Is it acceptable to mislead the jury in order to secure a conviction? No. And this shouldn't be debatable. Prosecutors should be required to keep a "fairness scorecard" of their own. And, since it's human to cheat — unconsciously if not consciously — there should be umpires.

Revision of RICO

The RICO family of statutes started with a worthy purpose and has achieved much. But RICO has been egregiously abused. Legislators, following the guidance of a panel of distinguished jurists, should revisit the laws and replace them with ones that are consistent with what the public needs and expects. If new laws are needed that fall in between existing statutes and the RICO howitzer, that's fine. But any outcome should eliminate the mile-wide discretion currently afforded to prosecutors.

Guidelines on Recusal and Venue

The courts already recognize the need for recusal, and actually apply it in cases where political hysteria isn't dominant. But Ohio's Supreme Court should accept that local politics sometimes makes necessary broad recusal to the point of requiring a new venue for prosecution as well as trial. Such situations will be extremely rare. And, when they do occur, they aren't likely to be more expensive. If Noe's case had been investigated from the beginning in another place, for example Dayton, it's reasonable to believe the costs would have been at most marginally higher than they were in Toledo. In any case, new guidelines on recusal and venue should be explicit in describing the problem of subconscious bias and how it affects all parties – jurors, prosecutors, and judges.

FINAL THOUGHTS

Some will argue that releasing Noe will be embarrassing for the State of Ohio, and that there's no value in revisiting Coingate in order to determine how things could have gone so wrong.

But such defensive approaches are dangerous. Putting the issues out in the open is a far better choice.

Reconsidering Coingate begins with an acknowledgment that justice doesn't simply mean determining guilt or innocence. Equally important is making sure that punishment is consistent with the crime. Anything else and two things will happen. First, public confidence in the integrity of the law will be weakened and replaced with a perception that the law isn't fair. Second, those who wish to use legal structures for political gain will be emboldened and we'll have more political prisoners.

If you approach the story of Coingate from a skeptical perspective, for example from a different political point of view than Noe's, it might help to strip the specifics from the story and consider it in the abstract. Doing that may help to allow the most important principles to emerge.

First the abstract sequence:

1) a key player in the media is angry at someone who we'll call "the target;" 2) the political establishment needs the media's support and dances to its vibes, so government officers violate essential values by using a phony search warrant against the target; 3) the seizure aspects of the warrant put the target out of business, deprive him of income and assets, and detach him from political relevance; 4) government officers twist the investigation and bend the law in order to hit the target with the most serious charges possible, including RICO; 5) the judicial system, which because of its own links to politics also dances to the media's music, sustains the mutated legal strategy; 6) the public, strongly influenced by the media, provides a complaisant jury; 7) the appeals process doesn't function outside a narrow, technical envelope; and 8) the target goes to jail for a long time.

Presented this way, few will agree that such a process is fair. And, when people think of this "Coingate process" not as what happened to Tom Noe but as what could happen to anyone, its importance grows.

We often hear the expression that "life isn't fair," and its companion, "the law isn't fair."

Some of us certainly do believe that life isn't fair, but if there's any sentiment that goes against the grain of American thinking, it's the idea that it's acceptable for anything intrinsic to the "system" to be unfair. As humans, we do understand that nature is capricious and that disaster happens, but as Americans we recoil at the idea that unfairness can be embedded in the structure of government. We love to use the expression "you can't fight city hall," but our history throbs with the conviction that not only *can* the "little guy" enter the lists against the powers that be, but that he *should.* And he should win.

Not fighting city hall and accepting that the law isn't fair[379] are old world beliefs, tightly connected to monarchical systems in which people were not viewed as equal and therefore not deserving of the same treatment by government. The prevalence of this way of thinking was a principal driver of many Europeans' decision to emigrate, and they carried their fierce opposition to unfairness across the Atlantic.

The concept of "American exceptionalism," incorporates a number of ideas,

248

but at its core is the idea that we don't accept that things done by government can be unfair. Or, rather, we accept that they happen but don't accept that they should be tolerated. And we firmly believe that individual Americans can make change happen.

The presence of these core values, the fundamentals that make America what it is, explain why what happened in Coingate is so directly in conflict with our thinking, why it must be undone, and why changes to the legal structure must be made.

Appendix A: Sections of the Audit and Contract

THE CONTRACT

Cited below are some relevant sections of the Capital Coin Fund I contract; Capital Coin Fund II was the same in these areas. the entire contract is available on the website at https://drive.google.com/open?id=0B9Sf_NQ6t8KJWURaNUpqQzZZcGs ; the contracts are at the end of the document.

Section 5.1 (Page 10)

Subject to the limitations imposed by the Ohio Act and this Agreement, the Managers in their full and exclusive discretion, shall manage and control and make all decisions affecting the business and assets of the Company, including without limitation, the power to:

(a) Acquire, invest in, maintain, finance, refinance, own, encumber, sell, exchange and otherwise manage the coins and other assets of the Company and to enter into other business arrangements with respect to Company assets deemed prudent by the Managers in order to achieve successful operations for the Company.

(b) Borrow money and to make and issue notes, obligations and evidences of indebtedness of all kinds, whether or not secured and to secure the same by necessary action, including, without limitation, the execution of notes and security agreements in order to secure a loan(s), make, enter into, perform and carry out any arrangements, contracts and/or agreements of every kind for any lawful purpose, without limit to amount or otherwise, with any party; authorize or approve all actions with respect to distributions from the Company and generally to make and perform agreements and contracts of every kind and description and do any all things necessary or incidental to the foregoing for the protection and enhancement of the assets of the Company.

Sections (c)-(g) follow.

Section 6.3 Other Rights (Page 16)

(a) Members shall not in any way be prohibited or restricted from engaging in or owning an interest in any other business venture of any nature including any venture which might be competitive with the business of the Company...

Garrison Walters

Comment: Section 5.1 makes it clear that Noe and the other manager, Frank Greenberg, can make loans or any other kind of indebtedness, which would include advances on behalf of the fund. Section 6.3 makes clear that the managers own companies, or companies they have an interest in, are to be treated like any other company. In other words, the managers' own companies can receive loans from the coin fund and be a party to other indebtedness issued by the fund. (Noe was the only manager in CCF II.)

Section 6.4 Prohibitions. (Page 16)

The Members shall not have the right:

Sections (a)-(e) list specific things members may not do; receiving loans and advances are *not* included in this list of prohibitions.

Section 7.1 Distribution of Profits (Page 16-17)

The Company's profits shall be distributed to the Members on an annual basis, or more frequently, in the sole discretion of the Managers… A Member who knowingly receives a distribution which is in violation of either the Agreement or the Ohio Act* is liable to the Company for a return of such distribution for a period of two years after such distribution is made.

Sections 7.2 and 7.3 follow.

Article IX (Page 19-20)

Termination of the Company

Provisions in this section make clear that Members (i.e., OBWC) cannot terminate the business without the approval of the Managers.

*"The Ohio Act" refers to Ohio law on regulating securities. It is part of a category known nationally as "blue sky laws" because they protect investors from instruments backed by nothing more than "the blue sky."

"Blue sky laws legitimately exercise state police powers in the prevention of fraud and deception in the sale of securities within a state's boundaries." Milton C. Boesel, Jr., "Analysis of the Ohio Securities Act." *Case Western Law Review*, Volume 5, Issue 4, 1954, page 353. http://scholarlycommons.law.case.edu/cgi/viewcontent.cgi?article=3364&context=caselrev

THE AUDIT AND "USE OF CASH"

Crowe's description of their "use of cash" approach is as follows; note that they don't mention deposits from other sources *after* the CCFI deposit:

In addition, we performed an analysis of how VCC used the CCFI monies it received as a result of these unsupported inventory transactions. Our "use of cash" analyses were based on the information included within the VCC check registers. In order to determine which VCC expenditures were funded with CCFI monies, we relied on the assumption that monies from non-CCFI sources were used (or "applied") to fund the earliest VCC checks or wire transfers and that the CCFI monies would be applied subsequently. For example, if there was a preexisting positive cash balance in the VCC check register when the CCFI deposit was recorded, we assumed that the amount of any preexisting cash balance applied to the first checks written after which the CCFI would be applied to checks written subsequently.

In 13 of these 16 CCFI cash disbursement transactions characterized as inventory purchases, we noted that the VCC check register reflected a negative cash balance prior to the CCFI monies being deposited. Therefore, in our "use of cash" analyses for these transactions we applied CCFI monies to VCC checks written prior to the day VCC recorded the CCFI deposit.

This is clear enough and entirely logical, but the problem comes when VCC receives deposits from businesses other than CCFI.

For example, here's a typical, not problematic situation:

1) The VCC account is in deficit.
2) A CCFI deposit based on a fraudulent transaction goes into the VCC account; let's say it's $10,000.
3) Crowe says that the next $10,000 in checks written from the VCC account are stolen money.

This is OK, but here's the problem:

1) The VCC account is in deficit.
2) A CCFI deposit based on a fraudulent transaction goes into the VCC account; let's say it's $10,000.
3) VCC receives a deposit from a different source (i.e. *not* CCFI) that is a valid transaction amounting to $15,000 the same day as the $10,000 and before any checks are written;.
4) Crowe ignores the $15,000 deposit and still says that the next $10,000 in checks written from the VCC account (in days after the $15,000 deposit) are stolen money (and/or money laundering).

Garrison Walters

Appendix B: Counts and Verdicts

G= Guilty; NG= Not Guilty; F+# = felony level

#	Type	Verdict/ Sentence in years	Type	Notes
1	Pattern of Corrupt Activity	G/ 10 years	F1 (Felony 1)	This is the RICO count, which connects other counts to a pattern of activity and to a felony level (in turn normally connected to a dollar amount). As the Ohio Supreme Court pointed out, understanding this statute is incredibly difficult – 3 of the 7 justices would have voided it for that reason.
2	Aggravated theft	G/ 4 years	F3	Theft via "unsupported inventory purchases" at various times.
3	ML (money laundering)	NG	F3	Payments in April of 1998 to people to whom Noe owed money; based on the activity in count 2 that resulted in guilty verdicts.
5	ML	NG	F3	Same as #3.
7	ML	G/ 4 years	F3	Paid off a line of credit in April of 1998. • There is no difference here than in the other ML counts for which NG verdicts were given. • The money laundering counts are to be served concurrently with each other.
9	ML	NG	F3	
11	ML	NG	F3	
13	ML	G	F3	9, 11, which were NG, only differ from 13, which was G, in the dates.

15	ML	NG	F3	
17	ML	G	F3	The same as #7 – the key difference is that the payment is to a bank.
19	ML	NG	F3	
20	ML	G	F3	As in #7 and #17. No legal rationale for this being G and others NG.
22	TR (tampering with records)	G	M1 (Misd emea nor 1)	This refers to the falsification of inventory records just prior to the raid on Vintage Coins and Collectibles in May of 2005
23	TR	NG	M1	There appears to be no substantive difference between #22 and #23 from the point of view of the facts or the law.
24	TR	G/ 6 months	M1	Tampering counts are to be served concurrent to each other.
25	TR	G	M1	
26	TR	G	M1	
27	TR	NG	M1	From the point of view of the facts or the law, there appears to be no substantive difference between #27, 28, 29, and 31 which are NG vs. other ML counts which are G.
28	TR	NG	M1	
29	TR	NG	M1	
30	Aggravated theft	G/ 8 years	F1	Theft of more than a million dollar – this is the main area in which the "unsupported inventory purchases" are charged.
31	ML	NG	F3	Connected to #30, theft.
32-49, 52	Forgery	G/ 11 months	F5	Forgery was an issue of interpretation, not one of fact; sentences are to be served concurrent to each other.

Sources: Bill of Particulars (*LC Docs*, Bill of Particulars, 4/18/2006,) and testimony. The Executive Application for Clemency contains both the indictment and the judgements. Note that some of the original 53 counts in the indictment were dropped; mostly because of consolidation ordered by the judge but also for other reasons (e.g. one person named in a forgery count had died before the trial).

Garrison Walters

Appendix C: Table of Persons and Organizations*

*Presented alphabetically by first name

Name	Identification
AG	See Ohio AG
Bernadette Restivo (Bernadette Noe at the time of the trial)	One-time chair of the Lucas County Republican party and controversial head of the County elections board; Tom Noe's wife at the time of Coingate
Beth Deisher	Editor of *Coin World* magazine; wrote an editorial about the liquidation
Bob Bennett	Head of the Ohio Republican Party during the Coingate period; outspokenly hostile to Noe in the heat of partisan conflict but changed his view and has supported clemency.
Bob Taft	Governor of Ohio, 1999-2007
BWC	See OBWC
CCF I and CCF II	The two coin funds set up to invest OBWC money
Craig Calcaterra	Defense attorney, Thompson Hine
Crowe Chizek	The external accounting firm hired by the Auditor of State to do a special audit of the coin funds
David Buchman	Assistant Franklin County Prosecutor; assisted in the trial
David Tripp	An expert from Sotheby's who did part of the valuation of the coin inventory
Deneen Day	Lead investigator for OBWC who knew about DVRC taking $1.5 million as the same time as Noe's VCC but didn't investigate it
DSI	Development Specialists, Inc. – the company hired to liquidate the assets of CCF I and II
DVRC	Delaware Valley Rare Coin – Co-Manager of CCF I Frank Greenberg's business
Emlyn Neuman-Javornik	The lead staff person for the external accounting firm, Crowe Chizek; she testified extensively
Frank Greenberg	Co-Manager with Tom Noe of CCF I

Fritz Wenzel	*Blade* reporter accused of suppressing information on Noe prior to the 2004 election
George Voinovich	Governor of Ohio, 1991-1999
Henry Hudson	Ohio Highway Patrol officer who signed the search warrant
James Bates	Senior Judge in the Lucas County Court of Common Pleas; Julia Bates' husband
James Petiniot	Jury foreman; later said that the jury acted inappropriately
Jeff Lingo	Assistant Lucas County Prosecutor; active in the trial
Jim Petro	Ohio Attorney General during the trial period; a candidate for the Republican nomination for Governor in 2005-2006. Outspokenly hostile to Noe in the heat of partisan conflict but changed his view and has supported clemency. Petro was later Chancellor of the Ohio Board of Regents and has become a leading national opponent of the death penalty and advocate for those falsely imprisoned
Joe Kidd	Assistant to Bernadette Noe at the elections board; went to prosecutors to reveal Noe's illegal campaign donations
John Mitchell	Co-lead defense attorney, Thompson Hine
John Robinson Block	Co-publisher, *The Blade*
John Ulmer	A Toledo area developer who was found to be running a Ponzi scheme and was sentenced to a long prison term; Noe's investment drew attention to Ulmer's firm
John Weglian	Assistant Lucas County Prosecutor; lead prosecutor in the trial
Jud Sheaf	Defense attorney, Thompson Hine
Judge Thomas Osowik	Trial judge for Noe's case in the Lucas County Court of Common Pleas
Judge William Bodoh	Retired bankruptcy judge hired by Attorney General Petro to oversee liquidation of the coin funds
Julia Bates	Lucas County Prosecutor; did not participate in the trial but was critical to deciding charges
Keith Elliott	Assistant auditor at the OBWC; raised concerns about the coin funds
Kenneth Blackwell	Secretary of State during the trial period; won

	his party's nomination for Governor against Petro but lost badly in the general election
Kevin Pituch	Assistant Lucas County Prosecutor; active in the trial
Larry Kiroff	Assistant Lucas County Prosecutor; active in the trial
Lora Manon	An attorney for the OBWC who assisted in the trial
Mark Chrans	Received investment money from CCF I and lost a substantial amount; a focus of the *Blade*
Mike Storeim	Managed a coin fund investment in Colorado; involved in key disputes with Noe
OBWC	Ohio Bureau of Workers' Compensation; often used as "BWC" in legal documents and news accounts
Ohio AG	Ohio Attorney General's office; also AG
OIG	Ohio Office of the Inspector General; tasked with a wide array of oversight of state operations
Paul Mifsud	Chief of Staff to Ohio Governor George Voinovich for much of his two terms in the period 1991-99; later convicted of accepting bribes
Perry Silverman	A Columbus attorney whose fraud and RICO conviction was used by the prosecution as a comparable to justify Noe's 18 year sentence
Rick Kerger	Toledo criminal lawyer who has represented Noe since the Supreme Court appeal
Sue Metzger	An assistant to Noe at VCC who testified early in the trial; she made the "ATM" comment
Terrence Gasper	Head of investments for the OBWC; later sent to prison for soliciting bribes
Thomas Moyer	Chief Justice of the Ohio Supreme Court who said that Judge Osowik didn't need to recuse himself and refused an appeal of Osowik's rejection of a change of venue
Thompson Hine	Cleveland-based law firm for which defense lawyers Wilkinson and Mitchell worked
Tim LaPointe	Vice President at Noe's VCC during the coin funds period; testified for the prosecution.

	Charged with RICO, sentenced to 18 months but served only three months
Tom Charles	Head of the Ohio Inspector General's office during the trial period
Tom Wersell	In charge of investigations for the OBWC; testified in the trial
VCC	Noe's personal business
William "Bill" Wilkinson	Lead defense attorney, Thompson Hine
William Brandt	Head of DSI, the firm appointed by Judge Bodoh to manage liquidation

About the Author

Garrison Walters was trained as an historian. He received bachelor's and master's degrees in history from Boston University in 1967 and 1968 respectively and, after a year as a Fulbright Scholar in Romania, was awarded a Ph.D. in the history of Eastern Europe and Russia from Ohio State in 1972.

Walters worked in various administrative and teaching roles at Ohio State from 1972 to 1985, when he joined the staff at the Ohio Board of Regents. His principal responsibilities there were in academic programs and research. He also led the initial development of the OhioLink library system and the planning for the Third Frontier fiber optic network, and was in charge of the very contentious statewide review of doctoral and professional programs in the early 1990s. He was a Vice Chancellor from 1990 to 2007 and served a year as Interim Chancellor from 2006-2007.

Walters was Executive Director of the South Carolina Commission on Higher Education from 2007 to 2012, retiring in that year. He is the author of a number of books:

- ***Ion C. Brătianu: The Making Of A Nationalist Politician, 1821-1866.*** Columbus, Ohio: Ohio State University, 1972.
  https://etd.ohiolink.edu/!etd.send_file?accession=osu1486737899171796&disposition=inline
- ***The Other Europe.*** Syracuse: Syracuse University Press, 1987. Also published by Barnes and Noble. *http://www.amazon.com/The-Other-Europe-Eastern-1945/dp/0815624409/ref=sr_1_1?ie=UTF8&qid=1398496375&sr=8-1&keywords=garrison+walters+the+other+europe*
- ***The Essential Guide to Computing.*** Upper Saddle River New Jersey: Prentice Hall, 2001. http://www.amazon.com/The-Essential-Guide-Computing-Information/dp/0130194697/ref=sr_1_6?ie=UTF8&qid=1398494283&sr=8-6&keywords=garrison+walters
- ***Total F*ing Magic.*** Amazon Kindle, *2013.*
  http://www.amazon.com/Total-ing-Magic-Garrison-Walters-ebook/dp/B00B39SRCU/ref=sr_1_4?ie=UTF8&qid=1398494413&sr=8-4&keywords=garrison+walters+total
- ***Killing Justice.*** Amazon CreateSpace, 2010.
  http://www.amazon.com/s/ref=nb_sb_noss?url=search-alias%3Daps&field-keywords=garrison%20walters%20killing%20justice
- ***A Riddle.*** Amazon CreateSpace, 2017.

In addition to general writing about higher education, Walters has published a number of articles on the need to create an "education culture" in communities, especially low-income ones. He believes that improving an individual's attitudes about his or her ability to succeed as a learner will be the most important factor in resolving America's education problems. Further, he considers that an education culture can't be created in schools alone, but will require volunteer-led peer to peer community action involving parents and caregivers and supported by organizations such as the Boys and Girls clubs, religious organizations, athletics programs, and more. See: "Change Education Attitudes, Not Just Management" in *Education Week*-http://www.edweek.org/ew/articles/2015/01/28/change-education-attitudes-not-just-management.html?qs=garrison+walters

In a related area, Walters and his wife, Professor Sylvia Marotta-Walters, are pursuing a project, called "From History to Hope," that is aimed at helping to prevent the inter-generational transfer of ethnic hatred that plagues many areas of the world.

Walters is interested in helping individuals with biographies or autobiographies and has a business with that focus: Partners for Writers (http://www.partners-for-writers.com/). He currently splits time between Mt. Pleasant, South Carolina and Alexandria, Virginia.

Information about the location of sources is given at the end of the Introduction. All of the references below are copied on the website to that a reader wanting to follow links on a computer or tablet can do so easily. Some newspaper links are not available because the articles disappeared online between initial research and final writing.

---

[1] [Cesare] Beccaria, *Des délits et des peines*. Paris : Guillaumin et Cie, Libraires, 1870. Second Edition, available via Google Scholar. See pages 16 and 41 in the book's Introduction by Faustin Hélie.

[2] Sam Sheppard was a Cleveland-area physician who was convicted of murdering his wife in 1954. The US Supreme Court overturned the conviction because of the effects of media bias. The television series *The Fugitive* was loosely based on the Sheppard story.

[3] An experienced litigator at a major law firm took exception to the idea that a civil court judge would necessarily have read everything. His experience is that some judges are fairly casual with written submissions and suggested describing this level of diligence as "aspirational."

[4] Sources report that there were actually more than 200 such boxes used in the trial.

[5] Complete Application for Clemency, Petiniot Letter to the Governor of Ohio, August 11, 2008, p 2.
https://drive.google.com/open?id=0B9Sf_NQ6t8KJMFNlVDJfdDI1REU

[6] Complete Application for Clemency.

[7] Tina Rosenberg. *Join the Club*. New York, W.W. Norton & Company, 2012.

[8] Rosenberg, *Join the* Club, p. 32.

[9] Editorial Board, "Bennett's Specious Claim. The *Blade*, June 19, 2006.
http://www.toledoblade.com/Editorials/2006/06/19/Bennett-s-specious-claim.html

[10] James Drew and Steve Eder, "Noe Says Ohio Rare-Coin Funds Made $11M; State Questions Claim." *The Blade*, December 22, 2005.
http://www.toledoblade.com/State/2005/12/22/Noe-says-Ohio-rare-coin-funds-made-11M-state-questions-claim.html

[11] Jim Provance "Judge Removed From Ex-Lawmaker's Appeal Justice Cites Appearance Of Conflict." *The Blade*, April 29, 2017.
http://www.toledoblade.com/Courts/2017/04/29/Judge-removed-from-ex-lawmaker-s-appeal.html Note that in the Knaus case the local prosecutor did recuse himself.

[12] Blade Staff, "Why O'Connor Was Right." *The Blade*, May 15, 2017.
http://www.toledoblade.com/Editorials/2017/05/15/Toledo-Blade-editorial-Why-

O-Connor-was-right.html

[13] *Transcripts*, 10/11/2006, p. 272.

[14] To illustrate what happened in the automobile industry, the international consulting firm McKinsey reports that the hours of labor required to assemble a vehicle at Chrysler, the principal employer in Toledo, fell from about 52 to only about 30 from 1979 to 2002. Most of this change, according to McKinsey, was the result of the adoption of Japanese-style "lean production" techniques. McKinsey&Co, *Increasing Global Competition and Labor Productivity: Lessons from the US Automotive Industry*. November 2005. file:///Users/garrisonwalters/Downloads/MGI_Lessons_from_auto_industry_full_%20report.pdf, p. 13.

[15] This text is extracted from messages sent by Noe to the author.

[16] https://en.wikipedia.org/wiki/Block_Communications

[17] George Gurley "Allan Block Is Worth More Than $100 Million and He's Seeking a Wife in New York." *Observer*, August 2, 1999. http://observer.com/1999/08/allan-block-is-worth-more-than-100-million-and-hes-seeking-a-wife-in-new-york/

[18] The *Blade* did not endorse a candidate for President in 2016, but coverage of Donald Trump was very favorable.

[19] Dave Murray, "The Late Paul Mifsud is Credited with Making the Skyway Reality." *The Blade*, June 17, 2007.

[20] Blade Staff, "Blade Wins Pulitzer: Series Exposing Vietnam Atrocities Earns Top Honor." *The Blade*, April 6, 2004.

[21] There have been suggestions that both papers are unprofitable: "Allan Block talks of sale of both papers and declines to say if either is profitable." Joe Strupp, "Block Hints At Possible Sale of Toledo, Pittsburgh Papers." *Editor & Publisher*, February 17, 2006. http://www.editorandpublisher.com/news/block-hints-at-possible-sale-of-toledo-pittsburgh-papers/

[22] Bob Fitrakis and Harvey Wasserman, "Dramatic New Charges Deepen Link Between Ohio's 'Coingate,' Voinovich Mob Connections, and the Theft Of The 2004 Election." *Detroit Free Press*, July 29, 2005. Dramatic new charges deepen link between Ohio's "Coingate," Voinovich mob connections, and the theft of the 2004 election

[23] Fritz Wenzel, "Lucas County Elections Board Is Told To Resign; Blackwell Threatens Firings If Necessary." *The Blade*, April 7, 2005. http://www.toledoblade.com/Politics/2005/04/07/Lucas-County-elections-board-is-told-to-resign-Blackwell-threatens-firings-if-necessary.html April 7

[24] http://www.gallup.com/poll/116500/presidential-approval-ratings-george-bush.aspx

[25] Editorial Board, "A Petty Reaction" *The Blade*. November 3, 2004. http://www.toledoblade.com/Editorials/2004/11/03/A-petty-reaction.html

[26] https://en.wikipedia.org/wiki/Bruce_McNall

[27] *Transcripts*, 11/2/06, p. 3587.

[28] The most comprehensive story is that from the *Detroit Free Press*, cited above.

[29] Explicitly stated by Noe to OBWC auditor Keith Elliott. *Transcripts*, 10/19/06, p. 1760.

[30] Mike Wilkinson and James Drew, 'Ohio Agency Sinks Millions Into Rare Coins" *The Blade*, April 3, 2005. http://www.toledoblade.com/frontpage/2005/04/03/Ohio-agency-sinks-millions-into-rare-coins.html

[31] Operating Agreement, p. 10. https://drive.google.com/open?id=0B9Sf_NQ6t8KJWURaNUpqQzZZcGs .

[32] Erica Blake, "Ulmer Given Ten Years Behind Bars." *The Blade*, 3/25/2009. http://www.toledoblade.com/local/2009/03/25/Ulmer-given-10-years-behind-bars.html Note that Ulmer had no ability to repay from other parts of his business but got out of jail after five years.

[33] Ohio Bureau of Workers Compensation, "BWC's Emerging, Minority Managers Continue Outstanding Investment Performance." OBWC, January 15, 2004. http://www.ohiobwc.com/home/current/releases/2004/011504.asp.

[34] *Transcripts*, 6/14/06, pp. 18-23.

[35] The author was responsible for research and technology transfer programs at the Regents from 1985 to 2007. He can think of no occasion in which Regents authority extended to faculty-run but legally separate businesses.

[36] Ohio History Connection, *State Archives*, Series 7005- Office of the Governor, Box 57,725, folder 9.

[37] *LC Docs*, Change of Venue, 5/19/2006; entry on 5/15/05 in the PDF, which is organized chronologically. ("Lucas County Documents" cited after this as "*LC Documents*".)

[38] James Drew, "Noe Sent Funds From State to Bankrupt Coin Associate. *The Blade*, May 22, 2005. http://www.toledoblade.com/frontpage/2005/05/22/Noe-sent-funds-from-state-to-bankrupt-coin-associate.html

[39] *Lucas County Documents*, Motion to Suppress…Search Warrant, 6/12/2006, pp. 12-13.

[40] *Transcripts*, 10/16/06, p. 971, p. 976. OIG head Tom Charles and OBWC lead investigator Tom Wersell both testified in the trial that they had no evidence of criminal activity when they started their investigations. Charles said that he sought the search warrant because the Governor (in a press release) had said, in effect, "To get into the coin shop and get the coins."

[41] *Transcripts*, 10/17/06, p. 1128.

[42] Mike Wilkinson and James Drew, "Ex-Coin Fund Associate Has Felony Record." *The Blade*, April 22, 2005.

[43] Mike Wilkinson, "Lucas County Judge Keeps Most Noe Charges, Merges Others." *The Blade*, August 23, 2006.

[44] *LC Documents*, Findings of Fact. 8/22/06, p.20.

[45] Christopher D. Kirkpatrick and Steve Eder, "Paper Trail Offers a Glimpse

into Search's Timeline." *The Blade*, June 1, 2005.
http://www.toledoblade.com/frontpage/2005/06/01/Paper-trail-offers-a-glimpse-into-search-s-timeline.html

[46] The OBWC made a number of other alternative investments at the same time it invested in CCF I in 1998. One was in a hedge fund run by a firm called MDL. Beginning around 2004, MDL made a series of very bad bets in the market, eventually losing nearly $215 million. But the problem wasn't just losing money. Evidence emerged that MDL's CEO, Mark Lay, had misled OBWC about the high risk nature of the hedge fund and had also regularly exceeded guidelines with respect to the amount of debt he could assume in the fund's name. It also emerged that MDL had inappropriate links to OBWC: the daughter of a member of the Bureau's oversight board was a vice president at MDL, and it was widely alleged that Lay got special treatment because of the relationship. Despite losing some 17 times more money than the charges against Noe, Lay got a substantially lighter sentence (see Part IX). See: 1) "Lay Gets 12 Years in BWC Scandal." *Columbus Dispatch*, July 8, 2008.
http://www.dispatch.com/content/stories/local/2008/07/08/lay09_web.html and 2) United States of America, Plaintiff-Appellee, v. Mark D. Lay, Defendant-Appellant. No. 08-3892, Appeal from the United States District Court for the Northern District of Ohio at Cleveland. No. 07-00339-001—David D. Dowd, District Judge. Argued: April 27, 2010. Decided and Filed: July 14, 2010.
http://www.opn.ca6.uscourts.gov/opinions.pdf/10a0201p-06.pdf

[47] For the official report of Wilkinson's words, see the affidavit of Kent M. Shmeall in *LC Docs,* Motion Opposing Defendant's Motion In Limine Regarding Attorney Statements, 9/29/2006, pp. 14-16.

[48] *LC Docs*, 9/29/2006, Motion Opposing Defendant's Motion In Limine Regarding Attorney Statements, p. 6.

[49] James Drew and Steve Eder, Franklin County Prosecutor Faces Conflict Questions, *The Blade*, January 15, 2006.
http://www.toledoblade.com/Politics/2006/01/15/Franklin-County-prosecutor-faces-conflict-questions.html

[50] One of the aides, Douglas Talbott, testified that he did not know about Noe's deal with the OBWC until many years after he had left the Governor's Office. OEC, *Report of Investigation, H. Douglas Talbott*, 11/29/2005 p. 24.

[51] James Drew and Mike Wilkinson, "Kidd's 'Wrong Choice' Led to Noe's Downfall." *The Blade*, October. 8, 2006.
http://www.toledoblade.com/frontpage/2006/10/08/Kidd-s-wrong-choice-led-to-Noe-s-downfall.html

[52] "Tom Noe: Contrite to a Point." *Columbus Dispatch*, October 2, 2010.
http://www.dispatch.com/content/stories/local/2010/02/28/tom-noe--contrite-to-a-point.html

[53] Drew and Wilkinson, "Kidd's Wrong Choice…"

[54] James Drew and Mike Wilkinson, "Allegation Against Kidd Came Back to Bite Noes." *The Blade*, October. 9, 2006.
http://www.toledoblade.com/frontpage/2006/10/09/Allegation-against-Kidd-

came-back-to-bite-Noes.html

[55] Drew and Wilkinson, "Allegation Against Kidd..."

[56] Joshua Boak, "2 Sue Over Disclosure of Noe Book Proposal." *The Blade*, September 29, 2007. http://www.toledoblade.com/Politics/2007/09/29/2-sue-over-disclosure-of-Noe-book-proposal.html

[57] James Drew and Mike Wilkinson, "Taft: Coin Deal a 'Bad Decision." *The Blade*, May 28, 2005. http://www.toledoblade.com/State/2005/05/28/Taft-Coin-deal-a-bad-decision.html

[58] Steve Eder, "Political Fur Flies Among Officials." *The Blade*, February 14, 2005. http://www.toledoblade.com/Politics/2006/02/14/Political-fur-flies-among-officials.html

[59] Mike Wilkinson and James Drew, "Noe's Racketeering, Theft Trial to Begin Today." *The Blade*, October 10, 2006. http://business.toledoblade.com/frontpage/2006/10/10/Noe-s-racketeering-theft-trial-to-begin-today.html

[60] James Drew and Steve Eder, "Petro: Noe stole millions." *The Blade*, July 22, 2005. http://www.toledoblade.com/State/2005/07/22/Petro-Noe-stole-millions.html

[61] Both Petro and Bennett later changed their minds and wrote letters in support of clemency for Noe. Ohio Parole Board, Application for Executive Clemency. https://drive.google.com/open?id=0B9Sf_NQ6t8KJMFNlVDJfdDI1REU

[62] Editorial Board, "Liquidate in the Open," *The Blade*, May 26, 2005.

[63] Jeff Starck, "Strong Market Helps Ohio Recoup Funds Investments." *Coin World*, October 16, 2006.

[64] Mike Wilkinson and James Drew, "Ex-Coin Fund Associate Has Felony Record," *The Blade*, April 22, 2005. http://www.toledoblade.com/news/State/2005/04/22/Ex-coin-fund-associate-has-felony-record.html

[65] Christopher D. Kirkpatrick," Coin Fund Profits for State Hinged on Graders' Opinions, *The Blade*, August 5, 2005. http://www.toledoblade.com/news/State/2005/04/22/Ex-coin-fund-associate-has-felony-record.html

[66]Christopher D. Kirkpatrick, "State Experts Trace Origin Of Missing Gold coins," *The Toledo Blade*, July 5, 2005

[67] Steve Eder And James Drew, "Coin, Cigars, Wine Seized in Colorado, Authorities Raid Home of Former Noe Associate." *The Blade*, June 7, 2005. http://www.toledoblade.com/State/2005/06/07/Coin-cigars-wine-seized-in-Colorado.html

[68] Christopher D. Kirkpatrick, "Colorado Man Traded Coins to Feed His Expensive Tastes." *The Blade*, August 5, 2006. http://www.toledoblade.com/State/2005/08/05/Colorado-man-traded-coins-to-

feed-his-expensive-tastes.html

[69] In the Court of Appeals of Lucas County, Ohio Sixth Appellate District, C.A. No. L-06-1393, C.P. No. CR06-1348, p. 26. Appeals, p. 26.

[70] Mike Wilkinson And James Drew, "Letter claims Noe had link to bank in Caribbean." *The Blade*, November 11, 2005. http://www.toledoblade.com/local/2005/11/11/Letter-claims-Noe-had-link-to-bank-in-Caribbean.html

[71] James Drew and Steve Eder, "Noe Says Ohio Rare-Coin Funds Made $11M; State Questions Claim." *The Blade*, December 22, 2005. http://www.toledoblade.com/State/2005/12/22/Noe-says-Ohio-rare-coin-funds-made-11M-state-questions-claim.html

[72] Drew and Eder, "Noe Says Ohio…"

[73] Drew and Eder, "Noe Says Ohio…"

[74] George Nelson, "Noe Attorney Argues Coin Fund Made Money for BWC." *The Business Journal,* December 21, 2005. http://archive.businessjournaldaily.com/content/noe-attorney-argues-coin-fund-made-money-bwc

[75] The head of DSI, William Brandt, sent a number of memos with attached "crib sheets" (spreadsheets) describing expected coin fund recovery. A review of the available versions of these shows that, even as early as June of 2005 (less than a month after the seizure of assets), DSI was predicting around $48 million of recovery (including the prior profit distribution). Source: Ohio History Connection, *State Archives*, Series 6771, Box 57,499, Folder 17.

[76] Eric von Klinger, "Spectrum CEO Responds to Claims," *Coin World*, December 19, 2005.

[77] Editorial Staff, "No News, Much Spin." *The Blade*, December 26, 2005. http://www.toledoblade.com/Editorials/2005/12/26/No-news-much-spin.html

[78] James Drew and Steve Eder, "Noe Stole BWC Cash For Home, Petro Says Check Forgery and False Profits Also Alleged." *The Blade*, September 30, 2005. http://www.toledoblade.com/State/2005/09/30/Noe-stole-BWC-cash-for-home-Petro-says.html

[79] Editorial Staff, "No Deal," *The Blade*, March 22, 2015. http://www.toledoblade.com/Featured-Editorial-Home/2015/03/22/No-deal.html

[80] Jack Lessenberry, "When Did Reporter Know of Noe Scandal?" *The Blade*, October 16, 2005. http://www.toledoblade.com/JackLessenberry/2005/10/16/When-did-reporter-know-of-Noe-scandal.html

[81] Bill Frogameni, "Saving Ohio." *Salon.com,* October 6, 2005. http://www.salon.com/2005/10/06/ohio_32/

[82] The same issue surfaced in 2006 in the context of the Blade's nomination for a Pulitzer. Dave Murray, "Anonymous Letter to Pulitzer Board Spurs Investigation by The *Blade*." *The Blade*, May 28, 2006.

[83] *Audit*, p. 3.

[84] WTOL Staff, "Ohio Law Keeps Noe Coin Fund Files Secret." March 13, 2006. http://www.wtol.com/Global/story.asp?S=4624753

[85] The prosecution even noted that the coin inventory in Colorado was about "a third off." *Transcripts*, 10/16/06, p. 898.

[86] *Audit*, Page 43.

[87] *Transcripts*, 11/03/06, p. 3883. Ms. Day must have been well aware of the DVRC/Greenberg transaction since she spontaneously recalled that the $1.5 million was recorded as coin inventory.

[88] A document from Greenberg's lawyer to the liquidator DSI, dated July of 2005, proposes ("in accordance with our prior discussions") that DVRC be allowed to repay its $1.85 million debt with about $800,000 upfront (in a period of three months) with the balance of $1,045,482 paid in monthly amounts of $50,000 and a final installment of $45,482 – with interest of 6% per year. No reply or agreement can be found. Since this (apparent) agreement was well in advance of Crowe Chizek's audit, it may explain the reason for Crowe's oblique reference to Delaware Valley's "inventory purchase." Source: Ohio History Connection, *Archives*, Series 6771- Office of the Governor, Box 57,499, Folder 17.

[89] Ohio History Connection, *Archives*, Series 6771- Office of the Governor, Box 57,499, Folder 17.

[90] Ohio History Connection, *Archives*, Series 6771- Office of the Governor, Box 57,499, Folder 17.

[91] James Drew and Mike Wilkinson, "Gasper Pleads Guilty in 2 Courts." *The Blade*, June 8, 2006. http://www.toledoblade.com/frontpage/2006/06/08/Gasper-pleads-guilty-in-2-courts.html

[92] Steve Eder and Joshua Boak, "Firm Fired After Losing $71 million from BWC," *The Blade*, July 8, 2005.

[93] Tom Troy, "Should Noe Have Taken Deal?" *The Blade*, August 16, 2015. http://www.toledoblade.com/Courts/2015/08/16/Should-Noe-have-taken-deal.html

[94] There are about 64,000 document pages in a gigabyte. The cost of a GB on a hard drive today is about $0.03. Twelve years ago, it was about 20x higher, but that's still less than a dollar. http://www.mkomo.com/cost-per-gigabyte Maintenance of storage over time is not much higher than the initial cost of the drive space and is also falling fast.

[95] Salon.com "Saving Ohio" October 6, 2005.

[96] http://www.sconet.state.oh.us/rod/docs/pdf/10/2013/2013-ohio-3627.pdf

[97] *LC Documents*, Affidavit of Disqualification, 3/2/2006,.

[98] Mike Wilkinson and James Drew, "Noe Wants 10 County Judges Off Coin Case." March 1, 2006. http://www.toledoblade.com/local/2006/03/01/Noe-wants-10-county-judges-off-coin-case.html

[99] *In Re Disqualification of Osowik Et Al. The State Of Ohio V. Noe*. 2006-Ohio-7224 NO. 06-AP-019. 113 Ohio St.3d 1209 (2006)

http://supremecourtofohio.gov/rod/docs/pdf/0/2006/2006-ohio-7224.pdf

[100] *In Re Disqualification of Osowik.*

[101] *In Re Disqualification of Osowik.*

[102] It's also odd that Chief Justice Moyer recused himself on a later case with a very tangential relationship to Noe (public records), but felt able to rule in this one that had a direct role in Noe's fate.

[103] Editorial Board, "Bennett's Specious Claim." The *Blade,* June 19, 2006.
http://www.toledoblade.com/Editorials/2006/06/19/Bennett-s-specious-claim.html

[104] Editorial Board, "Zeroing in on the Conduits." *The Blade,* January 11, 2006. See: *LC Documents*, "Thomas W. Noe's Motion to Change Venue," 5/19/2006.

[105] Mark Reiter, "Judge Upholds Investigation Fee for Four Conduits." *The Blade,* November 1, 2006.
http://www.toledoblade.com/frontpage/2006/11/01/Judge-upholds-investigation-fee-for-4-conduits.html

[106] *LC Docs*, "Memorandum in Support of Thomas W. Noe's Motion to Change Venue," 5-19-2006.

[107] *Transcripts*, 6/14/06, pp. 38-39.

[108] *Transcripts*, 6/14/06, p. 40.

[109] *Transcripts*, 6/14/06,., p. 43.

[110] Mark Niquette, "Noe Seeks to Have State Trial Shifted." *Columbus Dispatch.* May 20, 2006.

[111] *Transcripts*, 6/14/06,., p. 52.

[112] *LC Documents*, Change of Venue, 5/19/06, 3/17/06 ABC 13 Toledo. To find the article, it's necessary to scan through the PDF, which is organized chronologically.

[113] *LC Documents*, Change of Venue, 5/19/06, 3/29/2006 ABC 13 Toledo. To find the article, it's necessary to scan through the PDF, which is organized chronologically.

[114] *LC Documents*, Motion For Change of Venue Hearing/ Denied, 7/3/06.

[115] *Transcripts*, 6/14/06, pp 12-13.

[116] *Transcripts*, 6/14/06, p. 16.

[117] *Transcripts*, 6/14/06, p. 26. The Noes estimate that they eventually paid Thompson Hine more than $2 million.

[118] Steve Eder and Erica Blake, "Judge Blocks Statements by Noe Lawyers; Audit OK." *The Blade,* October 7, 2006.

[119] *LC Documents*, Motion to Compel a More Specific Bill of Particulars, 4/28/06, p. 7.

[120] *LC Documents*, More Specific Bill of Particulars, 4/28,/06, p 6.

[121] *LC Documents*, 8/22/06, p. 10.

[122] *LC Documents*, 8/22/06, p. 10.

[123] *LC Documents*, Motion to Dismiss, 6/12/06, p. 5.

[124] *LC Documents,* Motion to Dismiss, 6/12/06, p. 7.

[125] *LC Documents,* 7/3/06.

[126] Steve Eder And James Drew, "Judge Tells Petro To Stop Misleading Public On Noe Ruling." *The Blade,* September 23, 2005. http://www.toledoblade.com/frontpage/2005/09/23/Judge-tells-Petro-to-stop-misleading-public-on-Noe-ruling.html

[127] James Drew and Mike Wilkinson, "Noe Owes $13.5M to State, Audit Finds; Coin Funds Fueled Lavish Lifestyle, Officials Say." *The Blade,* February 23, 2006.

[128] Jeff Starck, "Strong Market Helps Ohio Recoup Funds Investments." *Coin World,* October 16, 2006.

[129] It's interesting that, when the *Coin World* reporter questioned Judge Bodoh about the valuation for the October 16 story, he was referred to the liquidator, DSI, which refused comment. But a month later the same firm announced an overall profit. Did that much change in four weeks? Or did DSI decide to help the prosecutors by keeping silent?

[130] Mike Wilkinson and James Drew, "Noe's Racketeering, Theft Trial to Begin Today." *The Blade,* October 10, 2006.

[131] Mike Wilkinson and Steve Eder, "Noe Guilty Of 29 Felony Counts; Convictions Include Racketeering, Theft, Forgery. *The Blade,* November 13, 2006. http://www.toledoblade.com/Editorials/2006/11/13/Noe-guilty-of-29-felony-counts-convictions-include-racketeering-theft-forgery.html

[132] But the *Blade* still made links to Noe whenever possible. See: Mike Wilkinson and James Drew, "Westhaven Firm Ordered To Stop Selling Securities," *The Blade,* November 22, 2005. http://www.toledoblade.com/State/2005/11/22/Westhaven-firm-ordered-to-stop-selling-securities.html

[133] James Drew and Steve Eder, "Noe, Wife Maintain Low Profile in Florida: Much Has Changed in Year of Upheaval." *The Blade,* December 27, 2005.

[134] Mark Niquette, "Noe: Contrite, To A Point." *Columbus Dispatch,* February 28, 2010. http://www.dispatch.com/content/stories/local/2010/02/28/tom-noe--contrite-to-a-point.html

[135] *Transcripts,* 10/16/06, p. 882.

[136] *Transcripts,* 10/16/06, p. 885.

[137] *Transcripts,* 10/16/06, p. 888.

[138] *Transcripts,* 10/16/06, p. 888.

[139] *Transcripts,* 10/16/06, p. 888-889.

[140] *Transcripts,* 10/16/06, p. 890.

[141] OBWC's holdings are given by various sources during this period as from $16-18 billion. It's likely the value of its holdings did vary within that range.

[142] *Transcripts,* 10/16/06, p. 929.

[143] *Transcripts,* 10/16/06, p. 915.

[144] *Transcripts*, 10/16/06, p. 917.

[145] *Transcripts*, 10/16/06, p. 924.

[146] *Transcripts*, 10/16/06, p. 924.

[147] *Transcripts*, 10/16/06, p. 937.

[148] *Transcripts*, 10/16/06, p. 919.

[149] *Transcripts*, 10/16/06, p. 945.

[150] *Transcripts* 10/17/06, p. 1097.

[151] *Transcripts*, 10/16/06, p. 1074.

[152] *Transcripts*, 10/17/06, p. 1205.

[153] *Transcripts*, 10/17/06, p. 1255.

[154] *Transcripts*, 10/18/06, p. 1498.

[155] *Transcripts*, 10/18/06, p. 1589.

[156] *Transcripts*, 10/18/06, p. 1609.

[157] *Transcripts*, 10/25/06, p. 2406.

[158] *Transcripts*,10/25/06, p. 2406.

[159] *Transcripts*, 10/25/06, p. 2432.

[160] *Transcripts*, 10/25/06, pp. p. 2444-2457.

[161] *Transcripts*, 10/25/06, pp. 2468-69.

[162] *Transcripts*, 10/25/06, pp. 2466-67]

[163] *Transcripts*, 10/25/06, p. 2422.

[164] *Transcripts*, 10/25/06, p. 2387.

[165] *Transcripts*, 10/25/06, p. 2254-5.

[166] *Transcripts*, 10/25/06, pp. 2461-2462.

[167] *Transcripts*, 10/19/06, pp. 1732-1733.

[168] *Transcripts*, 10/19/06, p. 1750.

[169] *Transcripts*, 10/19/06, p 1881.

[170] *Transcripts*, 10/19/06, p. 1788.

[171] *Transcripts*, 10/19/06, p. 1878.

[172] Important revisions after Elliott's May of 2000 review included: 1) no more advances to "joint venture partners;" 2) formal documentation of joint ventures; 3) full documentation of collateral, including current value; 4) purchases from related parties to be at wholesale or less; and 5) Plante Moran (the coin funds' auditor) would do auditing of the value and existence of assets such as coins and collectibles as well as financial instruments.

[173] "The Ohio Act" refers to Ohio law on regulating securities. It is part of a category known nationally as "blue sky laws" because they protect investors from instruments backed by nothing more than "the blue sky." "Blue sky laws legitimately exercise state police powers in the prevention of fraud and deception in the sale of securities within a state's boundaries." Milton C. Boesel, Jr., "Analysis of the Ohio Securities Act." *Case Western Law Review*, Volume 5, Issue 4, 1954, page 353. http://scholarlycommons.law.case.edu/cgi/viewcontent.cgi?article=3364&context=caselrev

[174] *Transcripts*, 11/2/06, p. 3622-3623.

[175] *Transcripts*, 11/2/06, p. 3634.

[176] *Transcripts*, 11/8/06, p. 4286.

[177] *Transcripts*, 11/2/06, p. 3572.

[178] *LC Documents,* 10/16/2006.

[179] *LC Documents,* 10/16/06, *Motion in Limine,* pp. 6-7.

[180] The "with the purpose to keep it for his own use" quote here is important. If the meaning of "keep" is intended to describe permanent holding, Noe clearly didn't do that.

[181] *LC Documents*, Memorandum in Opposition, 10/27/2006

[182] *LC Documents*, Memorandum in Opposition, 10/27/06, p. 2.

[183] *LC Documents.,,* Memorandum in Opposition, 10/27/06, p. 3.

[184] *LC Documents*, Memorandum in Opposition 10/27/0,6, p 4.

[185] *LC Documents*, EVT:J.E. Filed and Journalized, 10/31/2006.

[186] *Transcripts,* 10/17/2005 pp. 1371-1372.

[187] *Brief of Plaintiff-Appellee,* In the Court of Appeals of Lucas County, Ohio Sixth Appellate District, C.A. No. L-06-1393, C.P. No. CR06-1348, p. 35.

[188] *Transcripts*, 11/7/06, p. 4100.

[189] *Transcripts*, 11/7/06, pp. 4100-4101.

[190] *Transcripts*, 11/7/06, p. 4101.

[191] *Transcripts*, 11/7/06, P. 4123-4124.

[192] *Transcripts*, 11/7/06, p. 4136.

[193] *Transcripts*, 11/7/06, p. 4136.

[194] Interestingly, though, Wilkinson had described it as a "dumb contract" when meeting with the jurors just after the voir dire was completed. Transcripts, 10/12/06, p. 818.

[195] *Transcripts,* 11/7/06, p. 4149.

[196] *Transcripts,* 11/7/06, p. 4163.

[197] *Transcripts,* 11/7/06, p. 4159.

[198] *Transcripts,* 11/7/06, p. 4166.

[199] *Transcripts,* 11/7/06, p. 4177.

[200] *Transcripts,* 11/7/06, p. 4182-83.

[201] *Transcripts,* 11/7/06, p. 4192.

[202] *Transcripts,* 11/7/06, p. 4199-4200.

[203] *Transcripts,* 11/7/06, p. 4203.

[204] *Transcripts,* 11/7/06, p. 4204.

[205] *Transcripts,* 11/07/06, pp. 4243-4246.

[206] *LC Docs, State of Ohio's Sentencing Memorandum,* 11/16/2006, Case No. CR06-

1348, p.5.

[207] *State of Ohio's Sentencing Memorandum*, p.8.

[208] *State of Ohio's Sentencing Memorandum*, pp.16-18.

[209] The *Blade* article Wilkinson refers to cannot be found. However, Prosecutor Bates did make a similar argument later, in the context of the 2015 clemency plea. Tom Troy, "Should Noe Have Taken Deal?" *The Blade*, August 16, 2015. http://www.toledoblade.com/Courts/2015/08/16/Should-Noe-have-taken-deal.html

[210] *Transcripts*, 11/20/06, pp. 21-22.

[211] Ohio does have an early release possibility in some cases, but the amount in Noe's case would be small and would require the approval of a Lucas County Judge. It's doubtful that any judge needing to be reelected would approve given such past Blade editorials as "Keep Noe in Prison" (June, 2011) and "No Deal" (March, 2015).

[212] Mike Wilkinson, "Auditor Testifies OBWC Allowed Noe to Spend State Money As He Desired." *The Blade*, October 20, 2005. http://www.toledoblade.com/frontpage/2006/10/20/Auditor-testifies-BWC-allowed-Noe-to-spend-state-money-as-he-desired.html

[213] *Blade* Staff, "Osowik for Appeals Court." *The Blade*, November 11, 2006. http://www.toledoblade.com/Editorials/2006/11/01/Osowik-for-appeals-court.html

[214] One version is that the sentence was only eight years above the maximum; this is hard to determine given the many counts and the fact that some were served consecutively and some not. In any case, the difference is small in the larger context.

[215] Sources report that there were actually more than 200 such boxes used in the trial.

[216] Complete Application for Clemency, Petiniot Letter to the Governor of Ohio, August 11, 2008, p 2. https://drive.google.com/open?id=0B9Sf_NQ6t8KJMFNlVDJfdDI1REU

[217] Mike Wilkinson and James Drew, "Judge Cites 'Elaborate Scheme' to Defraud State." *The Blade*, November 21, 2006. http://www.toledoblade.com/frontpage/2006/11/21/Judge-cites-elaborate-scheme-to-defraud-state.html

[218] Jeff Starck, "Ohio Recovers 40.8 Million From Its Two Rare Coin Funds." *Coin World*, December 11, 2006.

[219] Jeff Starck, "Ohio Recovers 40.8 Million From Its Two Rare Coin Funds." *Coin World*, December 11, 2006.

[220] Russ Buettner and Charles V. Bagli, "How Donald Trump Bankrupted His Atlantic City Casinos, but Still Earned Millions." *The New York Times*, June 11, 2016. https://www.nytimes.com/2016/06/12/nyregion/donald-trump-atlantic-city.html?hp&action=click&pgtype=Homepage&clickSource=story-heading&module=a-lede-package-region&region=top-news&WT.nav=top-news

[221] In The Sixth District Court of Appeals Lucas County, Ohio CASE NO. CL-06-1393 State of Ohio, Plaintiff-Appellee, v. Thomas W. Noe, Defendant-Appellant.

On Appeal From Case No. Cr-06-01348 In The Court of Common Pleas, Lucas County, Ohio Brief Of Appellant Thomas W. Noe.

[222] *The Blade*, "An Outrageous Delay," 11/14/2007. http://www.toledoblade.com/Editorials/2007/11/14/An-outrageous-delay.html

[223] Ohio State Bar Association: https://www.ohiobar.org/ForPublic/Resources/LawFactsPamphlets/Pages/LawFactsPamphlet-5.aspx . A good summary can also be found in- http://www.americanbar.org/groups/public_education/resources/law_related_education_network/how_courts_work/appeals.html

[224] American Bar Association, *Criminal Justice Section Standards: Criminal Appeals.* http://www.americanbar.org/publications/criminal_justice_section_archive/crimjust_standards_crimappeals_blkold.html Accessed on April 4, 2017.

[225] *Brief of Appellant Thomas W. Noe*, In the Sixth District Court of Appeals, Lucas County, Ohio, On Appeal from Case No. CR06-01348, p. 9.

[226] *Brief of Plaintiff-Appellee*, In the Court of Appeals of Lucas County, Ohio Sixth Appellate District, C.A. No. L-06-1393, C.P. No. CR06-1348, p. 23.

[227] *Brief of Plaintiff-Appellee*, p. 23.

[228] *Brief of Plaintiff-Appellee*, p. 24.

[229] *Brief of Plaintiff-Appellee*, p. 24.

[230] *Reply Brief of Appellant Thomas W. Noe*, In the Sixth District Court of Appeals, Lucas County, Ohio. On Appeal from Case No. CR-06-01348, p. 2.

[231] *Reply Brief of Appellant*, p. 3.

[232] *Reply Brief of Appellant*, p. 20.

[233] *Reply Brief of Appellant*, p.21.

[234] *Reply Brief of Appellant*, p. 21.

[235] *Brief of Appellant*, pp. 17-18.

[236] *Brief of Plaintiff-Appellee*, p. 32.

[237] *Reply Brief*, pp. 5-6.

[238] *Brief of Plaintiff-Appellee*, p. 42.

[239] Ohio's money laundering statute seems very inconsistent with the definition used by the US Department of the Treasury: " Typically, it [money laundering] involves three steps: placement, layering and integration. First, the illegitimate funds are furtively introduced into the legitimate financial system. Then, the money is moved around to create confusion, sometimes by wiring or transferring through numerous accounts. Finally, it is integrated into the financial system through additional transactions until the "dirty money" appears "clean."

What happened with Noe's accounts wasn't "furtive," wasn't "moved around to create confusion," and wasn't integrated in a way to make "dirty money" appear clean. Instead, it was simply deposited and spent. Since Ohio's law doesn't require any of these three steps, it certainly does seem to an effort at double-jeopardy. See: United States Department of the Treasury, FinCen website.

https://www.fincen.gov/history-anti-money-laundering-laws

[240] Catherine Candisky, "Racketeering law poorly written but still enforceable, Ohio Supreme Court rules." *Columbus Dispatch*, June 11, 2013.

[241] *In The Court of Appeals of Ohio Sixth Appellate District Lucas County,* Nos. L-06-1393, Appellee Trial Court Nos. CR-2006-1348, p. 17.

[242] *Brief of Appellant,* p. 34.

[243] *Reply Brief,* p. 16.

[244] *Court of Appeals,* p. 35.

[245] *Brief of Appellant,* p. 25.

[246] *Brief of Appellant,* p. 27.

[247] *Brief of Appellant,* p. 28.

[248] *Brief of Plaintiff,* p. 18.

[249] *Brief of Plaintiff,* p. 18.

[250] *Transcripts,* 11/9/2006, p. 4357.

[251] *Reply Brief,* p. 33.

[252] *Reply Brief,* p. 7.

[253] *Reply Brief,* p. 9

[254] *Reply Brief,* p. 9.

[255] *Reply Brief,* p. 11.

[256] *Court of Appeals,* p. 25.

[257] *Court of Appeals,* p. 26.

[258] *Court of Appeals,* p. 26.

[259] *Brief of Plaintiff,* p. 38.

[260] *Reply Brief,* p. 13.

[261] *Brief of Appellant,* p. 14.

[262] *Court of Appeals,* p. 27.

[263] *Court of Appeals,* pp. 27-28.

[264] *Court of Appeals,* p. 31.

[265] *LC Docs, State of Ohio's Sentencing Memorandum,* 11/16/2006, Case No. CR06-1348, pp. 8-9.

[266]. http://www.supremecourt.ohio.gov/rod/docs/pdf/10/2006/2006-Ohio-3826.pdf

[267] Columbus Dispatch, "Strickland Clears Desk of Requests, Grants 152 Pardons, 1/7/2011. http://www.dispatch.com/content/stories/local/2011/01/07/strickland-clears-desk-of-requests-by-granting-152-pardons.html

[268] New York Times, "A Spirited Campaign for Ohio Court Puts Judges on New Terrain," 7/7/2000. http://www.nytimes.com/2000/07/07/us/a-spirited-campaign-for-ohio-court-puts-judges-on-new-terrain.html

[269] Staff, "Coin Dealer Noe Loses Final Appeal," *The Columbus Dispatch,* June 9/2010. http://www.dispatch.com/content/stories/local/2010/06/09/noe-loses-final-appeal.html

[270] Ohio Supreme Court press release, 2010-0294. State v. Noe. Lucas App.

Nos. L-06-1393 and L-09-1193, 2009-Ohio-6978. Discretionary appeal and cross-appeal not accepted. Brown, C.J., dissents and would accept the appeal on Proposition of Law No. IX and hold the appeal for the decision in 2009-1997, State v. Hodge, Hamilton App. No. C-080968, and would also accept the cross-appeal. O'Donnell, J., dissents and would accept the appeal on Proposition of Law No. I. O'Connor and Lanzinger, JJ., not participating.

271 *The Blade*, "Judge Denies Petition by Noe's Defense," 1/20/2012. http://www.toledoblade.com/Courts/2012/01/20/Judge-denies-petition-by-Noe-s-defense.html

272 *The Blade*, "Federal Magistrate Denies Noe's Request for a New Trial," 6/20/2013 http://www.toledoblade.com/Courts/2013/06/20/Federal-magistrate-denies-Noe-s-request-for-new-trial.html

273 *The Blade*, "Federal Judge Rejects Noe's Bid for New Trial. 10/1/2014. http://www.toledoblade.com/Courts/2014/10/01/Federal-judge-rejects-Noe-s-bid-for-new-trial.html

274 In The United States District Court for the Northern District Of Ohio, Petitioner Thomas W. Noe v. Respondent Francisco Pineda, Warden CASE NO. 3:11CV1173 Judge John R. Adams, Magistrate Judge Kathleen B. Burke, Report & Recommendation, p.1.

275 In The United States District Court for the Northern District Of Ohio, Petitioner Thomas W. Noe v. Respondent Francisco Pineda, Warden. Case No. 3:11cv01173 Akron, Ohio, Tuesday, April 1, 2014. Cited as Federal Court Transcript.

276 Kerger had replaced the Thompson Hine attorneys beginning with the Ohio Supreme Court appeal.

277 Federal Court Transcript, p. 5.

278 Petition Under 28 U.S.C. For Writ of Habeas Corpus by a Person in State Custody, Thomas W. Noe, Case 3:11-cv-01173. Filed 6/30/2011, p. 20.

279 Federal Court Transcript, p. 9.

280 Federal Court Transcript, pp. 9-10.

281 Federal Court Transcript, pp. 9-10.

282 Federal Court Transcript., p 12.

283 Federal Court Transcript, p 12.

284 Federal Court Transcript, p. 17.

285 Federal Court Transcript., p. 17.

286 Federal Court Transcript, p. 20.

287 United States District Court, Northern District of Ohio, Eastern Division, Memorandum of Opinion and Order, Case No: 3:11cv1173. Filed 9/30/2014, p. 3.

288 US District Court, Northern District of Ohio, p. 3.

289 US District Court, Northern District of Ohio, p. 3.

[290] US District Court, Northern District of Ohio, p. 2.

[291] US District Court, Northern District of Ohio, p. 2.

[292] *The Blade*, "Appellate Court Upholds Noe Conviction," 12/31/2009. http://www.toledoblade.com/local/2009/12/31/Appellate-court-upholds-Noe-conviction.html

[293] Blade Staff, "Federal Magistrate Denies Noe's Request for New Trial," The Blade, June 20, 2013. http://www.toledoblade.com/Courts/2013/06/20/Federal-magistrate-denies-Noe-s-request-for-new-trial.html

[294] Jennifer Feehan, "Federal Judge Rejects Noe's Bid for New Trial," *The Blade*, October 1, 2014. http://www.toledoblade.com/Courts/2014/10/01/Federal-judge-rejects-Noe-s-bid-for-new-trial.html

[295] Columbus Dispatch, "Noe Loses Final Appeal," 6/09/2010, http://www.dispatch.com/content/stories/local/2010/06/09/noe-loses-final-appeal.html

[296] Editorial Board, "Tom Noe's Predicament," *The Blade*, May 3, 2007. http://www.toledoblade.com/Editorials/2007/05/03/Tom-Noe-s-predicament.html

[297] Application for Executive Clemency, p. 12 of 14.

[298] The *Blade* has had at least three editorials on Noe and his appeals. The first, from August of 2008 ("A Vain Appeal") concerns the Court of Appeals and closely follows the prosecutions brief, including the argument that "the fact that the jury acquitted Noe on 11 other counts [is] … pretty good evidence they paid close attention, understood what they saw and heard, and were able to discern between charges." One wishes that a *Blade* editor would be put on the stand to describe exactly what "discernments" he thought the jurors made. As noted in Part IV, jurors seem to have simply skipped from place to place in order to quell internal dissent. The second editorial "Keep Noe in Prison" (June, 2011) concerns the federal appeal and is as sophisticated as its title suggests.

The strongest of the *Blade's* efforts to support its point of view is the last one and concerns the clemency request (March, 2015). This most recent commentary fits into a well-established pattern of boasting of the paper's own role in starting the investigation and also takes a favorite shot at Noe's education, pointing out that "[he served] as chairman of the state Board of Regents (*even though he lacked a college degree*)." Emphasis supplied.

Despite the boilerplate, this essay is well-argued and, like nearly all of the *Blade's* efforts, quite well written. In order to agree with it, however, you have to accept as given some things that the *Blade* considers established fact. For example, the *Blade* assumes that Noe "used his connections as a party activist and prolific fund-raiser to strike a deal with the Ohio Bureau of Workers' Compensation." This is something that the *Blade* has long argued but that Noe was never charged with and for which no evidence has been advanced – indeed, one of the *Blade's* criticisms of Noe is that he hasn't provided evidence to support the paper's claims. The editorial also brings up the idea of a Cayman Islands offshore account, suggesting that Noe has hidden money and shouldn't be allowed to "finance a lavish lifestyle [a favorite *Blade* phrase with regard to Noe] once he leaves prison." The *Blade* here advances two arguments that have the advantage of being unanswerable: it's almost impossible to prove a negative, which means in this case that Noe can't prove that he didn't use political influence or that he doesn't have an offshore account. Thus, the *Blade* can safely claim for all eternity that Noe hasn't satisfactorily answered its questions.

[299] Federal Court Transcript, p. 6.

[300] Christina A. Studebaker and Steven D. Penrod, "Pretrial Publicity : The Media, the Law, and Common Sense." *Psychology, Public Policy, and Law.* 1997. Vol. 3, No. 2/3, p. 433.

[301] Studebaker and Penrod, p. 434.

[302] Studebaker and Penrod, p. 434.

[303] Studebaker and Penrod, p. 435.

[304] Studebaker and Penrod, p. 436.

[305] Studebaker and Penrod, p.437.

[306] Studebaker and Penrod, p. 437.

[307] *Transcripts*, 6/14/06, p. 57.

[308] Les Robinson, *Changeology*. Totnes, Devon: Green Books, Ltd., 2012. Kindle Edition. "Family, friends, neighbors are the credible sources people turn to when deciding how to behave when challenged by new ideas, events, or threats." Chapter: Ingredient 1: First Start a Buzz.

[309] Studebaker and Penrod., p. 441.

[310] Studebaker and Penrod. p. 442.

[311] Studebaker and Penrod., p. 445.

[312] Studebaker and Penrod., p. 446.

[313] Studebaker and Penrod. p. 446.

[314] Studebaker and Penrod. p. 455.

[315] Mark W. Bennett, "Unraveling the Gordian Knot of Implicit Bias in Jury Selection: The Problem of Judge-Dominated Voir Dire, the Failed Promise of Batson, and Proposed Solutions." *Harvard Law & Policy Review*, Vol. 4, p. 149, 2010. https://papers.ssrn.com/sol3/papers.cfm?abstract_id=2505424

[316] Association for Psychological Science, "US Supreme Court Recognizes Role of Unconscious Bias in Disparate Treatment." https://www.psychologicalscience.org/news/releases/us-supreme-court-recognizes-role-of-unconscious-bias-in-disparate-treatment.html#.WOjpGGjyvb0 Accessed on 4/7/2017.

[317] Anthony G. Greenwald and Mahzarin R. Banaji, "Implicit Social Cognition: Attitudes, Self-Esteem, and Stereotypes." *Psychological Review* 1995, Vol. 102, No. 1 4-27, p. 4.

[318] Inferred from examples of race and gender. Greenwald and Banaji, p. 15.

[319] New York: Random House, 2016.

[320] *Transcripts*, 10/10/06 and 10/11/06.

[321] *Transcripts*, 10/11/06, p. 486.

[322] *Transcripts*, 10/11/06, p.349.

[323] *Transcripts*, 10/11/06, p.349.

[324] *Transcripts*, 10/10/06. p. 159.

[325] *Transcripts*, 10/10/06 pp. 200-201.

[326] *Transcripts*, 10/11/06, p. 302.

[327] *Transcripts*, 10/10/06, p. 155.

[328] *Transcripts*, 10/11/06, p. 262.

[329] *Transcripts*, 10/10/06, pp. 123-124.

[330] *Transcripts*, 10/11/06, p. 382.

[331] *Transcripts*, 10/10/06, p. 177.

[332] The *Blade's* initial story on jury selection was quite balanced. The paper highlighted the fact that many jurors had been strongly and negatively influenced toward Noe by pre-trial publicity. The story even reported the fact that people who said they had formed opinions about Noe's being guilty were left in the jury pool. Objectivity only goes so far, however – there was no mention of the many anti-*Blade* comments. Mike Wilkinson, "Many Potential Jurors in Noe Case Dismissed." *The Blade*, October 11, 2006. http://www.toledoblade.com/local/2006/10/11/Many-potential-jurors-in-Noe-case-dismissed.html

[333] "Kevin Pituch, one of four Lucas County assistant prosecutors who worked on the Noe case, agreed: "If you read the transcripts during jury selection, you'd know that's not so. Most of the people selected had no idea who he was. ... The people who were truly prejudiced against Tom Noe were excluded, and there weren't that many." *Columbus Dispatch*, "Noe Takes Fight to Federal Court," June 9, 2011. http://www.dispatch.com/content/stories/local/2011/06/09/noe-takes-fight-to-federal-court.html The "truly" is interesting here.

[334] *Transcripts*, 10/10/06, p. 70.

[335] Molly Mcdonough, "Rogue Jurors." *ABA Journal*, October 24, 2006. http://www.abajournal.com/magazine/article/rogue_jurors

[336] http://www.apa.org/monitor/2014/09/jn.aspx

[337] *Columbus Dispatch*, "Noe Takes Fight to Federal Court" 6/9/2011 http://www.dispatch.com/content/stories/local/2011/06/09/noe-takes-fight-to-federal-court.html

[338] Complete Application for Clemency.

[339] Tina Rosenberg. *Join the Club*. New York, W.W. Norton & Company, 2012.

[340] Rosenberg, *Join the Club*, p. 32.

[341] Josh Levin, "The Judge Who Coined "Indict a Ham Sandwich" Was Himself Indicted." Slate.com, November 25, 2014. http://www.slate.com/blogs/lexicon_valley/2014/11/25/sol_wachtler_the_judge_who_coined_indict_a_ham_sandwich_was_himself_indicted.html

[342] Stuart Diamond, "Steep Rise Seen in Private Use Of Federal Racketeering Law." *New York Times*, August 1, 1988.

[343] Russell D. Leblang, "Controlling Prosecutorial Discretion under State

RICO." *Suffolk University Law Review* 79 1990 80-115. Page 86.

344 In the Matter of Joseph Skupniewitz, Richard Posner, Barbara Crabb, and the United States Seventh Circuit, Petitioners, 73 F.3d 702 (7th Cir. 1996)

345 *In Re Disqualification of Osowik.*

346 New York: Cambridge University Press, 2013.

347 Jennifer Jones, "The Rationalizing Voter by Milton Lodge and Charles S. Taber. Cambridge University Press, 2013, 281 pp." *Political Psychology*, Volume 36, Issue 1 February 2015, Pages 137–140, p. 137.

348 Editorial Board, "Bennett's Specious Claim."

349 Drew and Eder, "Noe Says Ohio…"

350 Michael J. Ellis, "The Origins of the Elected Prosecutor." *The Yale Law Journal* 121 Yale. L.J. 1528.

351 Colin Taylor Ross, "Despite what many reformers believe, special prosecutors will only weaken police accountability." *Washington Post,* April 17, 2016.

352 Jim Provance "Judge Removed From Ex-Lawmaker's Appeal Justice Cites Appearance Of Conflict." *The Blade,* April 29, 2017. http://www.toledoblade.com/Courts/2017/04/29/Judge-removed-from-ex-lawmaker-s-appeal.html Note that in the Knaus case the local prosecutor did recuse himself.

353 Blade Staff, "Why O'Connor Was Right." *The Blade,* May 15, 2017. http://www.toledoblade.com/Editorials/2017/05/15/Toledo-Blade-editorial-Why-O-Connor-was-right.html

354 *Transcripts,* 10/11/2006, p. 272.

355 Blade Staff, "Broker: State May Recoup $6M." The *Toledo Blade,* November 15/2006. http://www.toledoblade.com/State/2006/11/15/Broker-State-may-recoup-6M.html

356 The Columbus Dispatch reported "professional fees, liquidation costs, and other related expenses so far are nearly $7.7 million, and total expenses could reach $9.5 million, according to figures released to The Dispatch this week [July, 2008] by the Ohio Bureau of Workers' Compensation." Mark Niquette, ""Millions Back After Coin Flap," *The Columbus Dispatch.* July 27, 2008.

357 Jeff Starck, "Ohio Official Has Guarantee of $7.5 Million in Coin Sale." *Coin World,* 2006; no further date available.

358 Beth Deisher, "Editorial: Ohio Sealed-Bid Coin Sale Bizarre." *Coin World,* 2006, no further date.

359 Beth Deisher, "Spectrum Bid Wins Items in Ohio Sale." *Coin World,* 2006; no further date available.

360 Christopher D. Kirkpatrick, "Batch of Noe Rare Coins Fetches $7.5M for State." The *Toledo Blade,* April 1, 2006. http://www.toledoblade.com/State/2006/04/01/Batch-of-Noe-rare-coins-fetches-7-5M-for-state.html

[361] Jeff Starck, "Strong Market Helps Ohio Recoup Funds' Investments." *Coin World,* October 16, 2006.

[362] The CEO of Heritage, Steve Ivy, wrote to Judge Bodoh in May of 2006: "Heritage is the largest auctioneer in the world and outsells its closest four competitors combined, none of which have a customer bases nearly as large and diverse as Heritage's."

. . .

"It is our belief that while other smaller competitors will indeed sell the coins, the prices realized for many of them will be at prices much less than they would bring from a Heritage sale. As a result, many of the coins will be purchased by savvy dealers at bargain prices." Ivy then pointed out that many of the coins purchased this way would almost certainly return and be auctioned by Heritage. Source: Ohio History Connection, *State Archives,* Series 6771, Box 57,499, Folder 16.

[363] Jeff Starck, "Ohio Supreme Court Ruling on Coin Funds." *Coin World,* July 17, 2005.

[364] Joshua Boak, "Turbulent Times in Columbus." *The Blade,* August 7, 2005. http://www.toledoblade.com/frontpage/2005/08/07/Turbulent-times-in-Columbus.html

[365] James Drew and Steve Eder, "Voinovich Avoids Political Fallout of Ohio Scandals." The Blade, July 3, 2005. http://www.toledoblade.com/frontpage/2005/07/03/Voinovich-avoids-political-fallout-of-Ohio-scandals.html

[366] Michael Hawthorne, "Voinovich's Ex-chief of Staff Pleads Guilty in Coverup." *Cincinnati Enquirer,* September 4, 1997. http://www.enquirer.com/editions/1997/09/04/loc_mifsud.html

[367] Michael Hawthorne, "Voinovich's Ex-chief of Staff Pleads Guilty in Coverup." *Cincinnati Enquirer,* September 4, 1997. http://www.enquirer.com/editions/1997/09/04/loc_mifsud.html

[368] Dave Murray, "The Late Paul Mifsud is Credited with Making the Skyway Reality." *The Blade,* June 17, 2007. http://www.toledoblade.com/frontpage/2007/06/17/The-late-Paul-Mifsud-is-credited-with-making-the-Skyway-reality.html

[369] James Drew, "Obituary: Paul Mifsud / Aide to Ohio Governor; Ridge Adviser." *Pittsburgh Post-Gazette,* May 28, 2000.

[370] "Case Closed." *Columbus Dispatch,* February 2, 2009.

[371] Michael Hawthorne and Sandy Theis, "Mifsud Gets Jail Term." *Cincinnati Enquirer,* October 10, 1997. http://www.enquirer.com/editions/1997/10/10/loc_mifsud.html

[372] *LC Docs,* Affidavit of Disqualification, 3/2/06, p. 5.

[373] https://en.wikipedia.org/wiki/Appearance_of_impropriety

[374] One legal analyst suggests that Judge Osowik should have recused himself with a statement of reasons that would have led other judges in Lucas County to follow his example.

[375] Joe Strupp, "Handicapping the Pulitzers: Experts Pick Front-Runners."

Editor & Publisher, March 2, 2006.

[376] Given the circumstances, Noe should not be responsible for the costs of prosecution.

[377] William D. Cohan, "Remembering (and Misremembering) the Duke Lacrosse Case." *Vanity Fair*, March 10, 2016. http://www.vanityfair.com/news/2016/03/duke-lacrosse-case-fantastic-lies-documentary

[378] M. Alex Johnson," Ex-Texas Prosecutor First In History To Be Jailed For Withholding Evidence." NBC News, November 8, 2013, 7:50 PM ET. http://www.nbcnews.com/news/other/ex-texas-prosecutor-first-history-be-jailed-withholding-evidence-f8C11566289

[379] Some who argue that the law isn't about fairness emphasize that law is instead based on a process that, because it is so carefully defined to offer balance to all parties, should lead to a just conclusion most of the time. On the other hand, the federal Brady Rule, which requires that prosecutors provide exculpatory evidence to the defense even if it's not requested, illustrates that the concept of fairness exists in law even when the standard adversarial process is fully carried out. For a short reference, see: http://www.yourdictionary.com/brady-rule .

Made in the USA
Lexington, KY
23 October 2017